BUSINESS COMMUNICATIONS:
a cultural and strategic approach

Michael J. Rouse and Sandra Rouse

THOMSON

LEARNING

Australia · Canada · Mexico · Singapore · Spain · United Kingdom · United States

Business Communications: A Cultural and Strategic Approach

For more information, contact Thomson Learning, Berkshire House, 168–173 High Holborn, London, WC1V 7AA or visit us on the World Wide Web at:
http://www.thomsonlearning.co.uk

British Library Cataloguing-in-Publication Data
A catalogue record for this book is available from the British Library

ISBN 1-86152-544-3

First edition 2002

Typeset by Techset Composition Ltd.

Printed by TJ International, Padstow, Cornwall

For Jeff and Matt

Contents

List of figures

List of Tables

Preface

Business Communications: A Cultural and Strategic Approach is aimed at university- and college-level students in management and business programmes and managers who want to improve their communications skills. The book works on two levels. Going through the chapters sequentially provides a systematic understanding of communications, how they work and how you can make them work for you in business and organizations. Alternatively, students and managers can dip in to particular sections for practical strategies that can be implemented quickly to help with a communication task.

The two key concepts of the book are (1) that all communication takes place in a cultural context and (2) the best approach to any communication task is the step-by-step development of an integrated communication strategy. Within those themes we combine theory and practice at every stage to link understanding with implementation.

Support material for the book can be found on the publisher's website: www.thomsonlearning.co.uk. Lecturers have access to teaching notes and overhead transparencies for each chapter, answers to discussion questions, activities and assignment and examination questions. Students can access learning notes, additional activities and answers, examples, and links to other communication sites.

Thousands of students have used the strategies in this book to improve communications in their academic, personal and business lives. Material in the book has been used by lecturers, tutors and students in the UK, Canada, Malaysia and India and has benefited from their feedback. We strongly encourage feedback from students and lecturers on any aspect of the book or support materials. Contact us through the publisher's website.

Acknowledgements

Our first and greatest debt is to all students and lecturers who have worked with the material in the book and provided constructive feedback and support. Their ideas and suggestions have made this book a much better one than it would have been otherwise. Our particular thanks go to Professor Gerry Wilson who has kindly allowed us to draw on his extensive communications experience. A number of other people have contributed directly or indirectly to the writing of the book: Urs Daellenbach, Professor Herman Konrad, Professor Paul Foley, Graham Watson, Agnes Koch, Professor Pushkala Prasad, Professor Bill McCormack.

We would like to single out our colleagues at the University of Calgary and De Montfort University who stimulated our ideas with lively discussion and debate and whose collegiality and friendship are continuing sources of support. We are very grateful to Anna Faherty and her colleagues at Thomson Learning for their enthusiasm and patience and to Michael Fitch for his careful copy editing. As always our biggest thank you goes to our sons, Jeff and Matt, to whom this book is dedicated.

Introduction

Communication is everything. That may seem a rather blunt and forceful statement, but think about it for a moment. Most of our needs and indeed most of what makes us human has communication at its root. Human needs for love and affection come about as a result of communication, for example, between a parent and child. Caring is communicated through words and actions. We are socialized and educated through a communication process. Whether we are working, chatting with friends in the pub, cheering at a football match, or praying to our god, we are communicating. Of the two certainties in life, death is meaningful to us as humans because of what it communicates to the living, and taxes are a direct result of communication processes involving governments and voters. We know ourselves and our roles in society, learn about others and organize ourselves into groups of various kinds directly as a result of communication. Communication is, therefore, an important subject in and of itself. The key purpose of this text is to reward your efforts to study communications with immediate and long term benefits for you in all areas of your life, but particularly in business.

Core themes: culture and strategy

In some ways business communications can be thought of as a rich tapestry. Rather than a patchwork of topics loosely related to a communications theme, our perspective on business communications is held together by the warp and woof of two threads. These threads that wind their way through all topics are:

- culture

- strategy.

Culture is key. Culture is interwoven throughout the text in two ways. Firstly, as we describe it in Chapter Three, culture is the context for communication. That is, we can only communicate because, as human groups, we have culture as a framework that enables communication.

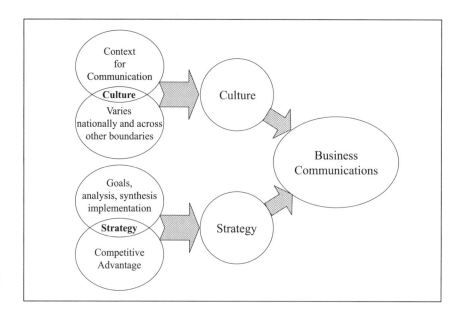

FIGURE 0.1 *Business communications: cultural and strategic perspectives*

Culture is also the framework for interpreting communication. Secondly, we look at culture as a phenomenon that varies across national, regional, organizational and other boundaries. Figure 0.1 shows how culture works on two levels.

Strategy is the other thread that draws our perspective on business communications together. As with culture, strategy is used in two ways. Both take their direction from the management discipline, strategic management. Firstly, we view communication strategy in terms of goals, analysis, synthesis and implementation. As you will see in Chapter Four, we promote an integrated communication strategy that starts with communication goals, sets out the kinds of analysis required, directs that all elements be synthesized into an integrated whole and then provides (Part II, Chapters Five–Nine) practical advice on implementation. Secondly, we believe that a thorough understanding of communications will provide competitive advantage not only for individuals who are able to apply communication strategies but also for organizations that can organize themselves for, and implement, business communications better than their competitors (e.g. Chapters Eleven–Twelve). Figure 0.1 illustrates the dual application of strategy to business communications.

Structure of the book

Business Communications: A Cultural and Strategic Approach is divided into three parts. The first part, Communication, Culture and Strategy, introduces the key themes of the book: organizations and communications, culture as the context for communication and taking a strategic approach to communication. Part II, Performance Communicating, deals with the practical aspects of common business communications tasks. Part III, Strategic Communications for the Corporation, focuses on communications at the corporate level, primarily dealing with external communications. At the beginning of each part is a diagram illustrating the structure of the book and highlighting the relationship between chapters and parts.

Communication flows in organizations are related to organizational structures. In Chapter One we explore the relationship between organizations and communication and how structure affects and is affected by communication. Organizations are socio-technical systems that are characterized by change and fluidity. We look at some of the social and technical aspects of organizational communication and discuss how communications might be related to an organization's competitive advantage.

Chapter Two presents models of communication and looks at forms of communication including a discussion of non-verbal communication. Communication is not always successful. Messages get distorted, are misinterpreted or fail to be transmitted. In the second half of the chapter we examine the barriers to communication – socio-cultural, psychological and organizational – and provide some concrete suggestions for overcoming or avoiding them.

Chapter Three explores one of our main themes, that all communication takes place in the context of culture. The basis of culture and the basis for communication are symbols. Language is a symbolic structure and we look at both language and culture from that perspective. Culture in the broader sense can be adapted to the organizational level. Chapter Three ends with a detailed look at organizational culture and its effect on business communications.

In Chapter Four we present our second core theme, a strategic communications model. We developed the strategy model by applying some aspects of strategy to the model of communication developed in Chapter Two. Our strategic approach is a step-by-step process that forms the basis for strategic communication discussions throughout the book.

In Part II: Performance Communicating we move to the practicalities of business communications. We start in Chapter Five with generating ideas and structure. Topics range from finding source material to conducting interviews for primary data collection and structuring ideas for writing.

Macro writing issues in Chapter Six deal with documents in their entirety: drafting and editing, style, tone and emphasis. Micro issues include constructing effective sentences and paragraphs, building transitions into your writing and acknowledging sources.

Most forms of business communications have standard conventions and formats. In Chapter Seven we look at specific forms of written communication: letters and letter styles including good-news, bad-news, persuasive and informative letters, electronic mail, facsimile messages, reports and press releases.

Oral presentations are a source of anxiety for most people, but can also be a source of personal and professional advantage. People who can give effective presentations are highly prized in most organizations. In Chapter Eight we apply communication strategies to constructing and delivering presentations.

In Chapter Nine we turn to meetings and negotiations. As with other communications they rely for success on applying the precepts of a good communication strategy. Practical issues discussed are planning and conducting meetings and preparing for negotiations that generate 'win–win' results.

Part III is Strategic Communications for the Corporation. Chapter Ten examines leadership, power and politics in organizations and issues related to communications and ethics.

How do companies project images of their products and of themselves? Marketing communications, advertising and public relations are synthesized in Chapter Eleven in a discussion of corporate image. The last part of the chapter explores reputation and communication as a source of competitive advantage.

Communicating across boundaries is a key concern of corporations. Chapter Twelve looks at how firms communicate externally with various stakeholder groups in their domestic environments and cross-culturally in the case of global or globalizing corporations.

Following Chapter 12 is a glossary of terms. Glossary entries are indicated in the text by bold-faced type.

In this book our focus is explicitly on business communications, though there are parallels and applications for communications for all forms of organizations. Many of the theories and practical applications you will learn are transferable to any type of communication and to most of professional and personal life. A deep understanding of communications and the ability to apply that understanding in a positive way is the most important professional transferable skill you can develop for success in business.

PART I

COMMUNICATION, CULTURE AND STRATEGY

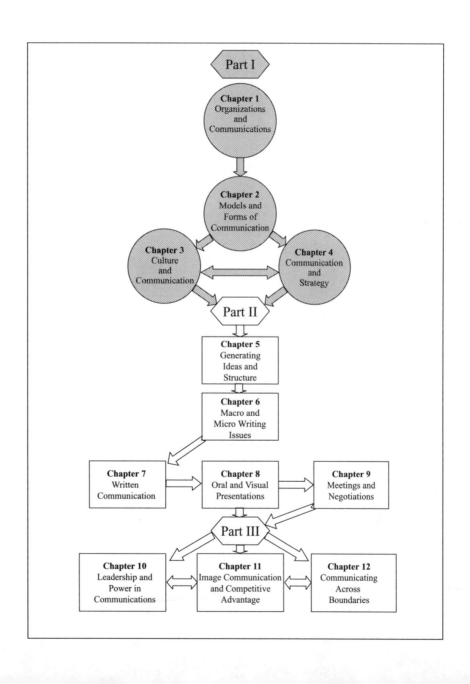

chapter one

Organizations and communication

Introduction

FAMILIES, COMMUNITIES, businesses, religions and governments are but a few examples of organizations that are a seemingly natural part of our everyday lives. All organizations are created and organized through a communication process and are maintained by people communicating with each other. Organizations and especially businesses are, therefore, contexts in which communication occurs. But they are more than that. They are also contexts which partly define what is communicated and how. In order to understand communications we must first understand a little about organizations as contexts for and of communications.

LEARNING OBJECTIVES

After studying this chapter you should be able to:

- Define organizations
- Demonstrate an understanding of the link between culture, strategy and communications
- Describe the main types of organizational structures
- Discuss the implications of organizational structure for business communications
- Demonstrate an understanding of organizations as socio-technical systems
- Discuss the link between communications and competitive advantage

WHAT ARE ORGANIZATIONS?

The human race has evolved and grown as a result of its ability to organize. We organize ourselves into families, tribes, clans, ethnic groups, religions, professions, nations, etc. We also organize ourselves into institutions such as businesses and public and not-for-profit organizations.

Why do we have organizations? To begin to answer that question we need to think about what organizations actually do, i.e., what is their function. Businesses manufacture products or provide services. Public-sector organizations also provide services that range from help for small businesses to health care and national security. Not-for-profit organizations provide services and sometimes products for those most in need in our society. All of these are the outcomes or outputs of organizations, and those outputs are valued by society. Organizations also tend to do things (produce products and services) that take groups of people to do. **Organizations** are society's way to generate value that individuals cannot generate on their own.

Examine this definition in a little more detail. Firstly, there is an emphasis on the social. That is, organizations are a social mechanism and they are social in composition. Organizations are made up of people and groups of people. People interact within the organization in order to produce goods and services. To do so they must communicate. In fact everything social depends upon communication. People have to communicate to organize in the first place, and then they have to communicate in order to co-ordinate and control their activities. An individual, for example, could not build a car. While one person could conceivably put all the parts together, no one person could construct all the parts – mine and process the ore into steel, craft the steel into shapes, drill, produce and refine petroleum into petrol, engine oil, greases and plastics of various kinds, design and make all the electronic components, turn sand into safety glass and so on. Automobile production requires a host of organizations and is almost entirely a socially-based process.

Whenever people come together over time another phenomenon occurs – culture. By defining organizations in social terms we implicitly identify culture as an important element. Culture is a core element not only of organizations (Chapter Three) but also a core element of communications. In fact, without culture there would be no communication.

Our definition states that organizations exist for a purpose and that purpose is generating value. Organizational goals need to be communicated not only within the organization, but also outside the organization in order to attract investors, employees, suppliers and managers and customers. The goals of the organization and its value-generation activities must be structured or organized within the organization. As we shall see (below), organizational structure also functions as a way to structure communication flows within the company.

Finally, we know from the management discipline 'strategic management', that organizations not only have to generate value, but they must have some form of competitive advantage. Without a competitive advantage there would be no reason to use that organization for value generation if there were advantages to having that value generated elsewhere by another organization.

Organizations are created as a direct result of people's desires to generate value. In organizing they set up structures of relationships to control organizational processes. Two kinds of organizational structures exist in all organizations – informal and formal. Both have related communication structures.

INFORMAL ORGANIZATION

The informal organizational structure is the unofficial part of the company. Informal networks may be groupings of colleagues or friends within a department, or groupings or networks of friends, colleagues or acquaintances throughout the organization. Not only could management not rid itself of its informal structure, since it exists in all institutions and groups, but it is actually necessary for the effective functioning of the company. The informal organization fills in the gaps left vacant by bureaucracy and formal structures. Indeed, it is common knowledge among managers that the surest way to bring production within the company grinding to a halt is to demand that employees strictly obey rules and directives without variance. There are just too many contingencies and variables in organizational processes for rules to handle. Without the information and intervention of the informal networks employees would not have sufficient information to do their jobs effectively.

INFORMAL COMMUNICATION

Related to the informal structure is the informal communication network. There are two related forms: the grapevine and informal groups. The grapevine is the core informal communication network. Via the grapevine people transmit information to each other outside of formal communication channels. To that end it tends to disregard not only formal reporting relationships but also the informal organizational structure. Davis (1953) identified several types of grapevine configurations. We illustrate three types in Figure 1.1.

The first of these is called a single-strand grapevine. It represents how one person passes a message on to another, who passes it to another, to another and so on in one long series of communications. The second configuration is the gossip chain. This is where one person tells everyone they meet and each of those people may or may not pass the message on. Third is the cluster

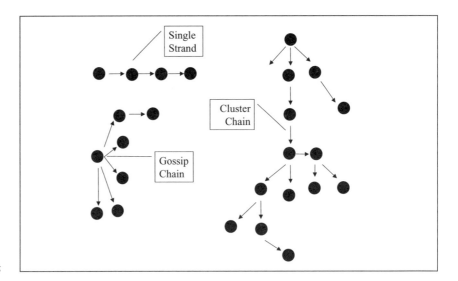

Single
Strand

Cluster
Chain

Gossip
Chain

FIGURE 1.1 *Grapevines*

chain which represents how one person tells selected others. One or some of those others will then pass on the information, once again, to selected others.

While managers cannot control the grapevine entirely, they do have a degree of control. By learning who key people are within a cluster chain, for example, a manager can ensure that those people receive the 'facts' to prevent rumours or to try to control interpretations of company actions. By having open communication channels managers can also position themselves to hear about rumours and inaccurate information to prevent them being passed on. The grapevine does not just carry inaccurate information, however. It carries information of all kinds and can be quite accurate when carrying facts. Interestingly, grapevine communication activity increases with increases in uncertainty and change within organizations.

Informal communications also occur within groups of employees who may get together outside of working hours. Informal groups are clusters of people within a company who share interests. For example, employees might get together for friendly inter-departmental football matches (or softball games in the US). Others might have a weekly poker or golf game, or may just meet occasionally at the local pub. In all of these examples topics related to the organization and what is happening in the company are inevitably discussed.

Informal communication networks can be very accurate sources of information. They can provide informal, low-cost information training for new employees. They can keep a large number of people informed and can do so very quickly. On the negative side, informal communication flows can distort information, are the source of rumour and innuendo, and can have a negative impact on motivation. A key feature of informal communications that can be both negative or positive is that messages received from the grapevine, for example, are considered as highly credible by those in the information chain. This is understandable given that generally rumours are received from friends or trusted colleagues (if you were not to be trusted you would not be told). This might particularly be the case if management is perceived to be highly self-serving or untrustworthy in its communications through the formal channels.

ORGANIZATIONAL STRUCTURE

Organizational structure is the formal organizing framework created to achieve the organization's goals. An example of a formal organizational structure which is often referred to as an organizational chart or organigram, can be seen in Figure 1.2. Remember that it is merely a representation of a formal structure. It is not a representation of the entire organizational structure, since there are, as we have seen, informal structures as well. What it does show is the formal, established pattern of relationships that *should* exist between departments, roles and individuals. How organizations are structured has implications for business communications. We will deal with those as we explore the structuring and bureaucratization of organizations.

Figure 1.2 not only represents a generic organizational structure, it also represents a bureaucracy. Bureaucracy is a social organizing and control system laid over a hierarchical organization structure. The German sociologist Max Weber studied bureaucracy in depth and identified it as not only one of the most efficient systems that could be instituted but he also saw it as a threat to basic liberties and humanity (Weber, 1947). In many ways he was

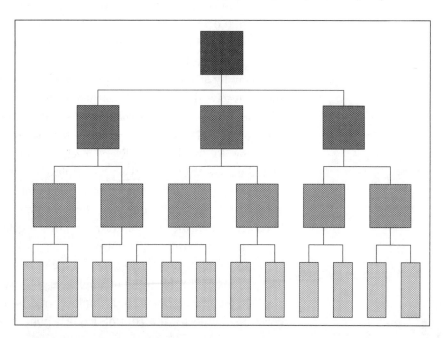

FIGURE 1.2

Bureaucratic organizational structures

right; bureaucracy has triumphed as the preferred organizing system and bureaucracies can be particularly dehumanizing places in which to work. What makes bureaucracies so efficient is the combination of the following six factors:

- division of labour

- hierarchy of authority

- uniform rules and policies

- standardized procedures

- structured career path and promotions based on merit

- impersonal relations.

Division of labour is defined as the way in which a company allocates people to functional organizational tasks and responsibilities in order to generate value. This means that the creation of products and services and the functions that support those activities (e.g. human resource management, procurement, etc.) are divided into specialized tasks which are then performed by people who do only that task. Compared to the situation of a craftsman in pre-industrial society, work in bureaucracies tends towards de-skilling. Instead of knowing the entire process each employee only knows a specialized part. The greater the division of labour, the greater the specialization.

Two kinds of division of labour are relevant: vertical and horizontal. Horizontal division of labour refers to division into functional tasks such as marketing, production, accounting and finance, etc. Vertical division of labour relates to the hierarchy of authority.

Hierarchy of authority refers to unity of command whereby any employee should receive direction and instruction from only one superior. Additionally, the principle of scalar chain means that the line of authority runs from superior to subordinate in a chain that stretches from the top of the hierarchy to the bottom. Every level is controlled by the immediately preceding level. Both of these principles (unity of command and scalar chain) are represented in the vertical division of labour shown in Figure 1.2. Vertical division of labour, therefore, is defined as the way in which bureaucracies distribute authority in the organization so that there is structured supervision and control.

Uniform rules and policies refers to the written rules set by management. The policies define the duties of employees and managers. Rules and policies also set out management and employee rights, especially with regard to governing authority and control. Explicit policies set out and define power relations which not only give managers legitimate authority to control, but also protect subordinates from power abuses of superiors.

Rules and policies work with other standardized procedures, such as standardized ways of manufacturing and assembling products. The goal in a bureaucracy, regardless of whether it produces products or services, is standardized output. In the tradition of scientific management developed in the early decades of the 20th century, bureaucracies seek to set up organizations in the image of machines (Morgan, 1986). Bureaucracies attempt as much as possible to standardize inputs, processes and, therefore, outputs.

Prior to the widespread development of bureaucracy, nepotism or favouritism was the basis for promotion. In bureaucracies there is a clear reward structure, salary structure and career path. Promotion is based on merit, especially in terms of technical competence. Bureaucracies originally promised lifetime careers in return for loyalty and rigorously fulfilling one's duties within the written rules and policies. In a bureaucracy, it is not the individual, but rather the role that takes on importance. As Figure 1.2 represents, bureaucratic relations ideally are based on and limited to the formal structure and its mapping of relations between specialized areas. People within those areas, therefore, have functional roles. In other words, people do not relate to Jane Smith as Jane Smith, they relate to her as a supervisor in the warehouse. Indeed, people are largely defined by their roles. Relationships are between roles – not people – and those relationships are impersonal, and unemotional.

Bureaucracies are very efficient. That is their attraction. The bureaucratic model is no longer used in many companies especially among firms that rely on multi-skilled, creative people for their competitive advantage. Still, bureaucracy is a part of all organizations and many of us continue to work in organizations that are quite heavily bureaucratized whether we work in the private sector, the public sector or in not-for-profit institutions. The implications of bureaucracy for communications remain highly relevant even in those organizations that are relatively low in terms of bureaucratization.

FORMAL COMMUNICATIONS IN BUREAUCRACIES

Just as the organizational structure has both vertical and horizontal divisions of labour, it has vertical and horizontal forms of communication. Figure 1.3 shows vertical and horizontal patterns of communication.

Vertical communication issues

Vertical communication refers to a communication that follows the chain of command of a bureaucratic organization (Figure 1.3). Of course, a vertical communication not only moves downwards through the hierarchy but also

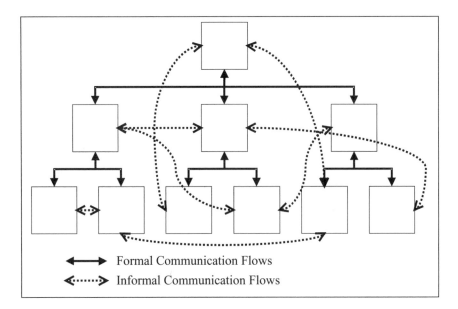

FIGURE 1.3 *Informal and formal communication flows*

⟷ Formal Communication Flows

⟵┈┈┈▷ Informal Communication Flows

can, and must, move upwards. Katz and Kahn (1966) identified five categories of downward communications:

- communication of organizational goals and mission
- task instructions and training (how)
- task rationale (why)
- communication about rules, policies, procedures
- performance and other feedback to subordinates.

Some of the basic assumptions of bureaucracy and organizing according to the machine metaphor are evident in these categories. It is assumed that tasks can be carried out by following systematic procedures and directives. However, as we discussed with informal communications, there are usually more task-related contingencies than can be anticipated by those who write the rules. The assumption is that information can be passed down the chain of command without distortion. Fisher (1993) identifies that information loss occurs and tends to increase with the distance that information has to travel down hierarchical levels. Figure 1.4 shows information loss using an inverted trapezoid. A message that begins with 100 per cent of its information intact, loses information content as it moves down the hierarchy. By the time it gets to the bottom, 50 per cent of the information has gone.

The effectiveness of downward communication is also a function of managers' span of control. Span of control refers to the number of subordinates that a manager directly oversees. This is represented in Figure 1.5

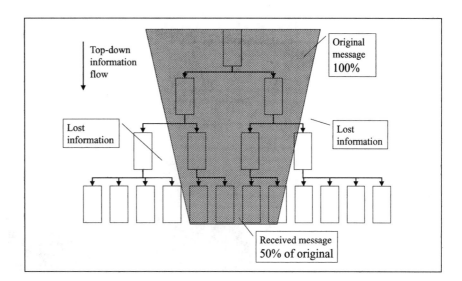

FIGURE 1.4 *Model of information loss*

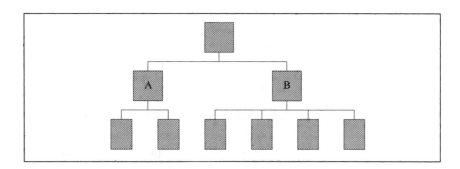

FIGURE 1.5 *Span of control*

where manager B has twice as many subordinates to supervise as manager A. Ideally a bureaucratic organization is structured so that a manager's span of control is as large as possible (therefore fewer managers and lower cost) without breaching the threshold of effective co-ordination, control and communication. It still remains, however, that the more subordinates a manager has to supervise, other things being equal, the greater the potential for ineffective communications.

Upward communication according to Katz and Kahn (1966) generally relates to subordinates' self-evaluation, problems with co-workers, comments regarding policies and procedures, and questions regarding tasks and task completion. The difference between downward and upward communication highlights the power differentials and the authority assumptions built into the bureaucratic model.

As a result of issues relating to span of control which, in turn, is related to organizational size (as measured by numbers of employees) organizations can be flat or tall (Figure 1.6). The height of organizational structures has clear implications for communications. All other things being equal, an organization that is flatter has the following communication advantages:

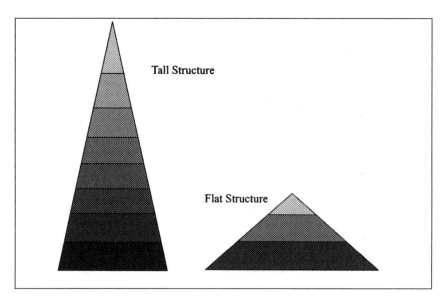

FIGURE 1.6 *Tall and flat organizational structures*

- faster communication – it will take less time for information to get down the hierarchy and to receive feedback

- more accurate communication – there will be less distortion the fewer the number of levels through which a message has to travel.

Horizontal communication issues

Horizontal communication refers to communication with colleagues and peers whose roles position them at the same hierarchical level of the organization. For example, the accounting and finance manager is engaging in horizontal communications when he or she is speaking with the manager of operations. Similarly, it is horizontal communication when a shopfloor worker in the manufacturing plant is talking on the telephone to a forklift driver in the warehouse.

Horizontal communication functions in a number of ways: between managers who are making inter-departmental decisions, for information sharing between divisions at many levels but especially among managers, for communications within committees and task forces. Horizontal communication is likely to be the dominant form of information exchange and negotiation between firms exploring or actually working in strategic alliances or other forms of inter-organizational relationship. Senior executives, when dealing with another company, expect to be dealing with others at their own level.

INTEGRATION AND INTEGRATING MECHANISMS

Division of labour is about dividing an organization's value-creating processes into pieces or chunks of specialized activity. When we divide an organization into divisions and departments that is precisely what we are doing – cutting it up. There also need to be mechanisms in organizations for keeping all the pieces working together. Division of labour is about dividing it up. Integration is about pulling it all together. One of the key tasks for organizations that wish to reap the benefits of both efficient bureaucratic structures and effective integration and communication is to strike a balance between divisions of labour and integration.

There are several integrating mechanisms which enable better communication and interaction between the parts of organizations (Galbraith and Kazanjian, 1986):

- direct contact
- integrating roles
- integrating departments
- liaison roles
- committees and task forces
- other organizational forms.

Direct contact between managers of different departments or divisions is one way to increase communication between those departments and divisions. By meeting occasionally they have the opportunity to discuss issues and interests that transcend departmental boundaries.

An integrating role is a senior management position usually held by an executive experienced in the issues and processes of two or more departments. The purpose of the position is to ensure communication and co-operation between departments. For example, there might be an integrating role linking production and processing functions in a large mining operation. Those fulfilling integrating roles are often responsible for leading task forces and teams from those departments.

In large, multi-divisional, or multi-national corporations, a whole department is sometimes established to perform the integrating role. As with an integrating role, integrating departments are responsible for co-ordination and communications at divisional level.

Rather than having one individual solely responsible for integration between departments as with the integrating roles, some organizations find it useful to select individuals within departments who liaise with each other from time to time. This improves communication especially if those who hold liaison roles do so for long periods of time.

Sometimes there is a particular problem within an organization that falls between departmental responsibilities but requires input from several departments. Temporary task forces and committees are often set up to handle these situations. Those on the committees have the responsibility of communicating to the task force the desires, issues and concerns of their departments and, in turn, report the committee's activities and decisions back to the department.

Finally, there are other organizational structures that enable better communications patterns to occur in response to different business environments. Organizations are not limited to a generic bureaucratic structure.

TYPES OF ORGANIZATIONAL STRUCTURES

The most familiar form of organizational structure is the functional design or U-form (unitary). The U-form (Figure 1.7) is similar to the generic bureaucratic structure that we have just discussed. U-forms have specialization and efficiency advantages but tend to encourage centralization, largely top-down communications, and limited or restrained relations between functional areas.

Usually as organizations grow in complexity they tend to adopt a divisional or M-form (for multi-divisional) structure. Figure 1.8 shows the M-form which is designed to focus organizational resources on specific areas.

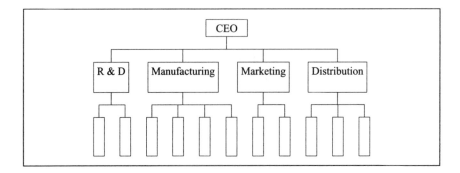

FIGURE 1.7 *U-form organizational structure*

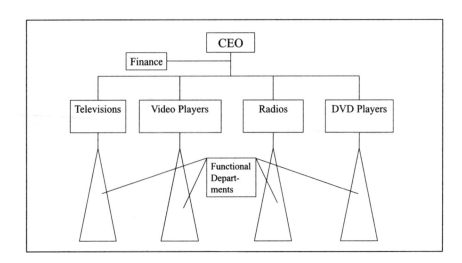

FIGURE 1.8 *M-form organizational structure*

M-forms allow better communication between functional areas which are duplicated in different divisions (except usually finance). Functional areas are then geared towards one single division. The breakdown by divisions could be based on a product, market, or technology.

Similar to an M-form structure is that of the holding company or H-form (Figure 1.9). In this example the company is organized into its different diversified businesses or strategic business units (SBUs). As with an M-form structure this enables the SBUs (divisions) to be focused within a particular industry, though communication difficulties as are identified for the U-form organization would remain with them in each SBU. The added communication element of the H-form organization is that generally the organization is structured so that there is no communication sharing or synergies between SBUs. Each SBU has full autonomy and is responsible solely for its own performance.

The matrix organization (Figure 1.10) is an attempt to combine the advantages of at least two organizational structures into one. Employees within the matrix are simultaneously members of both a functional department and a project team. Figure 1.10 represents part of the matrix organization at De Montfort University. As you can see, 'postgraduate programmes' has one or several members of each specialist academic department under the responsibility of the head of postgraduate studies. The Department of Corporate Strategy, for example, contains all of the academic staff in that department who are distributed amongst several programmes. The individual identified as 'A' on the matrix has, as do all others, two reporting relationships, i.e. two bosses. This is known as a multiple-command structure.

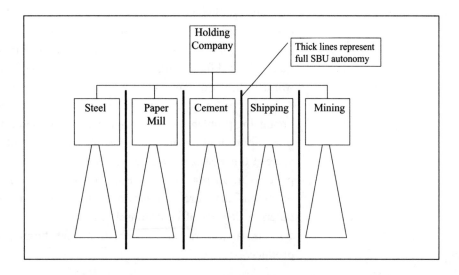

FIGURE 1.9 *H-form organizational structure*

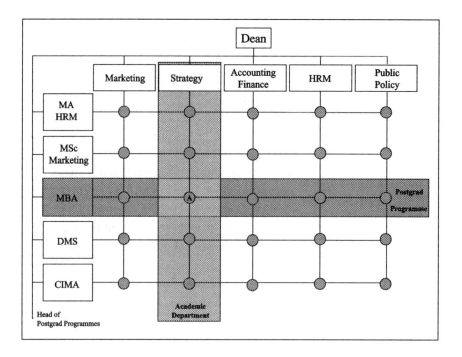

FIGURE 1.10 *Matrix structure*

The goal of the matrix structure is to enable quick and accurate communication and response to business environments that demand flexible and quick solutions. Matrix models were originally developed by firms in the electronics, aerospace and software industries. A matrix structure functions well given the types of people those industries needed to attract – professionals and other highly qualified specialists who tend to work best in flexible environments where they have high levels of autonomy. In essence every individual in the matrix is in an integrating role and is expected to communicate across programme or project and departmental lines. This can cause problems. Not everyone is capable of working for two bosses and communicating across overlapping structures. There is also the potential for increased conflict between the interests of departments and projects. It makes for a difficult communications environment, but when the structure works well, it can have substantial advantages.

Each kind of organizational structure solves some communication and organizing problems but may create others. Organizations need to adopt the most appropriate structure for communicating effectively and producing value at the least cost. Different structures generate different communication patterns in an organization. Even organizations with the same basic organizational structure will have variation in communication patterns and differing degrees of communication effectiveness. Organizations are social systems subject to all the variation that human societies and cultures produce.

ORGANIZATIONS ARE SOCIAL CONTEXTS

Organizations were defined in the opening section of this chapter as social entities. This simply means that they are constructed by people and are filled with people producing goods and services for people. Simple as this sounds, it has implications for communications.

Because organizations are composed of people, you can expect to find the whole range of human attributes in organizations – and the bigger the organization, the greater the variation. People have hopes, dreams, fears, biases, prejudices, strengths and weaknesses of all kinds. The whole range of human emotion and behaviour feeds into the structures of communication both within an organization and beyond its boundaries.

Perhaps even more important than the individual psychological attributes of people is social complexity. We have already discussed how people within organizations take on roles. A role is a social identity, not an individual one, yet people bring not only their individual psychological profiles to their roles, but also elements of their other social roles as well. For example, one person can have the following role identities: manager of marketing, friend, female, mother, sister, wife, aunt, Protestant, professional, Welsh, British, white, gourmet cook, Red Cross volunteer, bridge partner, aerobics instructor, MBA student, community activist, etc. At work, her predominant role will be that of marketing manager, but she will be influenced in her communications with others and her interpretations of others' messages by the multitude of social roles she carries. Precisely because organizations are social entities we deem it imperative to consider culture and other social systems in any discussion of communications.

ORGANIZATIONS ARE TECHNICAL CONTEXTS

Organizations are more than just social systems. They are also technical systems. Figure 1.11 illustrates the socio-technical model of organizations. Organizations create value by converting resources into products and services, but they do so through the convergence of social and technical systems.

Technical systems include all the technologies and processes used by the organization, e.g. machinery, management systems, communication systems, etc. The technical systems we are concerned with here are those that relate to communications. The main organizational technologies for communication are:

- IT systems

- telecommunications

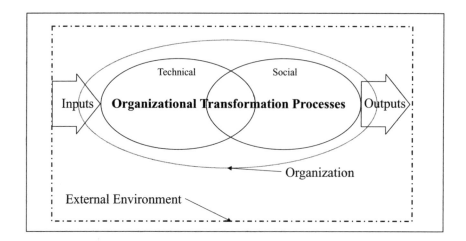

FIGURE 1.11

Organizations as

socio-technical

systems

- computer/communications networks

- internet.

IT is the acronym for information technology, which is the systems and related resources used by organizations to manage information. IT is not merely computers and computer software. Rather, it takes in the entire network of computers, storage devices, modems, servers, in-house specialists used to install and maintain the system, those who find and input the data, and those who interpret and organize the information. Part of the IT system at Wal-Mart (the giant US discount retailer) alerts the paper manufacturer Kimberly-Clark as soon as a toilet roll is sold at one of its checkouts, thus enabling the supplier to keep the product flowing to Wal-Mart's stores. In the UK, electronic point of sale (EPOS) systems in grocery chains like Tesco and Safeway enable management to see precisely what is selling where and when and to make decisions accordingly.   .

Other types of IT systems maintain student records and track their progress. Personnel files are stored on computers. Banks keep accounts, small businesses record invoicing and supplier payment systems, and even the person selling the fruit and vegetables at the local market has an IT system for recording sales and costs, though it might be a manual rather than an electronic system.

Telecommunications technology continues to advance rapidly and is becoming a major source of information exchange. Traditional telephones, mobile and cellular phones which can be used to receive email and the internet as well as telephone calls, FTP (file transfer protocol) sites and electronic bulletin boards, fax machines, voice mail and video-conferencing equipment are some of the technologies used everyday by organizations the world over. At De Montfort University MBA lectures are video-conferenced from Leicester in the UK to Kuala Lumpur in Malaysia, and video-conferencing is used by lecturers and administrators to co-ordinate activities among the university's distributed campus network.

Computers and telecommunications combine in multiple ways so that networked information systems not only enable people to communicate, but also permit people to 'talk' to their computers, and computers to 'talk' to computers for information exchange.

Finally, the internet is becoming indispensable for organizational communication. The internet is an unparalleled source of information and communication. Through the internet you can not only 'surf' for information but you can communicate with people anywhere in the world, put your writing, images, videos and sounds on web pages for the world to see, and in turn, see others'. Through the internet you can shop at the click of a button and this has opened up a whole new advertising and retailing universe. Internet bank accounts are almost totally electronic IT systems that enable you to save, transfer funds, set up direct debits, buy shares and unit trusts, borrow money and generally do everything that you could do in a branch without leaving home.

Students can learn on-line. They can communicate with their tutors or with friends, or 'go' to a chat room to talk in a virtual group situation. Quizzes can be answered on-line with the computer tracking your scores as you go. Lecture slides can be downloaded over the internet. Lecture materials may be posted on websites in the UK for students in South Africa, Malaysia, Singapore and Canada to download according to their own schedules and in the format they prefer.

Business to business (B2B) internet traffic accounts for the greatest volume of commercial transactions over the internet. Some automobile manufacturers, for example, will only buy from suppliers if they can buy on-line. Other supply chains are following their example and multi-divisional corporations are using the internet to purchase from each other as well as to transfer information.

Governments are using the internet to bring government closer to the people. Canada is one of the world leaders in this regard. The Community Access Program has been designed by Industry Canada to help establish access sites in 5000 rural and remote communities and up to 5000 access sites in urban communities by mid-2001. The internet allows Canadians to access federal, provincial and municipal information services. All schools and libraries are connected to the Internet. Even the not-for-profit sectors are on the Internet. In Canada over 10,000 not-for-profit and volunteer organizations are connected to the internet.

The UK is currently (2000) ranked about twelfth in the world (authors' research) in per capita internet usage with an estimated 18 million users in 2001. The UK government's aim, as set out in the 1998 Competitiveness

White Paper, is to help make the UK the best environment in the world for e-commerce. The UK government has set the following targets for 2002:

- 1.5 million small and medium-sized businesses connected to the digital marketplace

- 1 million small and medium-sized firms trading on-line

- UK small businesses should be at the level of the international best.

In the UK, in Canada and throughout the world, the internet is becoming a core technology for communications.

Communication and competitive advantage

Organizations that have effective communications are generally successful organizations. They communicate efficiently and thereby generate information and information flows at lower costs than their competitors. The savings translate into a cost advantage. Often these same firms have high-quality communications too. The result is that information is more clearly understood which allows managers and employees to work with better, more relevant information. In terms of competitive advantage this may mean better products and/or services and/or lower costs. Whenever organizational resources or processes, such as communications, are better-quality or lower-cost than competitors, the result is a competitive advantage and higher performance in terms of value creation (Figure 1.12).

Competitive advantage for organizations expressed this way seems relatively simple. Why is it, then, that only some organizations have a competitive advantage while the bulk of companies, for example, are only average or poor in performance? Everyone it seems pays lip service to the idea that communications are important. Business executives and commen-

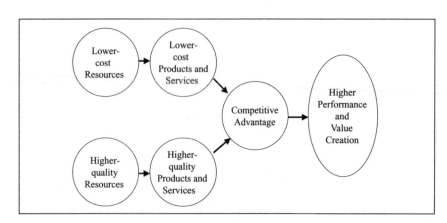

FIGURE 1.12 *Resources and competitive advantage*

tators agree that communication is highly valuable for organizations. Yet, communications is one of the more neglected areas of management. Good organizational communications are very rare. Where they exist they are very difficult to imitate. That combination of an organizational resource and process that is valuable, rare and inimitable is a powerful source of competitive advantage (Barney, 1997).

You will have seen some of the complexity of business communications in this introductory chapter. In the rest of the book, we provide practical strategies based on sound research for developing personal and organizational communication competencies. Study and learn these communication strategies and, armed with a solid understanding of culture which forms the context for and of communications, you will be well prepared to enjoy personal and organizational competitive advantage through superior business communications.

Discussion questions

1. Describe the link between culture and business communications.

2. What are some of the main types of organizational structures?

3. What is the impact of bureaucracy on organizational communications?

4. Discuss the advantages and disadvantages for business communications of companies' having a matrix structure.

5. Describe and discuss how superior business communications can lead to competitive advantage.

References

Barney, J. (1997) *Gaining and Sustaining Competitive Advantage*, Addison-Wesley, Harlow.

Davis, D. (1953) Management communication and the grapevine, *Harvard Business Review*, Sept.–Oct., 43–49.

Fisher, D. (1993) *Communication in Organizations*, West Publishing, St Paul, MN.

Galbraith, J. and Kazanjian, R. (1986) *Strategy Implementation: Structure, System and Process*, 2nd edn, West Publishing, St. Paul, MN.

Katz, D. and Kahn, R. (1966) *The Social Psychology of Organizations*, Wiley, New York.

Morgan, G. (1986) *Images of Organization*, Sage, London.

Weber, M. (1947) *The Theory of Social and Economic Organizations*, translated by A. Henderson and T. Parsons, Free Press, New York.

(Further reading)

Johnson, G. and Scholes, K. (1999) *Exploring Corporate Strategy*, 5th edn, Prentice Hall, Harlow.

Mintzberg, H. (1973) *The Nature of Managerial Work*, Harper and Row, New York.

Myers, P. (ed.) (1996) *Knowledge Management and Organizational Design*, Butterworth Heinemann, Oxford.

chapter two

Models and forms of communication

Introduction

IN THE last chapter we looked at how organizations are structured and the relationship between their structure and communication systems. Communication patterns in organizations may be formal or informal but all are based on a simple model of transmitting and receiving information. We begin this chapter by looking at variations on this basic communication model and the importance of information and interpretation in effective communication.

Communication can take many forms from face-to-face conversations to text messages on mobile phones, from gestures to clothing. In this chapter we will be looking at three general forms: oral, written and non-verbal. Whatever form communication takes its aim is to convey a message. For successful transmission of the message it is essential that all parties to the communication share understandings. Just as static on a radio can interfere with reception there are a number of potential forms of interference in any communication that can undermine the effective transmission of a message. The last section of this chapter deals with the most common barriers to successful communication and how to avoid them.

LEARNING OBJECTIVES

By the end of this chapter you should be able to:

- Describe basic models of communication
- Identify the difference between information and data

- Use feedback effectively

- Identify the different forms of communication

- Recognize barriers to communication and take action to overcome them

What is communication?

A manager's day typically involves telephone calls, and writing and receiving memos, facsimiles, e-mail and letters. It also includes attending meetings and reading or writing reports. Imagine a manager in different situations:

- privately rehearsing a presentation to be given later in the week

- dictating a letter into a tape-recorder

- providing detailed instructions to a salesperson by mobile phone and having parts of the information or instructions misunderstood because of a weak and intermittent telephone signal.

Which of these are communications? The first is not, because the manager is merely rehearsing and is not talking to another person (though when the presentation is actually given it will be a communication). The second is a communication since the manager is speaking to the person who will be typing the letter as well as communicating with the person to whom the letter will be addressed. But what about the third? Even though the manager's instructions may have been misunderstood communication still occurs.

Communication is the process of transmitting information from one person to another (Weick and Browning, 1986). It is important, however, that the information is understood. In the third example (above), while there is communication, there is no *effective* communication. **Effective communication** means that the information is received as accurately in terms of content and meaning as intended by the sender.

Information and data

The concept of effective communication highlights the difference between data and information. **Data** are raw facts and figures defined within a narrow context. For example, the fact that a company has 23 small competitors within a region is an item of data. What this means to management – i.e. the information interpreted from the data – is that their company is most likely operating within a context characterized as fragmented and highly competitive, and is probably in a growing market. This is information. **Information** is data in a meaningful form.

Imagine the following scenario:

You are driving in your car and realize you are lost. You spot a man walking down the road, pull up beside him and ask, 'Excuse me, can you help me? I don't know where I am.' He replies, 'You are in a car parked approximately two metres off the centre-line of the road and facing west. You are between 40 and 42 degrees North latitude, and between 58 and 60 degrees West longitude.' 'Thank you', you say, 'I am sure everything you have told me is technically correct, but I have no idea what to make of it, and the fact is I am still lost.'

In the scenario you sought information but received data. What you really needed was some information that was meaningful in the context of being lost and needing to find your way. We will talk in more depth about meaning later in the book but as you can see, in communication, meaning and context are highly important. Without meaning (or interpretation), information and data are of little use.

Even information that is meaningful can vary widely in its usefulness. Information is most useful when it is:

- accurate

- timely

- complete

- relevant.

Accuracy refers to the reliability and validity of information: in other words how reliable is the source of your information and how certain can you be that it is valid. Managers who act on inaccurate information can cause huge losses to their organizations. For example, a Canadian synthetic rubber company planned to build a factory in the US to produce components for the automobile industry. They hired a consulting firm to assess the market and were told that a Japanese firm which was the industry leader already had plans to build just such a plant. The Canadian firm changed their plans and invested their capital elsewhere. Later they discovered that although the Japanese firm had made enquiries about building a US plant, they had decided against it. A European firm, recognizing the gap in the market, took the opportunity instead and gained substantial market share as a result. The Canadian firm acted on information that was not accurate.

For information to be timely does not necessarily mean that it must arrive quickly – although in many cases speed is important – it means that information needs to arrive when it is needed. A stockbroker, for example, who does a high volume of stock trades every hour, needs instant information on the price of a company's stock to make the best decisions quickly for buying and selling. A company that is seeking to buy out another company needs the same information on stock values but not minute by minute. It needs to look at the variations in stock price, among other measures, over a long time to see if the company has good potential for take-over. What constitutes timely information is context-dependent.

Complete information may not be possible because people can never know everything about everything or even everything about almost anything. Information must be complete enough, however, that decisions can be made with reference to a picture of reality that is not too distorted. A UK electronics wholesaler seized the opportunity to buy video players at a very low price from an overseas producer. When the goods arrived it was discovered that while they had all the performance features claimed, the players were NTSC-standard and could not be used by UK consumers whose televisions are on a different (PAL) standard. The information on which the firm acted was incomplete, based only on price and performance rather than compatibility. With more complete information they would not have made the purchase.

Relevance is defined according to particular contexts. Information that is relevant in one situation or for one manager may be irrelevant in another situation or for another manager. Information regarding overseas expansion possibilities in Indonesia for a small, cash-strapped UK firm may be information that is not particularly relevant. For another firm with excess profits that cannot be used for organic growth in its home market, information about overseas opportunities in Indonesia may be very relevant.

Information that is accurate, timely, complete and relevant greatly enhances the effectiveness of decision-making. Effective communication must contain useful information. In business communications we can say that at a general level managers are interested in communication that contains useful information. In high-paced business environments, communication must be effective. It must perform and generate the outcomes managers and their organizations need. Before you can understand how to generate high-performing, effective communications, you must understand what communication is and how it works.

Communication models

Communication is a process, and like most processes it can be usefully modelled. Indeed, generating a model often helps in thinking about and understanding processes and systems. Communications in organizations can

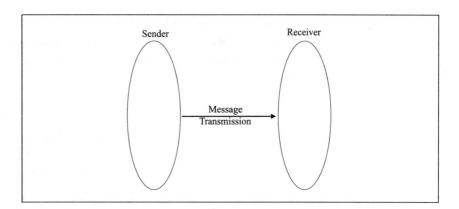

FIGURE 2.1 *Simple communication model*

take many forms but each instance or example of communication can be described in terms of the essential basic model of communication (Figure 2.1). In this model the sender transmits a message to the receiver. Figure 2.1 is a model of one way communication and represents the first element of the communication process. However, communication involves more than just the sender.

The communication process begins when the sender formulates an idea (Figure 2.2) or thinks of something to say. The idea is then encoded or transformed into meaningful symbols (symbols and language are discussed in greater detail in Chapter Three). For example, a person might be thinking of a small, soft-furred, four-legged domesticated mammal and speak or write the word 'cat'. Turning the formulated thoughts into spoken or written words constitutes **encoding**. Words are, therefore, an example of a code into which thoughts are encoded. Thoughts and ideas have to be in some form of code to form transmittable messages. These encoded messages (e.g. words which are the code or symbols for the thoughts) are then transmitted via voice, letter, e-mail, telephone or some other channel to the receiver.

Getting the message from the sender to the receiver is critical. Unless the communication goes from one person to another (or others) there is no communication. How does a message get from sender to receiver? Messages

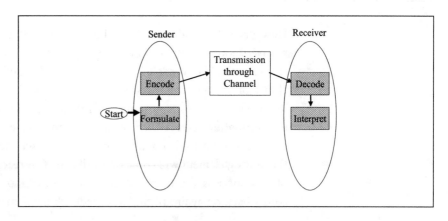

FIGURE 2.2

Communication model

travel via a channel. **Channel** refers to the particular technology or method used to get the message to the receiver. Major communication channels are letters, e-mail, face-to-face conversation, telephone, fax, newspapers, brochures, film, video, radio, television, websites and posters.

Another term that you will come across in communication theory is 'medium' or 'media' in the plural. Medium is not the same as channel in a communications context. **Medium** or **code** refers to the way in which a message is encoded. Thoughts can be translated into many codes or media, e.g. spoken or written words, other sounds, colours, images, smells, textures or any number of these in combination. You will be familiar with the word 'media' used in everyday language to refer to (usually commercial) mass communications such as television, radio, newspapers. Be careful not to confuse the two uses of the word. What most people call 'media' are what communication theorists refer to as 'channels'. To avoid confusion, rather than use 'media' we will instead use 'codes' (e.g. words) and 'channels' (e.g. television).

The sender sends a message (an idea in code) which is then transmitted via a channel to the receiver. Once the message gets from the sender to the receiver, the message has to be understood. Understanding occurs when the receiver decodes the message (Figure 2.2). **Decoding** is the act of interpreting the encoded message whereby meaning is attributed to and extracted from the symbols (sounds, words) so that the message is meaningful. Communication has occurred when the message is received and some degree of understanding occurs. This is not to say that the message as understood by the receiver has the same meaning as the sender intended. Indeed, the difference between intended and understood messages is partly how we define whether communication is effective or not. The greater the degree of shared meaning between the sent message and the received message, the more effective is the communication.

FEEDBACK AND NOISE

How does the sender know if the message was understood? How do the receivers know if their understanding of the message is the same as the sender intended? Feedback helps both sender and receiver determine the clarity of the message. **Feedback** is a response from the receiver. The term 'feedback' comes to communication theory from cybernetics where it refers to information required for control systems. For example, an oven thermometer utilizes a feedback mechanism. If you set the temperature to 200 °C the heating element will come on until 200 °C is reached and then it will shut off. As soon as the temperature drops below 200 °C, the heating element comes back on again. In this way feedback helps maintain some congruence between the desired state (in this case 200 °C) and the current state (more than or less than 200 °C). Similarly, in communication, feedback provides the opportunity to ensure that communication is effective by narrowing the difference between the intended meanings of sent messages and the interpreted meanings of received messages.

With feedback, the process becomes a conversation or two-way communication. Of course, once a message is received, decoded and interpreted, and a reply is formulated, the positions of sender and receiver are reversed. The receiver, having received the message, then becomes the sender by formulating, encoding and transmitting a reply. Figure 2.3 represents this process of a two-way communication.

There is another element in Figure 2.3 that is not in the previous models. That element is 'noise'. Think about attempting to have a conversation at a loud party. You cannot make your message heard and cannot hear the reply or only bits and pieces of it because of the noise from the party. But audio noise in speaking situations is not the only kind of noise in a system. **Noise** is anything that interrupts or distorts a message. Noise can be technological or human problems such as interruptions or gaps in mobile phone communications, faded photocopies or poorly printed documents, unattractive colours that 'turn off' your intended audience so that they do not read your brochure, or poor etiquette that people interpret as lack of credibility so they do not listen to what you have to say. Noise can even be having the person to whom you are speaking being called away before you have finished your conversation. Anything that disrupts the transmission and receipt of your encoded message with its intended meaning intact is noise. You can see from Figure 2.3 that noise can occur at many places in the communication process.

Since all messages are affected by noise, it is usually a good idea to put your message across using multiple channels where appropriate. Remember that people respond differently to different codes. Some people learn better

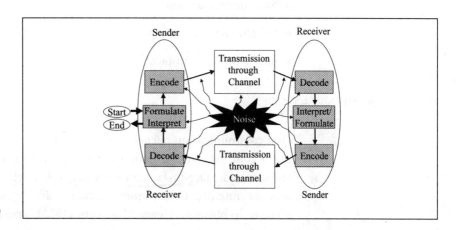

FIGURE 2.3 *Complete communication model*

from words or text than from pictures while for others pictures are more effective. Different codes and channels can be used to reinforce a message. Using different ways to send your message also may help it to be understood better. In a job interview you will be more successful if you not only say the right things, but also dress appropriately and have a professional c.v. (curriculum vitae) to present to the interviewer. Your message (hire me) will then be encoded in different codes: spoken words (saying the right things), written words (having a professional c.v.), clothing (wearing the appropriate style and colour), grooming (being clean and neat), body language (using eye contact and a firm handshake) and overall appearance (looking like the person for the job). It will also be transmitted through different channels, such as oral and written communication. If the message is consistent across all the codes and channels used, you will be strongly reinforcing your message.

For more successful communication, reinforce your message by:

- encoding your message using multiple codes (e.g. you might use pictures, words and sounds on a web page)

- transmitting your message using multiple channels (e.g. use face-to-face, telephone, letter).

Reinforcing your message thus involves multiple codes and channels which also means that it can take different forms.

Forms of communication

Each form of communication may rely on different codes and may be amenable to certain channels. In this section we discuss the following forms of communication:

- oral communication

- written communication

- non-verbal communication.

ORAL COMMUNICATION

Oral communication refers to conversations in which the spoken word is the major code for communication. Common channels for oral communication are telephone, face-to-face conversation, video, television, radio and sound over the internet. Oral communication is an important form of communication in business. Henry Mintzberg (1973), one of the world's foremost business strategists, discovered from his research that managers spend between 50 and 90 per cent of their time talking.

Oral communication has many advantages over other forms of communication. The primary advantage is that through conversation, questions and answers, people can receive immediate feedback and gauge if they are being understood. They can also ascertain that they are understanding others' messages. In addition, when oral communication is face-to-face, people can key in on symbolic and non-verbal communications (discussed below) such as facial expressions and body language which enables them to make a judgement about whether or not they should believe what they hear.

Little technology is involved in talking face-to-face. You do not need pen and paper, a computer, a printer or a telephone, for example. People are taught to speak from the moment they are born and most do it well enough that they really do not need to plan what they have to say ahead of time if the conversation is relatively informal. More formal face-to-face communication can benefit from a planned, strategic approach, but even if people have no formal communication training, most can probably hold a conversation without too much planning or effort. Talking for most of us is relatively easy and is assumed to be a rather unremarkable, daily activity.

Oral communication has disadvantages though. Precisely because talking is so easy, whether it is face-to-face or through a technological channel (e.g. telephone), people often do not think deeply enough about their message before delivering it. 'They put their mouth in motion before their brain is in gear' is a common expression related to the propensity to speak without thinking. The result is that sometimes people 'give away' more than they intend when speaking, or say things that they later regret. The sender might not consider carefully enough what meaning particular words might have for the receiver, which may result in misunderstandings. There are opportunities for other noise in an oral communication process, too. Words can be spoken but be unheard, telephone lines or mobile connections can be intermittent in quality and voice transmission is not perfect. The speaker might leave out some important details or answer a query without having enough time to determine the best response. Do you ever leave a conversation only to suddenly think of something you should have said?

The receiver might also forget or even intentionally 'forget' some of your message. In oral communication there is no permanent record, so both parties to the conversation have to rely on memory. Finally, although most of us are relatively comfortable speaking with our friends or even one-to-one with strangers, most people get nervous if they have to speak to large groups even if those groups are made up of family and friends rather than strangers. The stress of giving an oral presentation can negatively affect the quality and reception of your message.

WRITTEN COMMUNICATION

Written communication offers some advantages over oral communication. People tend to think more about what they put in writing than what they say when speaking. This is partly because, once written, the communication (e.g. the letter or fax) is a permanent record. Generally more time is spent preparing a letter. The sender gathers the information for the letter in an organized way and then can draft and re-draft the letter to get the wording just right. Similarly, the receiver can spend time digesting the information, re-read it and refer to it as many times as necessary. When the message has important details or it needs to be carefully considered by the receiver, the message generally takes the form of written correspondence.

Of course, written communication has its disadvantages too. Writing takes time. Think of the process of writing a letter, for example. The letter might be dictated, then typed, mailed, delivered, directed to the appropriate person within the organization, opened and, finally, read. E-mail is considerably faster, but it too takes more time than talking. Written feedback from your message can, therefore, take minutes (if you are lucky and the recipient gets your e-mail and replies instantly) to several days if it is a letter. Written communication has longer feedback times, is more difficult to generate and involves some kind of technology (even if only pen and paper) for transmission, whereas oral communication avoids these disadvantages.

At certain times it is better to use written rather than oral communication. When and why you would use one rather than the other or some combination of both will be discussed in greater detail in later chapters, as will how to produce various forms of written communications.

NON-VERBAL COMMUNICATIONS

Non-verbal communication tends to be under-appreciated by those not trained in business communications. Yet, non-verbal messages are given greater importance by receivers than written and spoken communication. **Non-verbal communication** refers to all intended and unintended meanings that are not in the form of written or spoken words (Hamilton, Parker and Smith 1982). Non-verbal communication refers, therefore, to such things as facial expression, eye contact, gestures, clothing and personal appearance, distance, personal space and tone of voice.

The more senses involved in the communication, the more impact the communication will have. Reading has least impact since it involves only sight whereas seeing and hearing together have a much greater impact. What we see, rather than what we hear, however, holds the most meaning. In fact, because seeing involves so much more neural processing, it greatly overrides what is heard. When seeing someone we note their body language, colour and style of clothing, body shape, size, hair colour, tone and inflection of voice and other physical details. After hearing a speaker, we will remember the appearance of the speaker more than the speaker's message unless the message has been strongly reinforced by other visual means.

Non-verbal communication is extremely powerful. Psychologist Albert Mehrabian (1968, 1971) suggests that the non-verbal parts of a message may outweigh the actual meaning of the words spoken. Mehrabian breaks a message into three components:

- verbal, meaning the words themselves

- vocal, meaning the tone in which the words are spoken

- facial, referring to the facial expression or body language accompanying the words.

The impact of each component is represented graphically in Figure 2.4. Only 10 per cent weighting is given to the actual words spoken, whereas 40 per cent is for tone of voice and 50 per cent is for facial expression and other body language.

The impact of non-verbal coding is so strong that when the tone of voice or body language contradicts the words spoken, the person(s) being addressed will believe the message delivered by the non-verbal cues rather than the actual words spoken. Try saying to someone that they have done a 'good job' with a scowl on your face or with an angry tone of voice. People will respond as if they do not believe what you are saying. Such responses indicate that your audience is confused as to your real meaning and may tend to believe the non-verbal cues rather than your words.

There are a number of categories into which we group the various components of non-verbal codes:

- paralanguage

- facial expressions

FIGURE 2.4 *Weighting of communication components*

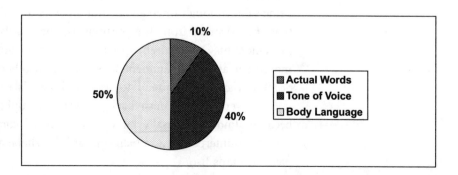

10%

50%

40%

- Actual Words
- Tone of Voice
- Body Language

- kinesics or 'body language'

- visual behaviour such as eye contact

Paralanguage refers to vocalizations (other than words) and pauses associated with speech, such as pitch, volume (loud or soft), intensity and hardness, or what people generally refer to as 'tone of voice'. Interruptions such as 'hmmm' or 'uh-uh' plus unfilled pauses and hesitations are also components of paralanguage. Any vocal noise that has no formal meaningful content qualifies for this category of non-verbal communication. Paralanguage may indicate emotions, doubt, reluctance to respond, indecision, uncertainty, or may simply be a cultural idiom of speech. Short utterances attached to the ends of sentences, for example, vary culturally. Canadians sometimes end a sentence with 'eh', where Malaysians may do the same with 'lal'. While these sentence endings may seem to hold little meaning, they do signal group identity or other social categories. Some paralanguage such as tone can provide depth of emotional meaning such as 'I am happy (or angry) with you'.

Facial language consists of facial movements, such as raised eye-brows, closed or half-closed eyes, flaring of the nostrils, the position of the mouth or the particular way in which people configure (often unconsciously) the muscles of their faces, including a totally relaxed expression. Meaning is conveyed with facial expression. A smile, for example, conveys meaning and while it is difficult to describe precisely what a smile is, it is recognizable as a smile. Seven primary emotions are expressed by the face: happiness, surprise, fear, sadness, anger, disgust–contempt and interest. Good actors can feign these emotions by making their faces express emotion, even if they do not feel it. But usually such a deception cannot be sustained except by particularly gifted actors. In addition to the face presenting a particular emotion, body language must also support the presented emotion to be believed.

Kinesics, or body language, is composed of a wide variety of signals. Body movements or positions tend to be more diffuse in meaning than facial language and therefore may be harder to read. Hand movements are particularly rich in meaning when they are used to emphasize what is being said, although when giving oral presentations they may be overused so that they distract from the meaning of the words. Also, excessive hand movement may be culturally specific, i.e. some cultures use much more hand movement as accompaniment to speech than others. People of British or Scandinavian ancestry tend to use hand signals less often than those of Italian, French or Spanish backgrounds. The uplifted middle finger has become almost universally known as a sign of contempt but has similar cultural counterparts, e.g. a palm-upwards 'V' shape made by the fingers or a palm-upwards fist.

Caution should be used in interpreting kinesics, since many are culturally specific and those cultural differences may lead to misinterpretation. Men kissing each other's cheeks in public means something different in Moscow and in San Francisco, for example, so you need to learn about other cultures to know what is appropriate in different cultural contexts. Similarly, a 'thumbs-up' signal in the US means 'okay', while in some Eastern European countries it can be considered rude and insulting.

Most body language, however, is more subtle. Crossed arms may indicate reservation or defensiveness. Leaning forward slightly while conversing may indicate interest or liking, as do signs of alertness and attentiveness in the face and body. Body language is powerful and tends to be given greater weight than words in conversations. Consider a manager whose words are 'I am open to your ideas', but said from too great a distance, with arms and legs crossed, and the face turned slightly away from the receiver. The receiver will think the manager is not sincere. The body language is saying something different from the words.

People tend to stand closer to each other when they have an intimate relationship than when they do not. Around each person is an invisible 'bubble' of space which expands and contracts depending on a number of variables: the relationship to the other person, emotional state, cultural background and the activity being performed. This is known as personal space. Personal space is a form of territory. People with an intimate relationship – such as parent and child – tend to sit or stand closer together than they would when with others. Formal relationships – e.g. with a bank manager – call for greater distance or larger 'bubbles' of personal space.

We tend to unconsciously adjust our position relative to others depending upon the variables. If someone is standing too close, we tend to unconsciously step backwards to regain that comfortable bubble. If the other person is too far away people tend to step forward or lean forward in order to regain the appropriate space. We do not like those who are not close in terms of our relationship with them to come too close spatially. Few people are allowed to penetrate our mobile personal space and then only for short periods of time. Changes in personal space brought about by cramped quarters or crowding cause people to feel uncomfortable or aggressive.

There are cultural differences in personal space expectations too. In northern Europe, the bubbles are quite large and people keep their distance. In southern France, Italy, Greece and Spain, the bubbles are smaller, so that the distance that is perceived as intimate in the north can overlap normal conversational distance in the south. When people from markedly different cultures (in terms of personal space expectations) are having a conversation, it is interesting to watch as one person takes a step backwards to regain their personal space only to have the other step forward to regain what is for them the appropriate distance. Unless one or the other consciously forces themself to stop, the conversation ends up being a mobile one as each participant 'chases' the other around the room.

In some societies, visual behaviour such as eye contact between strangers or mere acquaintances that is too direct or prolonged is offensive, particularly between the sexes. It is often socially improper in some cultures for those of different socio-economic status or gender to look each other in the eye, though such a cultural prohibition may work in one direction only, e.g. superiors may look subordinates in the eye, but not *vice versa*. Making eye contact is particularly advantageous in some situations. Giving an oral presentation, being interviewed or attempting to get someone's attention are all appropriate situations for eye contact in Western European countries. However, numerous factors may be involved, making it difficult to know what is appropriate eye contact outside of one's own culture. Direct and prolonged eye contact that is comfortable for both participants usually indicates mutual liking or respect. On the other hand, eye contact that results in the glance being averted, or discomfort being felt by one or both participants, will often indicate anger, aggression, disliking or suspicion.

There is no universal guidebook to non-verbal communication that would allow us to definitively interpret every sign that confronts us. The complex nature of non-verbal communication, plus its lack of universality, requires careful and prolonged observation and study. On the other hand, it is relatively easy to learn the non-verbal repertoire of those with whom we have direct and frequent social contact. As managers within a particular social context, the number of individuals whose non-verbal vocabulary you will need to learn will be relatively small. Observe carefully what non-verbal signs those around you tend to use. If necessary, ask what they are feeling (if the circumstances allow such intimacy) when they engage in particular behaviour. You may find that often people's body language is tacit. Those you ask may not even be aware that they are communicating their feelings with their body language.

Barriers to communication

Barriers to communication include anything that prevents a message from being received or understood. Barriers are, therefore, synonymous in many ways with noise (Figure 2.3) though technological noise (e.g. static on telephone lines, etc.) is less of a barrier and more of an obstacle. A technological problem does not usually stop communication, though it may block it temporarily. Technological problems are also perhaps the easiest problems to solve. When equipment fails, is unsuited to the task for which it is used, or when the problem is as simple as an incorrect telephone number, this can usually be quickly identified and remedied. Technological problems are, therefore, a form of noise but they are an obstacle rather than a barrier to communication.

Barriers are usually of human rather than technological origin. Human barriers are often less visible but generally more consequential. In this section we identify and focus on human barriers as a particular subset of noise of which managers need to be particularly aware. The barriers we focus on are:

- socio-cultural barriers

- psychological barriers

- organizational barriers.

SOCIO-CULTURAL BARRIERS

Communication always involves other people. As you will see in Chapter Three, culture is shared. An individual can be a carrier of culture but one person cannot create culture. Culture is a group or social phenomenon.

Culture is powerful. The language we use, the food we eat and how we eat it, how we dress, what we believe and so on, are all powerful cultural traits. We accept them as if they were non-confrontable and non-debatable. We implicitly believe in our culture and generally conform to its tenets. Culture is critically important to communication and will be covered in some depth in Chapter Three. For now, it is enough to know that culture which occurs at national, ethnic, regional and even organizational levels (the latter as corporate or organizational culture) can be a barrier to communication precisely because culture is both powerful and defining of groups.

By participating in a culture we are conforming to social norms, whether implicitly or explicitly. **Social norms** are tacit or informal 'rules' about what is done how, when, where, and by whom. For example, it is a social norm that in public restaurants we sit on chairs to eat at a table rather than sit on the floor or sit on the table. We also have norms about communication, e.g. gestures, the meaning of colour, tone of speech and the meanings of symbols. What is interesting from a communications perspective is that not only are social norms and cultural traits essential because they enable better communication, but also that these same norms and traits can be barriers to communication. The key socio-cultural elements that may be barriers are:

- groupthink

- conflicting values and beliefs

- stereotyping and ethnocentrism

- language and jargon.

Groupthink

Groupthink is the social phenomenon which occurs when group behaviour dominates and stifles the decision-making process (Janis 1982). It occurs when social norms or a group's desire for consensus overwhelms its desire to reach decisions that are in its best interest. It is what happens when shared values and conformity get out of control. Groupthink is a major problem in business, where people work extensively in groups and teams. Being aware of the key elements of groupthink can help you to recognize it and avoid it.

Groupthink is characterized by:

1. Similarity and hidden differences. Group members over-communicate or emphasize their similarities in beliefs and values while, at the same time, hiding or under-communicating their differences. This results in the appearance of tight similarity within the group.

2. Reliance on shared rationalizations. The group develops and maintains strong shared beliefs without questioning their accuracy or their underlying assumptions. Rather than recognizing some management or strategic error to explain failure, the group will rationalize or blame external forces.

3. Collective patterns of defensive avoidance. Defensive avoidance means that the group collectively avoids or refuses to confront any issue or information that threatens to challenge their shared views or decisions.

4. Lack of vigilance. One way that groups avoid having to confront contradictory evidence to decisions is through lack of vigilance. Group members simply stop looking for more information, and even ignore it when it is presented to them.

5. Suppression of worrisome defects. All groups, leaders and organizations have weaknesses. When groupthink is operating, such defects are specifically suppressed. This functions to maintain the appearance of group similarity and collective identity.

6. Unwarranted optimism. While optimism and enthusiasm are generally helpful for organizations, unwarranted optimism may be detrimental. If an organization does not have the competencies or the resources, or the strategies or other elements necessary for success, then overly enthusiastic optimism merely sets the organization up for debilitating, demoralizing defeat. Groupthink is often characterized by an optimism that functions more to impress other group members than to encourage the organization in its efforts.

7. Sloganistic thinking. Slogans are usually part of the optimism cited above. When management begins to think in terms of its own slogans or in clichés, it prevents analysis. Slogans trade upon shared values and ideas.

Since the ideas are shared and encapsulated in slogans, there is often no new thinking involved. This is particularly dangerous when organizations' environments are changing.

Conflicting values and beliefs
Culture is based on shared beliefs and values. When communication occurs across cultural boundaries, the potential for misunderstanding is magnified. Cultural and social norms are so ingrained that people act upon them without being consciously aware of doing so. When cross-cultural business ventures fail, the participants are often unable to understand why. It is usually a communication failure stemming from a lack of knowledge about each other's basic values and norms. In many cases deeply held values may have unknowingly been violated, leading to tension and conflict. In some cultures a successful business relationship is always preceded by the development of personal relationships, whereas in others it is strictly a commercial transaction. Organizations need to ensure they are familiar with potential cultural differences before attempting to do business across cultures (Chapter Twelve). Knowing the values, beliefs and norms of the other culture can avoid communication problems that could have serious consequences.

Stereotyping and ethnocentrism
There is a difference between being aware of another culture's beliefs and values and stereotyping all members of that culture based on your assumptions about them. **Stereotyping** is the attempt to predict people's behaviour based on their membership of a particular group. Stereotyping tends to be associated with superficial behaviours and inaccurate information rather than deeply held beliefs and norms. Stereotyping is a barrier to communication because it prevents people from being seen as individuals and their messages being heard. Stereotyping is dangerous. It can lead to prejudice, discrimination and racism. Make certain your communications are not influenced by stereotyping.

Ethnocentrism is related to stereotyping. Ethnocentric people see their own culture as the only valid one and find all others lacking by comparison. They measure all others by the standards of their own culture, which they believe to be superior. Like stereotyping, ethnocentrism is a breeding ground for prejudice and discrimination. Even in their mildest form communications with an ethnocentric bias are patronizing and condescending. Avoid them.

Language and jargon
Language can create barriers to communication in several ways. The most obvious is trying to communicate when there is a major language difference between the receiver and the transmitter of the message. As you will see in Chapter Three language is a means of encoding meaning that is culturally

specific. Anyone who can speak more than one language is aware that translation is not a straightforward process. Idiomatic expressions in a language do not easily translate and often lead to miscommunication.

Language can be a barrier to communication even when both parties speak the same language. Status and class differences result in different usage of language that is often the means of identifying or excluding groups of people. Jargon can serve the same purpose. Many professions such as engineering or medicine, for example, have their own jargon which serves to mark the boundary between professionals and their clients. Jargon tends to signal inclusivity, or who is an insider, and exclusivity, who is an outsider. For effective business communication avoid technical and scientific jargon where possible.

PSYCHOLOGICAL BARRIERS

Psychological barriers are those relating to the individual and the individual's mental and emotional state. Key psychological barriers are:

- filtering

- perceptions

- faulty memory

- poor listening skills

- emotional interference.

Filtering

People tend to hear what they want to hear and see what they want to see. People have differing degrees of attention. Some are more open to new ideas and information and see more than others. We are often unaware of our selective bias. At Beacon Research Associates, a mid-sized social survey company, leaders of each research team were informed by letter of their budget allocations twice a year. When the project manager received his allocation, he scanned the letter, took note of the amount of his budget and promptly filed the letter. What he did not notice was the paragraph which stated that the research allowance had to be used up in this budget period (within six months). Any surplus amount could not be carried forward into the next period. The manager selected from all of the information in the letter only the data in which he was interested – his budget allocation – and filtered out the rest. The result was that six months later he was very surprised to learn that the balance of his budget funds was recalled, which put severe pressure on some projects.

Often our filters and biases are a result of personal value systems or our cultural backgrounds. The key to avoiding filtering problems is to listen carefully, to read carefully and to be aware that we all have a tendency to be selective about the information and data with which we are confronted.

We are constantly bombarded with so much information that we cannot hope to process it all, so some amount of selectivity is always required. We are all limited by our cognitive powers. Indeed few, if any of us, could handle such a volume of information and data. This is referred to as **bounded rationality** (Simon 1962) and is caused by:

- limited time and other resources for collecting information

- differing expectations of managers and others regarding what constitutes relevant information

- limited ability to understand, process and use large amounts of information.

Given bounded rationality, business people often tend to rely on experience, tradition and 'rules of thumb' for selecting information and making decisions. This is not only the way that many business decisions are taken, but it is often the only way that people can make sense of a complex and chaotic world. Even so, we can all improve our engagement with information by knowing about bounded rationality, being sensitive to our filters and biases, and being more open to new ideas.

Perceptions

Like our filtering systems we each have our perceptions of how we view the world. We choose our friends because they tend to think like us, act like us, believe the things in which we believe and do the kinds of things we do. We often are not even aware that our perceptions influence so many areas of our life. We have perceptions of reality that we trust and we behave according to those beliefs which, in turn, influence our behaviour. We often do not realize that we filter out information that conflicts with our perceptions of the world. Our perceptions and filtering systems also affect how we communicate, including how we encode and decode messages.

Our perceptions can be barriers to communication. We can refuse to acknowledge or attend to what is being communicated because we have preconceived ideas about its relevance to our lives. When e-mail was being introduced to businesses people often would not use it because they 'knew' that computers were complicated and they 'knew' that they could not learn to use them. Computers and e-mail are now commonplace and no longer require a high degree of specialized knowledge to run most programs. E-mail is being readily adopted by many people who originally were predisposed to resist it. They are now part of a new world of communication and no longer perceive computers as outside their experience.

Faulty memory

If you do not remember what has been communicated to you, the communication is incomplete or ineffective. Memory plays an important role, therefore, in successful communication. We never actually lose what we have once experienced through action, hearing, reading, smelling or touching, though we may be unable to access those memories. Good memory skills can be learned and should be practised if you want to become an effective communicator.

Firstly, you have to focus your attention on the information you want to remember. You need to select it from amongst all the information you are receiving at any given time. Secondly, you have to store the information. You need to get it from your immediate (sensory) memory into your long-term memory. Thirdly, similar to using a computer, you have to be able to access the data/information when you need it.

Communications experts know that they need to consider how long their messages must be retained by the receiver for the communication to be successful. If that time is longer than a few seconds, they must consider how they are going to get their message into longer-term memory. There are a number of techniques that aid information retention by moving newly acquired information to long-term memories. Some of these techniques can be structured into communication tasks to help enhance memory of the material by the receiver(s) of the message. The key elements to better memory are:

- understanding

- breadth of knowledge

- active recall

- over-learning

- association.

Understand what you need to remember. Set up a frame within which to organize details and their relationship to each other. If the whole makes sense, the parts are easier to recall. For example, biology students forced to remember the names of nerves in the human body will remember more easily if they know the function of each nerve and how it interacts with the others. History students will better remember the names, dates and other details of an event when they have a thorough understanding of trends, philosophies and the broad sweep of historical events. Similarly, management students who know the social, historical and theoretical trends in their discipline will better remember details and how they fit into an integrated understanding of business, communications and strategic management. In other words, remember in the context of principles, theories, trends and important generalizations. Before you try to fix details in your mind, know the structure and main emphasis of what is being communicated to you. Similarly, when communicating with others try to structure the message and over-communicate the main points of emphasis.

Breadth of knowledge about the subject of communication is important because the more thoroughly and deeply you go into a subject, the better you will remember it. Broadening knowledge increases the number of associative links between one aspect of a topic and another, and makes the whole structure stronger. Your communications – both as sender and receiver – benefit from wider knowledge in the subject area. As a receiver of information, extra reading, doing extra problems and seeking out other points of view help just as much in business communications as in learning a subject at university. As a sender, you can try to make your message interesting so that people will engage with the information, think about it and perhaps seek further information.

Actively recall what you have just heard or read. If you want to remember information from this book, work at recalling material. Recalling the material is effective. Closing your book and going through the conscious effort of recalling the main points of what you have just read, while it is still fresh in your mind, seems to open the recall channel in your mind at a time when it is the easiest to open. The material seems closer to the surface and more easily accessible to review if the deliberate attempt to recall is made immediately after first reading or hearing the message. You can help receivers of your communications recall the message by restating at the end the main elements of your communication. In oral presentations it is conventional wisdom that you tell your audience what you are going to tell them, then tell them, and then tell them what you have told them. What you are doing is making it easier for the receiver to recall your message.

Over-learn material that you need to be able to produce on demand. In a business situation you might need to be able to remember detailed elements of business or marketing plans on a moment's notice. If so, then you need to over-learn such material. Similarly at university certain subjects – foreign languages, business, sciences, mathematics, statistics, for example – are more easily recalled and used when they are over-learned. **Over-learning** is knowing a subject well beyond the point of mastery. It is an extension of the conscious effort to recall, to the point where conscious effort is no longer needed. Over-learning results when a person continues to use a response repeatedly, with confirmation. Foreign languages, formulae, business plans, management theory – whatever it is you need to know without consciously reaching for it – should be over-learned. Knowing the material helps you communicate it to others and makes communication with you much more efficient and effective.

Build associations between what you already know and what you have to remember. Doing this is like constructing a chain which will lead you to the other end. Human minds vary greatly in the type of associative links to which response comes easiest. There is no one best method, but here are a few approaches that have proven utility.

Visualize. Some people have vivid visual memories, i.e. memories for how things look. If you remember better from charts and graphs than you do from the printed page, or if you remember how the page looked when you are trying to recall what was on it, you can make this tendency into an effective memory aid. If you want to remember a key business contact's name, you might visualize the name. Have you just been introduced to Mr Mason? Visualize some aspect of his appearance with the tools or raw materials of masonry. Have you just met Ms Henshaw? Thinking of her sitting in a rickshaw being pulled by a hen might help you remember her name. It is often the silliest mind pictures that produce the best recall results.

Use verbal mnemonic devices. In spelling, for instance, the saying, 'There is a rat in separate' – nonsensical as it is – has helped many people remember how to spell 'separate'. Students memorizing the colours of the spectrum in physics, for example, remember the nonsense-name 'Roy G. Biv': red, orange, yellow, green, blue, indigo, violet. In strategic management, some people remember SWOT PEST to remind them of the major elements in an industry analysis: strengths, weaknesses, opportunities and threats in the context of political, economic, social and technological environments.

Poor listening skills

Inadequate memory skills can also be attributed to poor listening. We may not remember someone's name, for example, simply because we were not paying enough attention when we were introduced. Day-dreaming, reading, listening to another conversation rather than the one in which we are engaged, looking around the room and just generally not concentrating on listening represent poor listening skills.

Few people listen with complete attention for more than a few seconds at a time. Unlike writing or talking skills, listening skills have tended to be given little priority. Yet, managers must listen to their customers, their employees, their shareholders and others. Students must listen to lectures. For most of us, learning, whether in university or in business, can be improved with enhanced listening skills. People can improve their listening skills to make it easier for others to communicate their ideas effectively.

Some listening problems are fairly obvious – problems caused by external distractions or lack of interest. Other listening problems are more subtle (Millar, Crute and Hargie 1992), such as:

- verbal battling

- fact hunting.

Verbal battling happens when, instead of listening and absorbing what the other person has to say, we start to debate the ideas in our heads. We may be more focused on coming up with counter-arguments or criticisms than on what is being said. When we do this, we lose track of the points the person is making.

Fact hunting occurs when, instead of listening for the main theme or general points in the argument, people concentrate on the detailed facts and lose sight of the overall message.

We can think much faster (typically four times faster) than we speak and this can either help us listen, or add to the distraction. The differential between thought speed and speech rate may encourage the listener to fill up the spare time with other unrelated thought processes (such as day-dreaming, verbal battling, fact hunting), which in turn may distract the listener from assimilating the speaker's message. Listening can be improved by using this extra thought-time positively, by mentally asking questions such as 'what are the main points being expressed by the speaker?', 'what reasons are being given?', 'in what frame of reference should these reasons be taken?', and 'what further information is necessary?'.

Sometimes someone appears to be listening to you but you suspect they are not. There are recognizable types of listeners:

- feigning listeners

- limiting listeners

- self-centred listeners

- positive or active listeners.

Feigning listeners are people who appear to be attentive and are making some appropriate non-verbal signals but their minds are elsewhere. Limiting listeners only give limited attention to what you are saying – they are focusing on specific topics or comments and may distort or misinterpret other things you say.

Self-centred listeners are only really concerned with their own views and may be simply looking for your agreement. They may appear to be listening to what is being said but rather than actually hearing what is said they are selecting only those elements of the communication that they can use to support their own views.

Positive or active listeners are those who internally absorb and process the information they receive but also encourage the other person to talk and demonstrate clearly that they are paying attention. To be a positive listener you need to develop three skills (Bolton 1987):

- attending skills

- following skills

- reflecting skills.

Attending skills relate to engaging with the speaker, being alert and appearing to take in what is being said. Following skills are to do not only with mentally following the conversation but also physically indicating that you are following. Your body language including head nodding and your verbal responses (e.g. saying such things as 'yes', 'uh-huh', 'hmm', etc.) all indicate that you are following the conversation. As an active listener you are also taking note of the speaker's body language and other non-verbal communication so that you can determine meaning and gauge the credibility of what you are being told. Finally, you need to reflect on the material so that it can go from your sensory to your short-term or long-term memory. All of these combine to create a positive listener who is actively engaged in the communication process.

Emotional interference

Emotions can be a barrier to communication both in sending and receiving messages. When people are angry, fearful or sad their communication skills can be impaired. This is not something you can necessarily control in others but you can control your own emotions to a degree. If you are angry you may say things you do not mean or refuse to communicate things that need to be said. If you are fearful or anxious, for example, in giving an oral presentation, your nervousness can affect how your audience receives your message. Your anxiety will be communicated to them and they will not be able to give full attention to what you are saying. Positive emotions can also be barriers to communication. Too much exuberance or overusing humour can detract from the seriousness of your message. A measured approach that conveys your message in a firm and calm manner works best.

ORGANIZATIONAL BARRIERS

Some communication problems are specific to organizations. Organizational barriers primarily relate to the organization's structure, culture, patterns of work and communication flows. The most common organizational barriers are:

- information overload

- message competition

- information distortion

- message filtering

- conflicting messages

- communications climate

- status differences

- structural problems.

Information overload

Information overload is a common complaint in our 'information society'. We are bombarded with information from all directions: letters, phone calls, e-mail, faxes, information over the internet, reports, advertising material, voice-mail, text messaging on mobile phones, radio, film, television and newspapers. New technologies for communication have not so much replaced traditional sources as added to them. Instant access to information leaves people sometimes feeling overwhelmed. People arrive at work and have to wade through dozens of e-mails before being able to start on more productive tasks of their day. Effective communicators have to strive harder all the time to get their messages heard.

Message Competition

Information overload leads to message competition. The amount of information we deal with every day forces us to make choices about what is important and what can be ignored. A manager can receive hundreds of messages a day in different forms. The result of such a communications and information assault is that messages have to compete for the manager's attention. Managers are put under more stress by the potential danger of missing or ignoring important messages and thus threaten their effectiveness.

Information distortion

A potentially bigger cost can be paid by organizations that suffer from information distortion. Taller structures mean that information has to pass through more departments and people before getting to its destination. This may cause the information to be distorted due to misunderstanding.

Sometimes information distortion can be less innocent. Information may be misinterpreted or even blocked on purpose. Managers who feel threatened by information may simply not pass it on, or they may misrepresent the information to superiors or subordinates. Of course, information distortion works both up and down the communication channels. Subordinates might pass information up to superiors only when it enhances their standing, or they may withhold information that threatens their position. In organizations where information is power and there is competition between divisional managers, information may be hoarded for divisional advantage rather than shared for organizational advantage. Flatter structures cannot eliminate all of these potential information distortion problems, but they can go a long way towards helping to cut down the bureaucratic costs associated with monitoring communication in taller structures.

Message filtering

Managers select the communications to which they pay attention by filtering or screening them. When passing on information managers once again filter information or reproduce it in abbreviated form for the consumption of others. This process happens at many levels in organizations. Administrative assistants may relay information in abbreviated forms. People tend to leave filtered messages on answerphones or e-mail. This filtering of messages means that communications can often become distorted and reduced. Drucker (1998) claims that every filter and relay of a message 'doubles the noise and cuts the message in half'.

Conflicting messages

What message do you take from a manager who says one thing one day and then says something contradictory the next? Unless there are other cues such as body language that you can interpret, you have no way to determine the nature of the message. Not only is there a communication problem surrounding that particular message, but there is also a credibility problem surrounding that manager. Future messages might be ignored (or selected out from consideration) because the source of the message is no longer believable. Similarly, what message do employees take from an espoused 'open door' policy when managers physically close their doors or show irritation when employees stop by to discuss something?

Conflicting messages can undermine communications and credibility. Leaders and managers should ensure that their messages are consistent. This is not to say that people cannot change their minds or their approaches or their ways of working. However, your messages should not change arbitrarily or randomly or according to emotional whims if you want to be taken seriously. When you do need to change policy, or when there are exceptions that are necessary, those differences in messages should be explained. Consistency builds credibility, makes messages stronger and enhances communication processes in organizations. Credibility is an important element of communications. In Chapter Four we will be looking at how you can increase your credibility for more effective communicating.

Communications climate

In many ways, good communication is dependent upon a management style or organizational climate that is relatively free and open to communication. Organizations need to open communication channels vertically both up and down the structure as well as horizontally across the organization. Too many communication channels means that messages will be distorted. Too few communication channels means the messages are blocked and too little information will flow.

Status differences

Status differences exist in most organizations. Status differences can be a barrier to communication because managers may listen less carefully to subordinates. Subordinates tend to read more into messages from superiors then is perhaps intended. The result is that messages coming down the organization are given too much interpretation while messages coming up the organization maybe unheard and unheeded. Even in companies where there is an open-door policy, status can be a barrier to communication. An open-door policy may unfairly rely on subordinates' overcoming status differences and their natural reserve in dealing with their managers.

Structural problems

An organizational structure for purposes of communication and co-ordination can be thought of in terms of a geographic metaphor. The greater the distance (physical, social or cultural) between two points, the longer it will take to get information from one point to the other. Similarly, the more hierarchical levels through which information must pass, the longer it will take to do so. This makes effective communication much more difficult and can put tall (hierarchical) organizations at a competitive disadvantage compared to those with flatter structures.

The very act of structuring an organization into specialized departments or divisions can create co-ordination problems simply because of the conflicts inherent in different functional roles within organizations. Figure 2.5 illustrates the potential conflict between marketing, for example, which might want customized products for its customers, and the production department, which may be striving for standardized products for long production runs in order to produce the products more cheaply. There is often conflict between the R&D department, which needs funds for long-term research, and finance, which is often more concerned with shorter-term measures such as return on investment and quarterly profits.

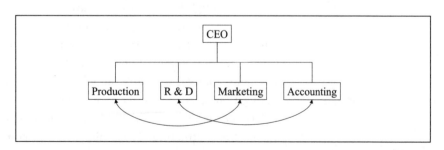

FIGURE 2.5 *Potential conflict in organizational structures*

Controlling such conflicts usually results in increased levels of authority and control which, in turn, creates taller structures. Tall structures tend, therefore, to be associated with tighter or more formalized communication channels which can add inflexibility to the problems of communication within tall hierarchies. Increasing control of communication also adds costs.

OVERCOMING ORGANIZATIONAL BARRIERS

A key way to overcome organizational barriers is to have people in the organization who are effective communicators. Effective communication requires:

- perception

- precision

- credibility

- control

- congeniality.

Perceptive people seem to be able to predict how a message will be interpreted. They anticipate a reaction and shape the message accordingly. They then key in on feedback, respond appropriately and correct any misunderstanding. Precise people are able to communicate in a way that provides the receiver with a clear understanding of the message. They create a shared mental picture because they communicate in such a way as to be understood. When they say something they mean it. This allows you to trust what they say, to trust their information and to be comfortable with their intentions. Effective communicators shape and control what they say. Their communications get results. They also are generally friendly people in organizations. They show respect for others, maintain good relations and are relatively easy to get along with. If you work with them you tend to want to work with them again.

An organization's communication climate is a reflection of its organizational culture, which we will be looking at in depth in Chapter Three. For now, it is enough to know that culture refers to the values and beliefs of an organization. Some organizations are very open while some tend to stifle communication. Research suggests that organizations whose cultures include such values as candour, honesty, openness, freedom to disagree with the boss, and ability for people at all levels to express their opinions, are organizations that have fewer communication barriers.

Barriers can often be reduced by lowering the number of levels in the organization's structure. Fewer links in the communication chain mean better communication. People should be offered the opportunity to communicate up and down the organization as well as across it. Instruments such as employee surveys, open-door policies, newsletters, intranets, memos, e-mail, task groups and open areas can all facilitate communication.

Feedback needs to be facilitated too. Feedback provides employees at all levels with wanted information on their performance. Managers need to know what is happening in their organizations. Employees need to know how they are doing. Managers who ask for feedback must be able to take criticism if they are to develop a communication climate that is useful.

Successful managers also tend to understand that, in a business context, communication and feedback tend to follow patterns that can be mapped onto organizational structures. The organization and its culture are the context in which all business communication occurs. The next chapter will look at culture, language and symbolism as the key elements of organizational communication.

Discussion questions

1. Videotape a TV interview from a news or current events programme. Replay the interview several times, each time watching the non-verbal communication of both interviewer and interviewee. What non-verbal cues are they giving? Are they indicating anxiety, nervousness, aggressiveness or evasiveness, for example? If so, how can you tell? Is their body language congruent with or contradicting what they are saying? Does their body language change when the topic changes to another subject?

2. Imagine you are the division manager of a large company. Your immediate supervisor has asked you to communicate some bad news to all 100 employees in your division. You are to advise them that the company is to be bought out by a foreign firm and there will be some redundancies but it has not been decided yet how many. What channel would you use to communicate the information? What barriers to communication might be an issue in this situation?

3. What kind of listener are you? Review the section on listening skills and at your next opportunity for a face-to-face conversation with a friend or family member, pay attention to how you listen. Do you turn off or tune out? Do you feign interest or do you show genuine interest in what is being said? What does your body language say about your listening style?

References

Bolton, R. (1987) *People Skills*, Simon and Schuster, London.

Drucker, P. F. (1998) Management's new paradigms, *Forbes*, October, 152–176.

Hamilton, C., Parker, C. and Smith, D. (1982) *Communicating for Results*, Wadsworth, Belmont, CA.

Janis, I. L. (1982) *Victims of Groupthink*, 2nd edn, Houghton Mifflin, Boston.

Mehrabian, A. (1968) Communication without words, *Psychology Today*, 2, Sept., 52–55.

Mehrabian, A. (1971) *Silent Messages*, Wadsworth, Belmont, CA.

Millar, R., Crute, V. and Hargie, O. (1992) *Professional Interviewing*, Routledge, London.

Mintzberg, H. (1973) *The Nature of Managerial Work*, Harper and Row, New York.

Simon, H. (1962) *Administrative Behavior*, Macmillan, New York.

Weick, K. E. and Browning, L. D. (1986) Argument and narration in organizational communication, *Journal of Management Studies*, Summer, 243–259.

Further reading

Argyle, Michael (1988) *Bodily Communication*, Methuen, London.

Hall, Edward T. (1973) *The Silent Language*, Anchor Books, Garden City, NY.

Handy, C. B. (1996) *Understanding Organizations*, Penguin Books, London.

Higbee, Kenneth (1989) *Your Memory: How it Works and How to Improve it.* Prentice Hall, New York.

Hoecklin, L. A. (1995) *Managing Cultural Differences: Strategies for Competitive Advantage*, Addison-Wesley, Wokingham.

Steil, L., Barker, L. and Watson, K. (1986) *Effective Listening: Key to Your Success*, Addison-Wesley, Reading, MA.

chapter three

Culture and communication

Introduction

IN CHAPTER Two we looked at models and forms of communication and barriers to communication. Before we go on to the strategic and practical aspects of communication we need to understand the cultural and symbolic basis of all forms of communication. In this chapter we look at language, culture and symbolism and their effects on culture and communication in organizations.

Signs and symbols are fundamental elements of communication. Systems of symbols form the basis of all communication systems including language. Language is one means of human communication, though the form it takes varies from society to society. In this chapter we examine the basic elements of language and how people make meaning in any language.

Meaning is related to culture which itself provides the context for understanding and behaviour in all societies. Understanding how culture influences communication helps make communication more effective in all social interactions and in particular in business situations. Learned and shared meanings and behaviours are basic elements of any culture and as such the concept of culture can be extended to organizations. Organizational culture occurs where individual organizations or groups of organizations develop a shared set of meanings and behaviours unique to them. In the last section of this chapter we will look in detail at organizational culture and its implications for business communications.

LEARNING OBJECTIVES

After studying this chapter you should be able to:

- Demonstrate an understanding of the symbolic nature of communication
- Discuss the basic components of language and its role in communication

- Describe the concept and basic attributes of culture and the cultural basis of communication

- Define the concept of organizational culture and explain its effect on organizational communication

Signs and symbols

All communication is based on signs. When we think of signs we normally associate them with road signs that indicate directions and hazards or with shops and companies that have exterior signs indicating the name of the business. Linguists, those who study language systems, use the term in a broader sense. In linguistics a **sign** is anything that transmits information such as a word, an object, a gesture, a picture or a sound. The word 'tree', whether written or spoken, is a sign. A simple pencil drawing of a tree or a coloured painting or a photograph of a tree are signs. All of these images are signs that communicate the concept of a tree (Figure 3.1).

Languages are examples of sign systems. Sign systems have a structure and rules that work together to produce a coherent means of communication. Sign systems may be open or closed. In closed sign systems signs cannot be combined to make new signs and each sign operates independently. Most animals have closed sign systems where the meaning of a sound or movement is genetically programmed. For example, birds often have specific mating calls that are pre-programmed and only used for that one purpose. Humans and to a lesser extent other primates have open sign systems. These are based on symbols. Human communication is almost entirely symbolic. A **symbol** is a sign with an arbitrary meaning. Different symbols can mean the same thing or a single symbol can have more than one meaning. A red cross on a white background can represent either the Red Cross foundation or the country of England. On the other hand a red light can mean 'stop' to a motorist whereas it has a different meaning in the 'red light' district of Amsterdam.

In human communication, unlike that of most other species, the meaning of a symbol is rarely genetically pre-programmed. The interpretation of symbols is learned. The meaning of words, for example, is learned from infancy. However, because symbols are arbitrary, different words in different

FIGURE 3.1 'Tree' signs

languages can mean the same thing. What is a 'dog' in English is a 'chien' in French and a 'Hund' in German – three different symbols with shared meanings. Objects such as flags, medals and logos are symbols, as are traffic lights and status goods such as expensive cars and watches. In most organizations symbols of top managerial rank might include large offices, personal assistants and company cars whereas symbols of lower-level positions might be small workstations, shared equipment and lower salaries. These symbols communicate clearly the relative position of employees in the organizational hierarchy and information about their socio-economic status.

An important property of symbols is their multivocality. **Multivocality** (literally 'speaking with many voices') means that symbols can have meaning on different levels. In other words they can say many things. Colours are multivocal symbols. Red may symbolize danger in one context and aggression in another whereas white can suggest purity, surrender, cleanliness or peace. An organization chooses the colours for its logo carefully to emphasize the values or image of its products or services. A garden design firm might want to have shades of green or bright flower colours whereas a medical supply company might use stark white and black lines to convey the purity of its products. A legal firm might choose dark wine reds or greys to suggest gravity and solidity.

Symbols and signs most often occur as part of sets. Meaning is dependent on the contrast between the items in the set, such as red and green for traffic signals. However, it is not only the contrast but the context of the communication that makes it meaningful. Red and green lights are only meaningful as traffic signals when they occur in the context of a road or street. In a different context, red and green can symbolize Christmas.

The success of any communication lies in its ability to relay a message from one person to another. Because symbols are arbitrary, interpreting a message involves not just decoding it but also putting it into context. Putting it into context involves assigning meaning. For example, there is a difference between a wink and a twitch. Though they may appear to be the same physically, their meanings differ. Observers of the gesture must interpret it in terms of what they know of the context of the communication. Only then can they make it fit with the sender's intentions, if any, and provide an appropriate response. A twitch is simply an involuntary physical act with no other meaning attached whereas a wink is symbolically loaded and can have many different meanings depending on the context (Geertz 1973). A wink may mean that the sender is making a joke or it could indicate a flirtation or it could be conspiratorial or simply indicate an acknowledgement of insider information. When interpreting the meaning of a sign or symbol, in this case the wink, it is necessary to be aware of the subtle cultural cues embedded in the context.

Language

Language is a symbolic system in that sounds or written symbols have shared meanings for members of a specific group. Each idea in language is associated with a sound. As in Figure 3.1, the sound of the word 'tree' is associated with a physical object in the natural world that has certain properties such as bark, trunk, leaves and branches. The sound 'tree' is the signifier and the idea or the physical object of the tree is the signified. Together they make up a linguistic sign or a unit of meaning in a given language. In the example of a dog, the sound, that is the signifier, can vary from language to language but the signified category of a domestic pet on four legs that barks is the same.

Those who do not share an understanding of a particular language cannot successfully communicate within it. Communication works the other way as well. The linguistic categories we have to work with influence our interpretation of the world around us (Leach 1976). In a human construct such as an organization we use language to cut it up into its different parts. We only see an organization in terms of its component parts because we have been socialized or trained to see things in categories such as hierarchies, departments and occupations. These are not things that have a fundamental physical reality like a tree or a dog but rather are symbolic descriptions of arrangements of people. We then match how we arrange people to how we understand the categories.

Artificially constructed categories can change or be changed at any time. They are simply linguistic categories used to mark the boundaries between groups and individuals in a specific context. In other words they are relative categories. We need to perceive things in their relative categories in order to see the relationships between them. Only then can we put them back together into a meaningful whole. For example, the categories of 'people' and 'plants' are relative categories that are too broad to be useful in many contexts. We have to break the categories down into understandable subcategories so we can more easily communicate specific things about them.

People use language to organize their understanding of the world and themselves within it. Different languages reflect different world views. Learning a second language usually provides the realization that the organization of the two worlds is significantly different. When learning a second language the student quickly realizes that successful communication depends not only on knowing vocabulary and grammatical rules but on a wide range of prior assumptions that native speakers share but are not easily apparent to an outsider. For this reason word-for-word translation does not often work because of the use of idiomatic expressions and different structures of meaning. Idiomatic expressions are combinations of words that make sense to a native speaker of a language but would lose their meaning if each word were understood literally. 'To take a break', 'to head the firm', 'to lead the charge' are all idiomatic expressions in English that would not translate literally into another language.

To communicate successfully in a new language is not simply a matter of applying new labels to familiar objects but of identifying familiar objects in a new way. In addition to vocabulary and grammar successful communication means recognizing that our assumptions about how the world works and how we understand our own experiences are not absolute or fixed but relative assumptions.

Components of language

Linguists have defined the components of language in various ways and with numerous features. We will be concentrating on the following four aspects of language:

- sounds (phonology)

- word structure (morphology)

- sentence structure (syntax)

- meaning (semantics).

All languages use only a limited number of sounds from the vast range of sounds the human voice is capable of making. Sounds used in one language may be completely absent in another language. For example, the language of the !Kung people in southern Africa includes a clicking sound which is not used in English. The Chinese use many tonal sounds that English speakers do not. Combinations of sounds are used in different ways in different languages. Some sounds by themselves do not convey meaning. They are only understandable when put together with other sounds. In any language the smallest sound unit that has meaning is called a **phoneme**. For example, 'd' as in 'day' and 'th' as in 'they' are both phonemes. That is, they make a single sound unit (Nanda 1984: 111). **Phonology** is the system of sounds (phonemes) in a language. Most languages have only about 30 phonemes. Ordinarily people do not consciously think about the system of sounds in their native language. As they learn to speak they unconsciously learn to distinguish between the sounds that are significant phonemes in the language and learn how to make them. Only when they try to learn a second language do people become aware of the phonetic structure of the language.

Morphology is the word structure of a language. A **morpheme** is the smallest unit in a language that has meaning. It is not necessarily a whole word. We know in English when we add 's' to the end of a noun such as 'tree' we are making it plural, which changes the meaning. In the word 'trees' there are two morphemes. The word 'zebra' has only one. In English to add 'un' to the beginning of a word changes it to a negative, so 'un' has meaning in itself even though it is not a complete word. You can both tie and untie your shoes. By adding 'un' to the word 'tie', the meaning changes to the opposite action.

Morphemes combine with other morphemes to make up whole words, phrases and sentences but the way they are put together is governed by a set of rules which we call grammar. Grammar dictates how morphemes are arranged to make words and sentences.

Syntax is an aspect of grammar that has to do with how words are arranged to form phrases and sentences. In English, word order is an important syntactic structure. The sentences 'The car was hit by the train' and 'The train was hit by the car' mean different things. In other languages such as German, the order might not be important as the endings of words convey the meaning of the action. The subject and object in English are indicated by their order in the sentence whereas in German they are conveyed by the word endings. The famous linguist, Noam Chomsky (1965) illustrates the importance of word order in the following example:

Colourless green ideas sleep furiously.
Furiously sleep ideas green colourless.

Both sentences are meaningless in English. However, an English speaker can easily recognize that the first sentence is grammatically correct. The first sentence has its elements in their proper relationship to each other whereas the second sentence does not. The second sentence is both grammatically incorrect and meaningless.

The study of meaning or **semantics** is a particularly important aspect of language which you will recognize as an important theme of this book. Effective communication is above all about conveying meaning. Linguists divide meaning into two types: denotation and connotation. **Denotation** refers to what a word in itself means, as in a dictionary definition. If you see sheep in a field and remark that they are sheep, you are stating what the word denotes. **Connotations**, on the other hand, are additional meanings that come from the context of a communication. We understand the connotation aspect of a communication by understanding its context. Understanding context comes from experience. Connotations point to experiences and understandings that go beyond the literal meaning of a word. For example, applying an animal description to groups of people, referring to them as 'sheep', attributes specific characteristics to people that are normally associated with the respective animal's behaviour. In this case it is not what the word denotes that is of importance but rather the connotation.

People and sheep are from two different linguistic categories, humans and animals. Linguists call these **semantic domains**. Semantic domains are domains of experience that are culturally meaningful. Examples of semantic domains are: colours, numbers, plants, occupations and industries. Within the domain of plants are sub-categories such as flowers, trees, shrubs, and grasses. Each of the sub-categories can be further subdivided. Flowers may be perennials, annuals or biennials. A primary colour such as red has a sub-category of related colours such as pink, fuchsia and wine.

People tend to accept as given the cultural domains of experience that their society recognizes. They take those experiences that their society pays attention to as typical and use them as a baseline for judging whether other experiences are typical. These typical experiences – what linguists call **prototypes** – are key to understanding meaning in language. Words in a language refer to prototypical experiences in a culturally relevant domain. In organizations, for example, a prototypical experience is promotion through a hierarchy of job positions as seniority and experience accumulate. In the semantic domain of an organizational structure terms such as assistant manager, regional manager and managing director are appropriate and understood within that context. They are thus culturally relevant to the semantic domain of organizations and understandable in that context.

METAPHOR AND METONYM

From our discussion of context and semantic domains you can see that language can deviate substantially from its literal meaning. It can become ambiguous, that is, it can be understood in more than one way. To convey a non-literal or figurative meaning we sometimes use linguistic forms such as metaphor and metonym.

A **metaphor** links two expressions from different semantic domains. In other words, metaphors are based on a similarity between two different realms. An example might be using sports terms to describe business situations – 'team playing' for working together to meet objectives or war terms to talk about an organization's business strategy – 'kill off the competition' and 'attack from the rear'.

A **metonym** is a part that stands for a whole as in the crown symbolizing the institution of monarchy or a mitre symbolizing the office of bishop. Any office that is habitually associated with a uniform can often be represented by a part of that uniform. The notation 'white tie' on an invitation indicates the level of formality of the event. The phrase 'white tie' conveys a substantial amount of information by means of a short two-word phrase.

Metaphor and metonym are powerful communication tools that allow meaning to be transmitted efficiently and effectively. Metaphor is particularly useful when there is a need to explain something unknown or less well-known. By relating it to a known semantic domain, the receiver of the message has a better grasp of its meaning. Metonym is useful as a shorthand. Powerful values and images can be transmitted by using a representative part of a larger domain. Marketing communications often use metonym to portray a target audience for a product. A young male watching football on television might stand for a whole age-related segment of the population that a beer company wants to attract as customers.

Language codes, classifies and prioritizes human behaviour. As such, it can be highly emotionally charged. Racist and sexist terminology in language are examples of highly charged symbols in contemporary Western society. Language is the primary medium for socialization of the individual into society and the means by which cultural information is transmitted from one generation to the next. An understanding of culture is important to effective communication as the context of a communication is culturally defined. In the next sections we look at the cultural basis of communication and the application of culture to organizations.

Culture and communication

The term 'culture' comes from anthropologists' studies of human societies. Culture is the particular configuration of behaviours, norms, attitudes, values, beliefs and basic assumptions that differ from society to society. This means that culture is not 'objective' in the sense that phenomena in the natural world are (or seem to be) objective. Culture can look different depending upon who does the looking, when they look and from what direction. This makes culture difficult to grasp.

Culture has been defined in many ways but a classic definition is:

culture consists of patterns, explicit and implicit, of and for behaviour, acquired and transmitted by symbols, constituting the distinctive achieve- ments of human groups ... the essential core of culture consists of traditional (i.e. historically derived and selected) ideas and especially their attached values.

(Kroeber and Kluckhohn 1952: 181)

Culture tells people what is, how it got that way, and what ought to be. Culture is not a rationally based belief system. Rather, culture refers to taken-for-granted beliefs, values, norms and basic assumptions that have proven useful in adapting to uncertainty and integration. It is for these reasons that cultures are often difficult to understand from afar. Culture is more emotionally charged and resistant to change than are rational beliefs because it gives people some sense of confidence in facing the threats posed by uncertainties, and because it arises in the very circumstances that cannot be fully understood or predicted by rational means.

Deep-seated belief in one's culture is also reinforced through culturally accepted ways of expressing and affirming beliefs, values and basic assumptions. There are sets of cultural forms, such as rituals, that groups use to express their cultures. In an organization these might include meetings, hierarchies, occupational groupings, uses of space, celebratory events, origin myths and legends. The location, duration, formality and interaction between people in a meeting (a type of ritual) can differ considerably between societies. Cultural forms imbue actions and things with meanings; they enable people to communicate and to celebrate their cultures in many different ways which generate feelings of identity and community.

Cultures are, therefore, collective social phenomena that embody people's responses to the uncertainties and chaos that are inevitable in human experience. These cultural responses fall into two major categories. First is the essence of a culture – shared, emotionally charged systems of value, beliefs and basic assumptions which are expressed in basic cultural characteristics. The second is cultural forms – observable behaviours and material objects through which members of a culture express, affirm and communicate the essence of the culture to one another. Out of these processes cultures make themselves, grow and re-make themselves.

Since culture is about people, their beliefs and their behaviour, culture is a highly important consideration in successful business communications. Operations in a foreign country will mean that customers, employees and business partners will, between them, share a culture that may differ widely from what is understood and lived by the customers, employees and business partners in the organization's country of origin. Sensitivity to and an understanding of how things work in a context different from one's own are essential to communication that gets results.

People generally believe strongly in their cultures. In addition, by endorsing some actions and forbidding others, culture channels people's actions so that most of the time they repeat apparently successful patterns of behaviour, integrate in predictable ways, and avoid certain kinds of dangers and conflicts, which in the process further reinforces their culture. This is possible because most human actions have dual functions – they both accomplish certain technical and practical outputs and they express some subset of cultural meanings (Leach 1968). In other words human behaviour has both practical and symbolic implications.

A company might choose to move its manufacturing division to another country for the practical reason that it may be able to reduce labour and overhead costs. However, the move communicates things about the firm's place in the social and moral order. For example, to employees in the home country who lose their jobs the company is communicating that it is uncaring and disloyal. To interest groups who protest against the exploitation of cheap labour abroad, the company communicates a degree of unethical behaviour. To its shareholders, the company is taking positive action to maximize their returns.

If a company decides to move into a new product area, its marketing department will devise a marketing campaign that will include the product but place it within the context of the lifestyle image it is trying to portray. Car advertisements are a good example. The car itself often figures as a small afterthought to the scenario presented in the advertisement. The practical objective is to sell cars, but the subtext is a cultural one that draws on people's deeply held beliefs about what they think their lives ought to be like.

That activities communicate cultural and social messages has implications for organizational communication. Effective communicators must consider not only what their activities accomplish but what their actions say about their organization. Corporate image, which we will look at later in the book, is reliant on what an organization is saying about itself through its actions.

THE ESSENCE OF CULTURE

It is important to understand that culture is a natural outgrowth of the social interactions that constitute human groups whether in societies or organizations. Whenever and wherever people come together over time, culture develops. The essence of culture is that it is:

- learned

- shared

- interrelated

- adaptive.

Culture is learned through social interaction. Learned behaviour is communicated from one member of society to another through forms of socialization such as observation, instruction, reward, punishment and experience. Culturally distinct ways of thinking, behaving, feeling and responding become habitual very early in life as a result of both explicit and subconscious or tacit socialization. The power of socialization in its conscious and unconscious forms is such that it makes much of what people learn about their culture seem 'natural' and 'true'.

Behaviour and ways of thinking or interacting must be shared within a group of people in order to be considered part of culture. Some cultural patterns are shared by nearly all people in some cultures, but most societies are less homogeneous than was once believed. It still holds, however, that shared cultural attributes not only define the culture, but also define membership of the group. Cultures are also about building and maintaining boundaries. Culture defines us (on one side of a boundary) as opposed to them (on the other side). This has negative as well as positive consequences. Wars, ethnic conflicts, racism and discrimination often have their origins in cultural differences and boundary-making activities.

Those who do not share a defined set of cultural attributes are considered outside the mainstream cultural boundaries, but may be thought of as members of sub-cultures contained within a dominant culture. A sub-culture refers to a system of perceptions, values, beliefs and assumptions that are different from those of the dominant culture. Nation states generally contain many sub-cultures that may be based on religion, region, occupation, social class, ethnicity, or even lifestyle. The degree to which sub-cultural variation is permitted within societies depends upon both the sub-culture and the mainstream culture and their relative value systems.

For organizations considering globalization strategies the existence of sub-cultures means that decisions have to be sensitive to their existence. For instance, a company must be aware that the proposed location of its overseas investment in a particular country may be dominated by a minority ethnic group, and is unlike other areas of the country concerned. For example, India has immense variation in culture and language in the different regions of the country. Any organization wanting to open new operations in India will need to have specialist knowledge of the area in which they propose to invest.

Precisely because culture is learned behaviour, it is adaptive. Adaptation refers to the way groups relate to their environment so that they can survive and grow. Culture is the major way in which human groups adapt. Culture changes in response to external forces. For example, there are identifiable cultural differences between East and West Germans as a result of political division after the Second World War which translated into structural, value-orientation and many other cultural differences in spite of a common, centuries-old, German heritage.

Culture strongly influences how its members communicate and interact. That interaction is visible in cultural forms. There are several cultural forms that seem to be in evidence in all cultures – though the forms express themselves differently in different societies. Some of these forms are family, religion, marriage, trade, education, art and music. The interaction of different configurations of these cultural forms has an impact on how businesses – especially international businesses – operate within different societies. Later in the book we will look at the implications of cross-cultural communication in an international business context.

A key essence of culture is that cultural forms are interrelated as a system. Although cultural analysis and discussion of cultural forms require that parts of a culture be studied or discussed separately, culture remains a complex whole that is interconnected much like a spider's web. All aspects of culture are related to each other either directly or indirectly.

Symbolism, culture and marketing

Symbolism and culture are intimately linked. Culture works in the symbolic domain which emphasizes meaning, rather than the technical/practical/rational side of human behaviour. Behaviour not only does, it also says. In that sense culture is subject to multiple meanings. As we noted above, all actions have symbolic content as well as being actions in and of themselves. Actions, like all kinds of behaviour, are interpreted and therefore communicate and symbolize other things. Things (actions, behaviours, etc.) always stand for something other than merely the thing itself. They always symbolize something else depending on the context. A red light is not simply a red light. In a particular cultural context it provides directions (i.e. symbolizes) to motorists to stop their vehicles. A car is not just a means of transport. It can symbolize socio-economic status and personality attributes.

Marketing campaigns trade on the power of symbols and culture. In the UK the newspapers you read are not just a means of keeping you informed on current affairs. They are cultural objects that symbolize specific things about you. Marketing surveys and polling agencies often ask their subjects which national newspapers they read. This simple marker or indicator tells a great deal about a person: age, class, political leanings, education, occupation, income categories and leisure interests. By compiling data on which newspapers their customers read, businesses can build a profile of their customer group and more closely target their markets for more effective marketing.

Marketing communications often use a 'lifestyle' approach in creating advertising campaigns. Lifestyle marketing trades on how people see themselves in relation to a complex mix of activities and objects, all of which are culturally based and symbolically loaded. When marketing analysts determine what kind of lifestyles their customers see themselves enjoying, they use that information to create advertisements that will symbolize and communicate that particular lifestyle.

For example, Levi Strauss, the American jeans manufacturers, wanted to extend their clothing range to other casual clothes and suits. They surveyed their customers and determined that they fell into four 'lifestyle' categories:

- classic independent

- mainstream traditionalist

- price shopper

- trendy casual.

They then surveyed the 'classic independent' category as the most likely customers to buy suits, to see if they were interested in the new line. The results indicated that the 'classic independents' would not buy a suit with the Levi Strauss logo. What Levi Strauss discovered was how powerfully their brand had come to symbolize a sub-cultural sector of American society. That symbolism was so entrenched that consumers would not associate it with a new and different set of social activities.

Culture is a very powerful determinant of what meaning should be applied to things and actions. Symbols are so much a part of action, behaviour and communication generally that they are considered the most basic unit of cultural expression. Culture and symbolism are also key aspects of organizations and their expression in an organizational context affects the whole of the organization, particularly its communications.

Organizational cultures

An understanding of organizational culture is imperative for effective communication in business. It is from the anthropological study of culture that the concept of organizational culture came to organization studies and from there to management. Organization studies began with Taylorism and scientific management principles. These principles were initially tested from 1927 to 1932 in the famous Western Electric Hawthorne Plant studies. The studies assumed that organization and job design should be based on strict scientific principles. It assumed, for example, that if lighting on the shopfloor were increased, production would go up – which it did. When lighting was reduced, it was assumed that production would go down, but, surprisingly, it increased again. The reason for the second increase was that the workers improved production when they felt that their welfare was being taken into consideration. With the help of anthropologists many of the principles of scientific management were discredited with the discovery that organizations are fundamentally social systems that cannot be regulated solely on scientific principles.

The human relations school then went on to dominate organization studies for the next quarter-century. It was at this time that culture was 'discovered' as an important dynamic within organizations. From there the idea that organizations have cultures developed into the concept of organizational culture which has become an important perspective in organizational theory, management and business studies.

There are numerous definitions of organizational culture. Most include such concepts as values, guiding beliefs, philosophies, standards and ways of thinking. A key ingredient is how these concepts develop over time in response to organizational needs for external adaptation and internal integration that are shared by members of the organization (Sathe 1985; Schein 1985; Smircich 1983). In essence, organizational culture is: 'how we do things around here'.

In its translation to a business context, culture has been necessarily narrowed in application and conceptualization. Organizational culture is focused at the organizational level and is generally concerned with organizational-level phenomena. A widely accepted definition of organizational culture is:

> a pattern of basic assumptions – invented, discovered, or developed by a given group as it learns to cope with its problems of external adaptation and internal integration – that has worked well enough to be considered valid and, therefore, to be taught to new members as the correct way to perceive, think, and feel in relation to those problems.
>
> (Schein 1985: 9)

Organizational culture, then, has to do with definable groups of people who share understandings about their group, its environment, and how to deal with that environment. It involves teaching (explicitly) or socializing (implicitly) newcomers to the group about accepted norms, values and basic assumptions and thus has important implications for communication in organizations.

To understand how communication in organizations works it is important to understand just what organizational culture is, what it is not, and how it is generated. Schein's definition includes the idea that culture arises partly as a result of groups adapting to their external environments. External environments for organizations may change for any number of reasons, but many can be traced to changes in economic or social conditions, technological developments, or the actions of competitors. Organizations must deal with different and often more demanding customers and a larger array of actual or potential new competitors. Certain stakeholder and interest groups ask organizations to deal with social problems of environmental pollution, environmental preservation, community employment, deterrence of drug and substance abuse, and elder and child care. Meanwhile, within organizations, management must try to co-ordinate the activities of groups with specialized expertise when each does not fully understand the other and when their diverse viewpoints are at odds.

Organizations are subject to many of these expectations simultaneously with intra-organizational demands such as changes due to mergers, alliances, internal restructuring, re-engineering and downsizing or 'right-sizing'. All of these dynamics lead to ambiguities and uncertainties. Within this environment, managers must decide on the best course of action to ensure organizational survival – at minimum – and they must be able to communicate their decisions and strategies effectively. If managers and their organizations fail, they face other threats and uncertainties, including loss of jobs for themselves and their employees, and loss of social standing and self-esteem. Thus, it is not surprising that, like people in other settings, people in organizations develop cultures to help deal with uncertainty. Culture provides organizational members with ways to cope collectively with uncertainties and ambiguities in their environments.

People in organizations, as in social life generally, develop mind sets or cultural models that tell them what is, how it got that way, and what ought to be. These are not rationally based belief systems. Rather, they are implicit and interpretative sets of taken-for-granted beliefs, values, norms and basic assumptions that have proven useful in adapting to uncertainty and integration. Culture may be likened to an iceberg in that the visible aspects of culture are only a fraction of its entirety. Just as the *Titanic* moved towards the iceberg and catastrophe without seeing its great mass so a lack of understanding of the taken-for-granted, submerged aspects of culture can lead to problems and misunderstandings (Figure 3.2).

Cultural models are more emotionally charged and resistant to change than are rational beliefs because they give people some sense of confidence in facing the threats posed by uncertainties, and because they arise in the very circumstances that cannot be fully understood or predicted by rational means. People believe strongly in their ideologies and cultural models. In addition, by endorsing some actions and forbidding others, cultural models channel people's actions so that most of the time they repeat apparently successful patterns of behaviour, integrate in predictable ways, and avoid certain kinds of dangers and conflicts, which in the process further reinforces their beliefs in their models.

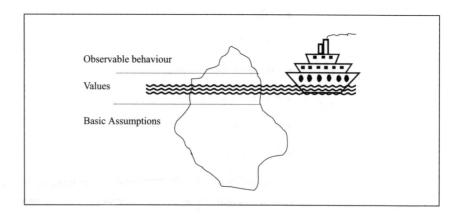

Observable behaviour

Values

Basic Assumptions

FIGURE 3.2 *The cultural iceberg*

Organizational cultures are, therefore, collective phenomena that embody people's responses to the uncertainties and chaos that are inevitable in organizational experience. These responses fall into two major categories:

- cultural essence

- cultural forms.

As in our discussion above about culture generally, the essence of a culture is shared, emotionally charged systems of value, beliefs and basic assumptions which are expressed in cultural models (Geertz 1973). For example, in business a basic assumption of an organization might be to maximize profits for shareholders or to generate sales increases. A basic assumption about life in organizations might be that they are hierarchically structured with the most powerful and well-paid positions at the top and the least powerful and lowest-paid at the bottom.

The second category, cultural forms, includes observable behaviours and physical or material objects through which members of a culture express, affirm and communicate the essence of the culture to one another (Schein 1985). An organization, for example, might use various means of transmitting its culture to new employees. Training sessions, meetings, mentoring, organizational charts and policy manuals are all cultural forms that will help the new employee become acculturated. Out of these processes cultures make themselves, grow and re-make themselves. Organizational cultures are a natural outgrowth of the social interactions that occur in organizations.

CHARACTERISTICS OF ORGANIZATIONAL CULTURE

Whenever and wherever people come together in groups over time, culture develops. This is as true of organizations as of societies. There are six major characteristics of cultures and in particular, organizational cultures (Trice and Beyer 1993):

- collective

- symbolic

- emotionally charged

- historically based

- dynamic

- inherently fuzzy.

Organizational culture cannot be produced by individuals acting alone. Culture originates as people interact with one another over time. Individuals may develop specific ways of managing their lives, but until these specific ways come to be collectively shared and practised they are not part of culture. Culture is shared. Persons who do not endorse and practise prevailing beliefs and values become marginal and may be socially sanctioned (i.e. punished or expelled either physically or symbolically). Belonging to culture involves believing what others believe and doing as they do and knowing that when you do not conform you are deviating.

Culture is infused with emotion as well as with meaning. Since culture is a way to deal with fundamental insecurities, people cherish established cultural models and practices because they seem to make the future predictable. Culture conforms with and represents the past which makes it seem 'right' and 'true' based on their experiences. People's deep-seated belief in their cultural models and assumptions springs from emotion rather than from rational analysis. It should not be surprising, therefore, that when cultural beliefs are questioned, people react emotionally.

Basic assumptions are so deeply held that members of a cultural group rarely question them. They may be able to generate rationales for why they believe or behave as they do, but the depth of feeling exhibited when culture is questioned is a clear indication that emotion rather than rationality is at work. This should not be mistaken, however, as self-evident criticism. It is the deep belief of culture that makes it so powerful.

Uncontrolled power can be dangerous, however. Cultural repertoires help to channel emotions in socially accepted ways. Performance of rites and rituals heightens the awareness and importance of shared beliefs. Rites and rituals also provide ways for individuals to avoid deviance; rituals remind people of the socially accepted order that is supposed to prevail (Leach 1968). An example of a ritual in organizations might be regular staff meetings to inform employees of the company's production and sales figures. Another ritual could be special events to celebrate employees' contributions to the organization such as long service, efficiency suggestions, or meeting new sales targets. Rituals might also be used to mark a change in status of an employee or manager from one level of the organizational hierarchy to another.

Organizational cultures are inseparable from the organizational histories from which they grew. When people spend time together they interact, organize and share common uncertainties and develop ways of coping with them. An organization's culture will, therefore, have developed within a set of physical, political, social, technological, economic and industrial circumstances. The culture that develops will then take on a 'life' of its own beyond the sum of the ideas and values of individual members. This is evidenced by cultural values that persist long after the circumstances that gave rise to them have changed or disappeared. Such cultural events that originated in the past, can nevertheless have powerful impacts on current behaviours. When people speak of how difficult it is to change organizations and organizational behaviour (sometimes referring to 'organizational inertia') they are speaking of the current impact of deeply ingrained practices that once were functional but have now become perhaps less so. Again, it is the symbolic domain that keeps these traditional behaviours (both negative and positive) alive.

New organizational members will hear stories of how 'heroines' and 'heroes' acted in particular circumstances in the past. These tales (whether positive or negative) will serve as a socializing guide to the priorities of the culture for newcomers, and as a reminder or reinforcement to members, regardless of whether or not the messages of the stories are the current priorities of the organization's management. Precisely because they represent deeply held cultural values, such stories are told and retold with powerful socializing and continuity effects. This accounts for the persistence not only of positive cultural survivals, but also of negative elements leading to organizational inertia which once again emphasizes the power of culture's symbolic domain (Schwartz and Davis 1981).

The concept of organizational inertia explains how organizations are difficult to change because of their cultures of deeply ingrained sets of behaviours and beliefs. One central cultural paradox is that cultures are not static (which is implied in organizational inertia) but dynamic. Cultures continually change primarily because of variation in:

- communication

- discretion

- tacitness

- symbolic imprecision

- demographics.

Communication is never perfect. Each individual does not learn the same things about a culture. This makes sense especially when one considers that even in a structured learning environment different students absorb different elements at different levels of depth, understanding and content. What does happen in the classroom, which is similar to what happens with cultural learning, is that most people learn the major elements at an average level of depth of understanding and content. This means that culture is never communicated perfectly. Not everyone learns precisely all cultural elements. The result is that even when members consciously intend to conform, their limited cultural understanding would make that impossible – and this is assuming that there were some 'real' or 'true' culture with which to conform. Since culture is in the domain of the symbolic and therefore the interpretative, culture changes depending upon who looks at it, when, and from what perspective.

Discretion is always present, therefore, in culture. Even in cultures with strong sanctions against deviance, there is considerable discretion in cultural behaviour and considerable variation in accepted behaviour. People can be innovative and creative in dealing with the complexities of organizational life. No culture could control behaviour to the extent that variation could not occur.

'Tacitness' describes the way in which much organizational socialization occurs. Not only does most cultural learning take place by 'osmosis' rather than by programmed instruction (though that does happen, too), but people are often unaware that even their simplest actions 'speak' tacitly of the culture. Managers might think they are simply performing a necessary task when disciplining a subordinate but the manner of their action 'speaks' about the culture of the organization. It might be the norm in one firm to have an informal talk with the employee about the problem whereas in another a formal letter of reprimand may be the accepted routine.

Symbolic imprecision is a direct result of the symbolic and interpretative nature of culture. As we discussed above, symbols always have more than one meaning (though one can be dominant). Cultural context does not provide 'laws' about how to interpret symbols, rather it provides a series of clues that must be interpreted and translated, and from which people must extrapolate meaning. This imprecision in interpretation contributes to cultural dynamism.

Demographics in this context refers to the changes in the make-up of the organization in time and space. As the membership of an organization changes with people quitting, being made redundant, retiring or being transferred, the mix of gender, age, ethnicity, training and life experience changes. People are carriers of culture. Not only do they carry their organizational cultures but people are always members of other cultural groups (national, ethnic, etc.). This other cultural 'baggage' is brought into the organization to varying degrees. Depending upon the importance of these cultures (and how elements of those cultures are used and interpreted in symbolic communication) people's other cultural identities will have an impact on the organizational culture and therefore the expression of culture in organizations.

Cultural persistence is imperfect and there is considerable change in how any particular organizational culture manifests itself over time. The irony, of course, is that culture is changing all the time and yet exhibiting continuity (organizational inertia) over time.

Cultures are inherently 'fuzzy' (Trice and Beyer 1993). Much of what we have described about culture suggests that while single cultures and dominant cultural elements can be interpreted at some level, all cultures have ambiguities, contradictions, paradoxes, ironies and a large element of confusion. Geertz (1973) describes culture as being deeply ambiguous and characterized by 'enormous multiplicity'. This is what we might expect given that culture develops in the context of and in response to internal and external environments that are themselves characterized by at least a similar degree of multiplicity, ambiguity, contradiction, paradox and general confusion. This gives culture its great power for adaptability and integration – the complexity of the context is mirrored in the culture. Culture, therefore, is very elusive. Add to this the impact of tradition, imperfect cultural learning, changing demographics, the influence of other cultures that are themselves dynamic, and the interactive, constantly emerging, and perpetually organizing aspect of culture. It quickly becomes obvious that culture is not a fixed or easily definable domain.

Finally, culture is not merely a way to describe organizations or other social groups. Cultures are a socially constructed reality as opposed to a natural reality, yet they occur naturally, which perhaps makes their influence even more consequential. Cultures are naturally occurring systems of values, beliefs and basic assumptions that have real consequences and are fundamental to understanding communication in organizations.

Discussion questions

1. Select a television or magazine advertisement. What kind of symbolism is used in the advert? What underlying assumptions or cultural norms and values can you discern from the advert? What is the target audience for the product being promoted?

2. What behaviours and activities in organizations might be related to culture? What rituals might you find in an organization? What are some of the shared norms and values that most organizations would want to promote?

3. Colour symbolism is an important tool in communication. Think of some ways in which colours might be used to convey specific meanings in a business context.

References

Chomsky, N. (1965) *Syntactic Structures*, Mouton, London.

Geertz, C. (1973) *The Interpretation of Culture*, Basic Books, New York.

Kroeber, A. L. and Kluckhohn, C. (1952) *Culture: A Critical Review of Concepts and Definitions*, Harvard University Press, Cambridge, MA.

Leach, E. (1968) Ritual, *International Encyclopedia of the Social Sciences*, 13, 520–526.

Culture and communication **73**

Leach, E. (1976) *Culture and Communication: The Logic by which Symbols Are Connected*, Cambridge University Press, Cambridge.

Nanda, S. (1984) *Cultural Anthropology*, Wadsworth, Belmont, CA.

Sathe, V. (1985) *Culture and Related Corporate Realities,* Irwin, Homewood, IL.

Schein, E. (1985) *Organizational Culture and Leadership: A Dynamic View*, Jossey-Bass, San Francisco.

Schwartz, H. and Davis, S. (1981) Matching corporate culture and business strategy, *Organizational Dynamics*, 10(1), 30–38.

Smircich, L. (1983) Concepts of culture and organizational analysis, *Administrative Science Quarterly*, 28(3), 339–358.

Trice, H. M. and Beyer, J. M. (1993) *The Cultures of Work Organizations*, Prentice Hall, Englewood Cliffs, NJ.

Further reading

Alvesson, M. (1993) *Cultural Perspectives on Organizations*, Cambridge University Press, Cambridge.

Deal, T. and Kennedy, A. (1982) *Corporate Cultures: The Rites and Rituals of Corporate Life*, Addison-Wesley, Reading, MA.

Peters, T. and Waterman, R. (1982) *In Search of Excellence: Lessons from America's Best-Run Companies*, Harper and Row, London.

Pickton, D. and Broderick, A. (2001) *Integrated Marketing Communications*, Pearson Education, Harlow, Essex.

Wright, Susan (ed.) (1994) *Anthropology of Organizations*, Routledge, London.

chapter four

Communication and strategy

Introduction

IN THE previous chapter we learned the importance of culture and symbolism in communications. In Chapter Two we looked at models and forms of communication. In this chapter we add a third key ingredient – a strategic approach to communication. We take the idea of strategy from strategic management. A good management strategy involves goals, analysis, synthesis and implementation. An effective communication strategy involves the same four concepts applied to communication tasks. When people or organizations communicate, they do so in order to achieve some result. We all communicate either because we want people to know and understand something, or because we want them to take some kind of action. In other words, all communication is results-oriented.

In this chapter we present a model of strategic communications that, when applied to any communication task, will enhance the success of the communication. To get the best results from your communication you need to develop a communication strategy. Developing a communication strategy involves a number of analytic tasks. These tasks are the same for all types of communication. You can use them in oral communications (face-to-face, telephone), written communications (letters, memos, reports, e-mails), or combinations of oral and written communications (presentations, adver-tisements).

The chapter begins with a brief introduction to communication strategy, what it means, and how you will benefit by taking a strategic approach to communications. Next we look at the key elements to an effective strategy: communicator strategy, audience strategy, channel strategy and message strategy. Unlike the way in which communications are often presented as discrete tasks we find it is more powerful to think about communica-tion holistically following Munter's (1987) framework. We see the commu-nication process as a cluster of integrated strategies that when applied step-by-step, generate desired results. Our approach is similar in some respects to what marketing experts refer to as an integrated marketing strategy.

After studying this chapter, you should be able to:

- Explain the core elements of a communication strategy

- Define your communication objectives

- Improve your credibility as a communicator

- Conduct an audience analysis

- Select an appropriate communication channel

- Construct an effective message strategy

Communication strategy

To get the results you want from your communication you need to develop a communication strategy. Many of us intuitively go through basic steps such as deciding how we want to communicate: face-to-face, by phone, mail, or e-mail. We also think in advance about the receiver of the message and what message we want to convey. However, we tend to do little more than is required to get the message across. The results are not always successful. We miscalculate how our audience will react or we put the message across in a confusing way. As we saw in Chapter Two there are numerous barriers that can distort our message. A well-developed communication strategy reduces the barriers to communication and increases the success of any communication task.

As you will recall from our discussion of culture and symbolism, all communications are culturally loaded and symbolic. All actions, including communication tasks, have meaning on more than one level and are performed in a cultural context. Each step in building a communication strategy needs to be considered in terms of its cultural and symbolic implications. As you go through the process of constructing a communication strategy, keep thinking about how cultural factors might affect each task.

There are four main elements in an effective communication strategy:

1. communicator strategy

2. audience strategy

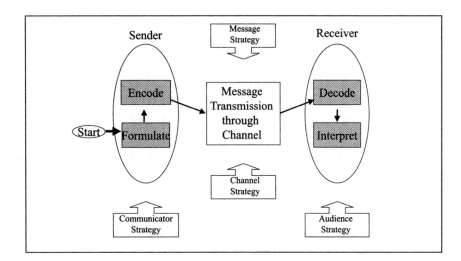

FIGURE 4.1
*Communication
strategy*

3. channel strategy

4. message strategy.

These four elements can be mapped onto our original communication model from Chapter Two (Figure 2.2). The transmitter of the communication is the communicator. The audience is the receiver of the message. The transmission of the message through a channel is where we apply channel and message strategies. In Figure 4.1 you can see how the four elements map onto the communication model.

Communicator strategy

Begin your communication strategy by looking at the first element in the communication model, the sender of the message. In your communication tasks you are the sender or communicator. What message do you want to send? How will you communicate (transmit) your message? What do you want to achieve as a result of sending your message? How does the receiver of the message view you, the sender? How much credibility do you have with your intended audience? Formulating answers to these questions constitutes your communicator strategy. For an effective communicator strategy you need to consider your objectives and credibility and/or those of your organization.

OBJECTIVES

When planning any communication the first thing you should do is think about the purpose of the task. Having an objective helps you decide what kind of approach to take and forces you to focus on the other elements of the communication process – your message, audience and channel. Your purpose might be clear and specific or more vague and general. If you are unsatisfied with mechanical work you had done on your car, for example, your objective would be clear: to get the work done properly. If you are the owner of a small software development company and you want your business to be more profitable your goal is less specific. You would have to decide between various options as to how to achieve your goal. Do you increase your advertising budget, decrease your costs, put up your prices or reduce your workforce? In this case you would have a general goal – to improve profits – and a specific one – whatever action you decide to take to achieve your main purpose.

Communication objectives also work on both levels. All communication tasks involve two kinds of objectives:

- general objectives

- specific objectives.

General objectives are the reason(s) you decide to communicate in the first place. These are straightforward statements about what it is you are attempting to accomplish or what precise problem you are trying to solve. In our car repair example your general objective might be to get the car repaired without incurring further costs. In the software company case it would be to improve profits. Turn your objective into a statement: 'My objective is to get my car repaired without costing me any more money' or 'My objective is to increase my profits this year by 10 per cent'.

Specific objectives define your general objective in more precise terms. Specific objectives are measurable steps that will be accomplished within a set time period. They set out what you are going to do to achieve your general objective. The specific objectives which would be tied to the general objectives in the above examples might be: 'I will contact the service manager and get him to agree to repair my car by the end of the week' or ' I will increase my sales by five per cent every month for the rest of the year by increasing my magazine advertising'.

The first step, then, in your communication strategy is to formulate clear goals for what you want to achieve by communicating. Write your goals on paper or type them into a computer file. Recording goals is an effective means of reinforcement and increases your chances of achieving them.

CREDIBILITY

When you have clearly formulated your goals, you can go on to the next step in your communicator strategy. As the communicator you need to consider how you are seen by your audience. What is your audience's perception of you? How will the audience react to you, the communicator? Your audience's response to you is based primarily on your credibility. Credibility is the measure of how believable you are. Your credibility is assessed by the receiver of your message on a range of both subtle and obvious measures. How these measures are assessed by your audience will affect their response to your message. Note that your audience's perceptions may not match your own perception of yourself on these measures. How you will be perceived on these criteria will also vary from message to message and audience to audience. Your credibility is a variable that is relative to the particular circumstances of each communication task. Credibility measures are always a factor in your audience's acceptance of your message whether you are writing a job application, an e-mail or annual company reports, or giving a presentation the. The difference is simply one of degree.

The following are the main characteristics that define your credibility (adapted from Ohanian 1990 and French and Raven 1959):

- trustworthiness and reliability

- fairness and integrity

- expertise and credentials

- image and attractiveness

- status and power

- shared values and beliefs.

Trustworthiness and reliability
Your trustworthiness and reliability are the most important factors in your credibility. How do you convince your audience that you are trustworthy? If you regularly communicate with the same audience they will learn to trust you over time. You will build up a reputation for reliability. Some large, established companies such as John Lewis Partnership have built their reputations for reliability over decades. Others, like the newly privatized train companies in the UK have been unable to build consumer confidence due to their unreliable schedules and a number of serious train accidents in the early years of privatization. It takes time to build a solid reputation for trustworthiness and reliability.

What if you are communicating with someone for the first time? Can they rely on what you are saying or promising to do? Persuading customers to do business with you when you have just started up your own graphic design firm, for example, means they will need reassurance or evidence of your trustworthiness and reliability. Testimonials from other satisfied customers, awards or plaudits for your designs, your credentials and local reputation or mutual contacts can help build your reputation. The accumulation of the goodwill of customers that a company builds over time is in large part due to its reputation for trustworthiness and reliability. So valuable is a firm's goodwill that when the company is bought or sold the price reflects the amount of goodwill the firm has generated over time.

What if your only contact with your audience is through a letter or e-mail? How does the receiver of the message know you are trustworthy? You may have to draw on your expertise, credentials or position in the organization. If your job title is congruent with the message you are conveying, you will be more convincing. If, for example, you are the Director of Human Resources and you are writing to employees to advise them of benefit changes, they will more easily accept the message than if your position was in the accounting department. Another way to generate trustworthiness and enhance your credibility is by showing fairness.

Fairness and integrity

Your audience will assess the fairness of your message, particularly if your message is not positive. If you are writing to inform someone of bad news such as a failed job application, the way you construct your message can greatly enhance your perceived level of fairness. If you explain the reasons for the rejection and praise the applicant's qualifications and experience, you will be seen as acting more fairly than if you simply state the rejection and abruptly end the communication. A fairer message will also enhance your trustworthiness and retain the goodwill of your customers, as will a direct and well-reasoned approach.

Even a hint of dissembling or hedging about an issue will bring your integrity into question. Your integrity is linked to your reliability and trustworthiness but also includes an honest and ethical approach to all business and personal transactions. A reputation for fairness and integrity will increase your credibility and thereby your success as a communicator.

Expertise and credentials

How can you convince your audience that you have the expertise and credentials to provide specialist information or services? If you are a doctor, lawyer, architect, accountant or other professional you will have credentials such as university degrees and professional designations from the accrediting bodies for your field. You will most likely have memberships in the nationally recognized associations related to your area of expertise. Other credentials might include awards such as OBE and MBE honours or government posts such as MP or MEP or professional titles such as doctor, reverend, and military or police ranks.

Your credentials combine with your expertise to give you professional credibility in specialist areas. If you are a chartered accountant sending out letters about your services to generate new business, you need to persuade potential clients of your expertise. Since you look after clients' financial affairs, expertise and credentials are essential to your credibility. You might indicate your expertise by listing your experience in particular areas such as tax advising and investment planning. Your credentials can be displayed in your letterhead or by indicating them with letters after your name. If you lack credentials you can enhance your credibility by emphasizing your experience and expertise or by noting your membership in relevant associations or licensing bodies. You must be careful not to over-emphasize your credentials. In some instances it might make you appear arrogant and thus undermine your credibility. Consider each situation carefully and decide whether it is appropriate to emphasize or under-play your credentials.

Image and attractiveness

Image and attractiveness are most important when you are physically delivering your message. Oral presentations, interviews, meetings, video and television are the most common situations where your image will be a factor in your credibility. In business communications you will most likely be representing either your own company or your employer in which case your image is closely linked with your organization's credibility. In marketing communications, for example, celebrities are used to endorse products. The credibility and attractiveness of the celebrity is key to the success of the advertising campaign. Consumers have to believe that the celebrity would use the product being advertised. The image of the celebrity has to match closely the image of the product for the advertisement to be successful (Ohanian 1990). Your image as a representative of your organization needs to match that of the company for optimum credibility. Lawyers and bankers, for example, tend to dress formally so that their clients feel more secure about entrusting them with intimate personal and financial information.

Image and attractiveness are also important in written communications. The way you present your message, its tone, structure and style can affect image. The type of lettering, logos, weight of paper, sophistication of graphics and print styles all affect image and attractiveness. Similarly, with telephone conversations, the tone and rhythm of your voice, your accent, and the emotion your voice carries say something about your image. Most of the factors affecting your image tend to be fairly superficial aspects that can easily be changed, controlled or improved. Matching your image to your message can improve its reception substantially.

Status and power

Your status can enhance or detract from your credibility. Your status is your position in the social system in which you live and work. Anthropologists divide status into two types (Nanda 1984):

- ascribed status

- achieved status.

Ascribed statuses are those you are born with. In Western society they are primarily sex, race and ethnic group. In societies where class or caste are fixed at birth and the individual has no opportunity of changing them, these would be considered ascribed statuses. In most Western societies individuals can move between classes, the most common change being from working class to middle class, in which case class is an achieved status. Achieved statuses are those you choose or achieve yourself. These are primarily related to socio-economic status such as occupation and wealth and social roles such as father, wife or grandmother.

Status is often associated with power. Power is the ability to make decisions and take actions that can change your own life or someone else's. Your status in society usually dictates the amount of power you have. Power and status are relative. The difference in power between a junior manager in an organization and its managing director is substantial. A bulletin coming from the managing director carries more weight than one coming from the junior manager because the MD has more power and status. Yet in her spare time the junior manager may be the president of a local interest group where her power and status would be greater than the other members'.

Status and power can affect your credibility both positively and negatively. Too much exercise of power or flaunting of status can cause your message to be ignored. To assess how your status will affect your credibility you will have to look at it in relation to the status of your audience. If you have very little status compared to your audience your credibility will be lower than if you share a similar status. You can enhance your relative status and power by appealing to your audience in a number of ways which we will look at below in the section on message strategy.

Shared values and beliefs

Culture is based on shared values, beliefs and basic assumptions. If you share the same culture and social background as your audience it will be easier for you to communicate with them. You will not have to worry about making wrong assumptions or taking an approach that may be offensive or create confusion. On the other hand, if you are from a different background than your audience, your credibility may be difficult for your audience to assess. If you take a too direct approach where an indirect approach is the norm, you may appear brash or aggressive, or in the opposite circumstance, too timid and ineffectual. In either case your message will not be clear and you reduce your credibility with your audience. When communicating cross-culturally, get advice from someone who is a part of or familiar with the cultural background of your audience.

Your audience will assess your credibility in several or all of the above areas depending on the type of communication you send. Once you analyse your credibility on each of the measures, you can decide how your credibility might be improved to increase the effect of your message on your audience.

Effective communication involves more than a self-assessment by the communicator. You can also improve your communication skills by analysing the other side of the communication equation, the audience; this is the next step in a communication strategy.

Audience strategy

Audience analysis will help you to meet your audience's needs and achieve your communicator objectives. By analysing your audience before you construct your message, you will be able to customize your communication to match your audience's interests and expectations. To analyse your audience, answer the following questions:

1. Who is your audience?

2. What do you know about your audience?

3. What does your audience know about you?

4. What does your audience know about your subject?

5. How will your message be received?

WHO IS YOUR AUDIENCE?

Can you construct a profile of your audience? Your audience may be a single person to whom you are writing a letter or making a phone call or it may be an audience of several hundred people listening to your presentation. In some cases you will be familiar with your audience and in others you may not know them at all. If your audience is someone you know well like a work colleague your analysis will be easy but if it is largely unknown you will have to do more research.

Divide your audience into primary and secondary levels. Your primary audience is the one with which you will have direct contact. If you are writing a letter of complaint to the managing director of a company, he or she is your primary audience. There is a good chance that your letter will be seen first by a personal assistant before the MD and subsequently by the person who will be assigned to look into your complaint. These and any other employees in the company to whom your letter might get shown are your secondary audience. When you apply for a job, the person who interviews you is your primary audience. Most hiring decisions are done by committee or require approvals by more than one person. The other people who will have to assess or approve your suitability are your secondary audience. Key decision-makers should be your primary audience where your goal is to have some action taken. Direct your communication to the appropriate audience, i.e. those who are in a position to help you achieve your objectives, but do not neglect any potential secondary audiences.

WHAT DO YOU KNOW ABOUT YOUR AUDIENCE?

Your audience may be determined for you or you may be able to choose your audience. If you regularly write monthly reports for your department and these are sent to the same people on a distribution list, your audience is fixed and well known to you. If you are distributing direct sales material to generate new business for your company, you will have to make choices about who you will target as your audience. In the latter case, you will have to do more research and analysis. You might choose to target a certain geographical area or aim your advertising material at a certain age group such as young, single, professional people or couples with children.

Any audience analysis should begin by assessing the size and composition of the audience. How many people are likely to be included? What is their age range, educational background, gender and socio-economic composition? Are there class, ethnic or other general social characteristics or indicators that you should know about your audience? What are their cultural attributes – shared norms, values, traditions, beliefs, standards of behaviour? If you are writing to someone in an organization, what is their position in the organizational structure? Are they the appropriate audience for your message? The more information you have about your audience, the easier it will be to make your message relevant and convincing.

WHAT DOES YOUR AUDIENCE KNOW ABOUT YOU?

In developing your communicator strategy you assess your credibility from your perspective as the transmitter of the message. What your audience knows about you will determine your credibility from their perspective. Your credibility is not fixed. If you have had no previous contact with your audience, they can only assess your credibility from what little they know about you. You can provide more information about yourself through your message, enabling your audience to adjust their view of your believability. Your before and after levels of credibility are what Munter (1987) calls 'initial' and 'acquired' credibility. You should aim to increase your acquired credibility by doing a self-analysis of your credibility on the criteria we discussed in the communicator strategy.

Your audience will always have some advance knowledge about you from the context of the communication. If you are giving an oral presentation on the sales projections for your company, for example, the audience will know your job position and area of expertise. If you are complaining about poor service in your bank branch, your audience will know you are a regular customer and may have some information about your dealings with the bank. In either case you have some initial credibility and have the opportunity by taking a strategic approach to your message to acquire more credibility.

The most important thing to convey to your audience is your sincerity. If you attempt to be something you are not, or pretend to have knowledge that you do not possess, your audience will spot it very quickly. You will undermine your credibility and your audience will lose interest in your message. Establishing rapport and a good relationship with your audience can only happen if you be yourself. To improve your credibility without compromising your sincerity, find out all you can about your audience's familiarity with your subject.

WHAT DOES YOUR AUDIENCE KNOW ABOUT YOUR SUBJECT?

What is your audience's level of understanding of the content of your message? If you share the same background with your audience, whether social, cultural, educational or occupational, you can assume they will not have difficulty understanding your message. You do not want to patronize your audience so be careful not to oversimplify your message or state the obvious. If you think your audience may be unfamiliar with your subject you will need to provide more basic information at a non-technical level. If you are dealing with a complicated situation such as resolving a dispute, or completing sensitive negotiations, your communication will have to clearly summarize all the relevant issues even though your audience is familiar with the situation.

You may not always have prior knowledge of your audience's familiarity with your subject or you may have a diverse audience with differing levels of background knowledge. How do you design a message that will engage an unknown audience? Research in organizational behaviour and psychology has generated some models of human motivation that you can draw on to improve audience engagement with your message in any communication situation.

MOTIVATING YOUR AUDIENCE

Motivation is what drives people to behave in certain ways. If sales representatives are paid on a commission basis, they are likely to work harder at selling their product than if they were paid a flat-rate salary. They are motivated by the increasing scale of the rewards based on their efforts. If you are working hard at learning a language or staying fit you may be motivated by the satisfaction you get from self-improvement. In each case the motivation is different. In the first example, the motivation is a reward. In the second it is the fulfilment of a need, i.e. for self-improvement. These two models of motivation we categorize as:

- reinforcement theory

- need/satisfaction theory.

Reinforcement theory

Reward and punishment schemes or reinforcement theory come from the work of behavioural psychologists such as B. F. Skinner. Reinforcement theory assumes that behaviour that has positive consequences will be repeated and behaviour that has negative consequences will be avoided. Positive reinforcement means rewarding desirable behaviours to strengthen the likelihood that the behaviour will be repeated. Positive reinforcement in organizations includes reward schemes such as weekly or monthly pay cheques, employee stock purchase plans, bonuses and commissions. In marketing communications, for example, including a discount offer with a mail-out flyer for membership in a new fitness centre may increase sales.

The threat of punishment can deter people from undesirable behaviours, though it is not as powerful as positive reinforcement. The threat of being sent back to prison will deter some offenders from re-offending but not all. Threats are seldom good practice in business communications. They can result in undesirable consequences such as resentment, withdrawal, hostility or retaliation. If you write a letter of complaint about incomplete work to a building contractor, threatening court action or non-payment, you may never get the work completed. If managers use threats to get more production from employees, the results are unlikely to last due to decreasing morale which leads ultimately to lower productivity. Threats should only be used as a last resort when more measured approaches have failed.

How can you motivate your audience by using rewards? Rewards work best when they are appropriate, immediate and meaningful to the audience (Munter 1987). An appropriate reward is one which is neither too large nor too small. An extravagant reward is suspect. The receiver will think there are hidden strings attached to it. Too meagre a reward will not be sufficiently motivating to produce the desired behaviour. Rewards work best when they are administered as close in time to the desired behaviour as possible. Too far from the event and people forget and tend not to make the association with the original behaviour. For a reward to be meaningful it must be suited to the audience. Different people are motivated by different rewards. One employee may find a higher salary more rewarding whereas another person would be motivated by more responsibility or more leisure time. Use your audience analysis to determine what reward schemes would be most motivating.

Need/satisfaction models

Need/satisfaction theories of motivation focus on needs and need deficiencies. They claim that people are motivated to satisfy needs or compensate for unmet needs or need-deficiencies. The two most important models are Maslow's hierarchy of needs and Herzberg's two-factor theory.

Abraham Maslow (1943) argued that people are motivated to satisfy different sets of needs which he classified in a hierarchy. Figure 4.2 shows the pyramid structure of Maslow's hierarchy. When the lowest-level needs in the hierarchy are met, only then do people go on to satisfy the needs of the next level. When one set of needs are met, they cease to be motivators for the individual. Maslow's five levels of needs, beginning with the most basic level, are:

- physiological

- security

- belongingness

- esteem

- self-actualization.

Physiological needs are the lowest level on the hierarchy. They include the most basic biological functions and survival needs such as food, water, air and sleep. Only once these needs are met do people turn their attention to satisfying the next level.

The second level, security needs, is the desire for a secure physical and emotional environment. Shelter, warmth, clothing and freedom from worry about money or financial security are prime considerations at this level. Insurance companies trade on our need for security. Their marketing communications often use terms such as 'secure', 'make provision', 'complete coverage' or 'no worries', to focus our attention on and appeal to our security needs.

Third on the hierarchy is belongingness needs. We are all social beings and need contact with other people. Our need for love and affection and acceptance by our peers are belongingness needs. A sense of belonging comes primarily from our relationships with our family, friends and co-workers and from being part of a community. Beer advertisements often appeal to belongingness needs by using scenes of groups of friends enjoying themselves in a pub or watching football. Telephone companies use belongingness needs in their adverts by appealing to our need to be in contact with friends and family.

The fourth category of needs is esteem needs. Our sense of self and self-esteem come from a positive self-image and self-respect. Acceptance and recognition from others increases our self-respect and builds self-esteem. Much advertising copy appeals to our esteem needs. A positive self-image includes looking and feeling attractive. Cosmetics, clothing and car retailers all trade on our need for a positive image, by associating their products with attractive people.

At the top of Maslow's hierarchy is the need for self-actualization. When all other needs have been satisfied we begin striving to realize our individual potential. Personal growth and accomplishment become important. Some people never reach the self-actualization level, though most people in Western society fulfil the needs of the first four levels.

How can Maslow's needs hierarchy be used to motivate an audience? As you can see from Figure 4.2, the top three levels of the pyramid are the most likely needs to appeal to in developing an audience strategy. The top level is the most difficult to aim at because personal growth and achievement are specific to the individual. Unless you know or have a very good idea of your audience's self-actualization needs, you would be better to appeal to belongingness and esteem needs. If you want people to attend a meeting you might appeal to their affiliation needs by stressing the need for team-work. If you are writing a letter to employees about an award programme for employee suggestions you are appealing to the need for recognition. If you send out a brochure to all employees about your firm's career development opportunities you are appealing to the need for achievement and personal growth. You can appeal to the need for responsibility by encouraging employees to use environmentally sound work practices.

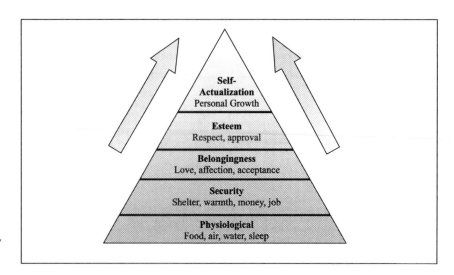

FIGURE 4.2 *Maslow's hierarchy of needs (adapted from Maslow 1943)*

Maslow's model should be used as a guide to motivation. The categories are not as discrete as the pyramid would suggest. Some needs straddle more than one category and in some cases people are motivated by higher level needs without fulfilling the needs of lower levels. Culture also comes into play in motivation theory. Whilst the basic levels of needs are universal, higher-level needs can vary cross-culturally. Make sure you are acquainted with the beliefs, values and basic assumptions of your audience before applying motivation theory.

The second needs-based motivation model is Frederick Herzberg's (1987) two-factor theory. Herzberg's theory came out of his research on job satisfaction. He interviewed accountants and engineers, asking them when they were most satisfied with their work and highly productive and when they were dissatisfied and least productive. He found that different sets of factors were responsible for high and low levels of production. For example, if employees were unmotivated by low pay, it did not follow that they would be motivated by higher pay. The deficiency of a need, in other words, produced one effect but the satisfaction of that need did not necessarily produce the opposite effect. A person might cite low pay as a source of dissatisfaction but not cite high pay as a source of satisfaction. Other factors such as recognition or accomplishment were often better motivators for higher production.

Herzberg's findings contradicted the popular view that satisfaction and dissatisfaction were at opposite ends of a continuum. Rather, Herzberg concluded that employee motivation operates in two different dimensions altogether: satisfaction to no satisfaction and dissatisfaction to no dissatisfaction. Factors that operate on the satisfaction continuum Herzberg called 'motivational factors' and factors on the dissatisfaction continuum he called 'hygiene factors'. Figure 4.3 illustrates the two-factor model.

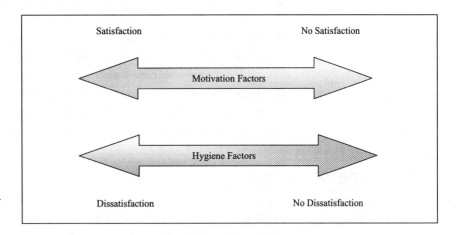

FIGURE 4.3 *Two-factor theory*

Hygiene factors in the workplace are related to the working environment. They include the physical environment, pay and security, company policies and relationships with colleagues. Any deficiencies of hygiene factors lead to worker dissatisfaction but meeting adequate hygiene needs does not necessarily lead to increased satisfaction. Only motivational factors such as achievement, additional responsibility, recognition, advancement and satisfaction with the work itself increase employee motivation. Much of the job enrichment movement of the last few decades began with Herzberg's findings.

Herzberg's and Maslow's work leads to the conclusion that the most effective way to motivate people is to appeal to growth needs rather than deficiency needs. As in reinforcement theory, the positive end of the spectrum is more motivating than dealing with negatives. Punishment as a deterrent and compensating for deficiencies are not as motivating as rewards and appealing to growth needs.

Use motivation to interest your audience in your message by appealing to their growth needs or offering some means of positive reinforcement, but remember what motivates one person may not motivate the next. Motivation theories are general models that do not take into consideration the wide variation in human populations.

Cost/benefit analysis

An alternative simpler approach you can take to motivating your audience is to ask yourself what benefit the audience will get from your communication. We are all motivated by self-interest. We all judge each action we take on the basis of what it means to us or what we can get from it. Your audience will make a calculation either consciously or subconsciously, whether the effort it takes to read your communication or listen to your presentation is worth it to them. Appeal to your audience by offering them a benefit to match the cost of their attention. If you are writing to complain about a company's service you might state that you regularly recommend the company to friends and would like to be able to continue to do so. You are more likely to get action taken on your complaint if there is a benefit to the reader that is at least equivalent to the effort involved. In this case the benefit of keeping a loyal customer and possibly acquiring new business would be a strong motivator.

When you have completed your communicator strategy, by setting your objectives and assessing your credibility, and you have analysed your audience and how to motivate them, you can go on to the third step in building a communication strategy – message analysis.

Message strategy

Message analysis deals with the content, style and structure of your message. The content will be relative to your communication objectives and how you intend to appeal to your audience. Message styles change relative to the task and context of the communication. Message structure allows the key ideas of your message to be emphasized appropriately for your audience.

WHAT GOES INTO YOUR MESSAGE?

Messages generally have one purpose: providing information, addressing a problem or answering a question. Message content can be anything from a request for the price of a product to a lengthy report on a legal decision to a book on communications. Your communication objective will form the core of your message content. It will also dictate length, level of formality, type of communication (letter, e-mail, report, phone call) and style. When developing the content of your message, always keep your communicator objectives in mind. In some cases you may need to generate new ideas or synthesize a large amount of material before you can construct your message. We will look in more detail at generating ideas and structure in the next chapter. Here we focus on some important generic strategies for ordering your message content and emphasizing important ideas.

SELECT YOUR EMPHASIS

An important part of message content is the ordering of ideas. Should you put your most important point at the beginning, middle or end of your message? You can identify the core ideas that need to be emphasized in your message by looking at your communicator objectives. Some of the ideas you have to communicate, or certain parts of the message, will be more important than others. You want to put the important ideas where they will have the most impact. The audience memory curve (Figure 4.4) illustrates where you should put ideas you want to emphasize.

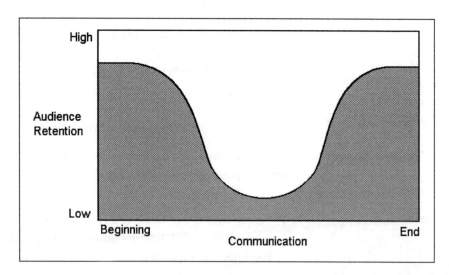

FIGURE 4.4 *Audience memory curve*

As the memory curve shows, the points at the beginning or end of a message have the most impact on your audience's memory. Thus important ideas should be placed at the beginning or the end of your communication rather than buried in the middle where audience retention is at its lowest. You can also see from the graph that you should make strong efforts to keep your audience's attention throughout the message – especially in the middle, where audience interest is low.

AUDIENCE AGREEMENT

You can take a direct or an indirect approach to your message. The choice should be based on your audience analysis which will tell you how your audience is likely to react to your message. Are they likely to agree with what you have to say? Will they be interested in your results or conclusions? Is your message good news? If so, or if your audience is extremely busy, choose a direct approach as part of your message strategy. If the culture of your organization, as one of its norms, tends to promote a direct approach, you will be better advised to use it in most cases.

When you use a direct approach state your purpose, conclusion or point at the very outset and then fill in the supporting evidence. For example, a company producing packaging materials might structure a direct approach as in the following:

Point:
    We now need to focus on increasing sales in the glass bottling division.
Support 1:
    We have penetrated the glass bottling market.
Support 2:
    We have first-mover advantages with our innovative bottling design.
Support 3:
    Increased market share is a critical factor in keeping other potential competitors out of the new bottling market.
Support 4:
    Only increased sales can provide the increased market share needed.

Such a direct approach has several advantages from a communication strategy perspective (Munter 1987):

1. People tend to assimilate and comprehend written and oral content more easily when they know the outcome, the point or the conclusion at the beginning of a message.

2. A direct approach is more audience-centred since it gives the results of your work first rather than the steps you went through to reach your conclusions.

3. Reports, memos and other communications where you want to get 'the facts' or the point across at the beginning are particularly appropriate for a direct approach.

4. The direct approach saves your audience time – it cuts to the important information quickly.

Present your ideas first when you are providing alternatives for your audience's consideration. If your audience is likely to agree they will be eager to see your support (paying less attention to alternatives). If your audience is very busy, they can skim through the document quickly since they agree with you from the outset. If your audience is likely to disagree use an indirect approach.

AUDIENCE DISAGREEMENT

Is your message bad news? Is your audience likely to disagree with you? Will you have to persuade them to accept your point of view? Will they be more interested in your analysis than your conclusions? If so, choose an indirect approach for your message strategy.

The indirect approach works by setting out your supporting arguments first followed by your point, conclusion or purpose. This is the exact opposite of a direct approach. Your indirect argument might go something like this:

Support 1:
   We have penetrated the glass bottling market.
Support 2:
   We have first-mover advantages with our innovative bottling design.
Support 3:
   Increased market share is a critical factor in keeping other potential competitors out of the new bottling market.
Support 4:
   Only increased sales can provide the increased market share needed.
Conclusion:
   We now need to focus on increasing sales in the glass bottling division.

There are a number of advantages to using an indirect approach (Munter 1987):

1. If you know from the outset that your audience is likely to disagree with you, an indirect approach may soften their resistance to your conclusion.

2. An indirect approach works best to arouse audience interest. They want to know the conclusion or 'punch line'.

3. If your credibility is low, leaving your views to the end can increase your audience's perception of your fair-mindedness.

If you are trying to bring your audience around to your point of view, you will need to explain your reasons and build interest in your argument before revealing your conclusion. Present your most convincing evidence last before stating your conclusion. Your views will appear the stronger when tied to the strongest support. Use the beginning of the communication to arouse audience interest. If you can, provide evidence first that they might agree with so they will be more amenable to your point. Next provide other supporting evidence from weakest to strongest and end with your solution, point, views or conclusion.

MESSAGE STYLES

Messages can be formal or informal. E-mails, conversations with friends and family and personal letters are examples of informal messages. Business reports, academic theses, business-to-business letters and legal documents are formal messages. Again, the context of your message will dictate its level of formality and tone. Remember that most communications in business should not use very formal or jargon-laden styles. Business communications are much less formal now than they were a few decades ago.

Your message style will depend on your purpose but most communications aim to do one of the following:

- persuade

- inform

- consult.

Persuasive messages attempt to influence people to take action or change their minds about something. Most persuasive messages are designed to sell something, elicit a favour or generate support. Persuasive messages tend to use the indirect approach as they assume audience disagreement from the beginning.

Informative messages simply provide information without trying to sell, persuade or advise. They explain or instruct. The audience is meant to learn something from the message. It is not necessary to be indirect as the audience will be either receptive to your message or neutral about it.

Consultative messages require your audience to join with you in taking action. They may also solicit advice. When you want to consult with someone you can use either a direct or an indirect approach depending on the context and your communicator objectives. If the issue is relatively simple, use a direct approach. If it is more complex or sensitive in content, use an indirect approach.

We will look at different styles used in specific communication tasks in Chapter Seven which deals with the practical aspects of communication.

Channel strategy

The fourth element in your communication is choosing a channel. Communication channels are the means you use to get your message across. You will not always have a choice of channel for your communication. If you are asked to give a presentation or write a report, your channel is fixed. When you do have a choice you should base your decision on your objectives, your audience analysis, and the appropriateness of the channel to your message.

Choose your channel carefully to ensure that your message gets heard. If you want to send a message to the CEO of an organization who does not know you, you would be more likely to get a hearing if you use a letter rather than a phone call. A phone call from a stranger probably would not get put through. If you are a division manager and want to talk to all of your regional managers your preferred channel would be a face-to-face meeting of the group.

Some other considerations for channel are time, cost and the necessity for having a record of the communication. Where a record is necessary, as in contract details, a formal letter is the norm. If time is important and a quick response is needed, choose phone calls or e-mails. Where cost is an issue, as in phone calls to foreign countries, e-mails and faxes would be better choices. Whatever channel you choose, match it to your objectives, audience and message.

An integrated communications strategy

With the four basic elements of a communication strategy in place we can now tie it all together with what is perhaps the most important but often most neglected aspect of communications – culture. There is no aspect of human life that is not touched and altered by culture. This means how problems are solved, how cities are planned and laid out, how transportation systems function and are organized, as well as how economic and government systems are put together and function. Culture even has an impact on personality, how people express themselves (including shows of emotion), the way they think, and how they move their bodies. Culture influences behaviour in the deepest and most subtle ways.

When we discuss communication and culture, we should be aware of the total spectrum of communication including symbolic communication other than just language: e.g. non-verbal communication, customs, rituals, perceived values, and concepts of time and space. The central point about culture is that culture has meaning. Communication is about communicating meaning. The best communication strategy will still allow you to produce a message that is misunderstood if you do not consider the importance of culture. Figure 4.5 illustrates an integrated communication strategy showing how the four elements are linked with the basic communication model, the whole operating within the context of culture.

In this chapter you have learned the components of an integrated communication strategy: communicator strategy, audience strategy, message strategy and channel strategy. The communicator strategy provides a structure for examining and setting out your objectives (general and specific) and for assessing and establishing your credibility.

The audience strategy provides a framework for analysing your audience, what you know about them, and what they know about you and your subject.

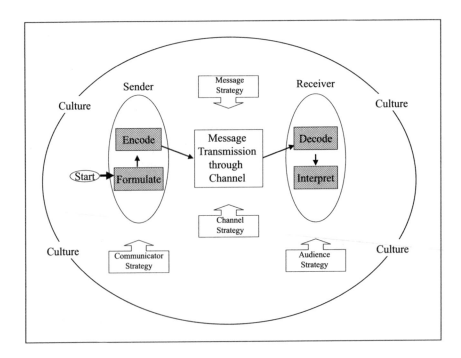

FIGURE 4.5 *An integrated communication strategy*

It also provides some suggestions for ways to appeal to and motivate your audience. Consideration of your audience is so important to the success of communications that it is worth the extra time and effort to understand audience analysis and motivation.

Message strategy affects the structure, style and ordering of ideas in your message. You need to decide on the degree of formality, whether to use a direct or indirect approach, and whether you aim to persuade, inform or consult.

Channel strategy gives you tools to decide which means you will use to transmit your message. Issues of time and cost and the need for a permanent record of your message are all considerations in an appropriate channel choice.

These four strategies are the kinds of strategies in which expert communicators engage – whether intuitively or through socialization and training. These are the strategies used by marketing and media communicators to make their messages memorable and to get you to buy their products. Teachers and trainers in managerial development use the same strategies to help students acquire and retain learning. Some people may find the process of targeting and planning communications to get people to do what you want somewhat unethical. It is not. Communication strategy is a neutral concept. It is only unethical if used for unethical ends. Using proven strategies to get constructive results from your communication is simply applying the principles of effective communication.

Discussion questions

1. Imagine you are a junior public relations officer for a large glass manufacturer. You have been asked by your manager to prepare a short presentation to be given to a consultation meeting of employees and community members on the benefits of a proposed plant expansion onto an adjacent plot of land within three blocks of a new residential development. Develop a communication strategy for your presentation using the four elements of an effective strategy.

2. How would you use motivation theory to appeal to an audience of consumers for a line of non-stick cookware products?

3. Assume you are applying for an important new position in a different company from your present job. How would you assess your credibility and how might you improve it?

References

French, J. and Raven, B. (1959) The bases of social power, in D. Cartwright (ed.), *Studies in Social Power*, University of Michigan Press, Ann Arbor.

Herzberg, Frederick (1987) One more time: how do you motivate employees? *Harvard Business Review*, Jan.–Feb., 109–120.

Maslow, Abraham (1943) A theory of human motivation, *Psychological Review*, 50, 370–396.

Munter, M. (1987) *Guide to Managerial Communication*, 2nd edn, Prentice Hall, Englewood Cliffs, NJ.

Nanda, S. (1984) *Cultural Anthropology*, 2nd edn, Wadsworth, Belmont, CA.

Ohanian, R. (1990) Construction and validation of a scale to measure celebrity endorser's perceived expertise, trustworthiness and attractiveness, *Journal of Advertising*, 19(3), 39–52.

Further reading

Conger, J. (1998) The necessary art of persuasion, *Harvard Business Review*, May–June, 84–95.

David, W. (1995) *Managing Company-wide Communication*, Chapman & Hall, London.

Jay, R. (1999) *The Seven Deadly Skills of Communicating*, International Thomson Business Press, London.

Maslow, A. (1954) *Motivation and Personality*, Harper and Row, New York.

War, P. (1996) *Psychology at Work*, Penguin Books, London.

PERFORMANCE COMMUNICATING

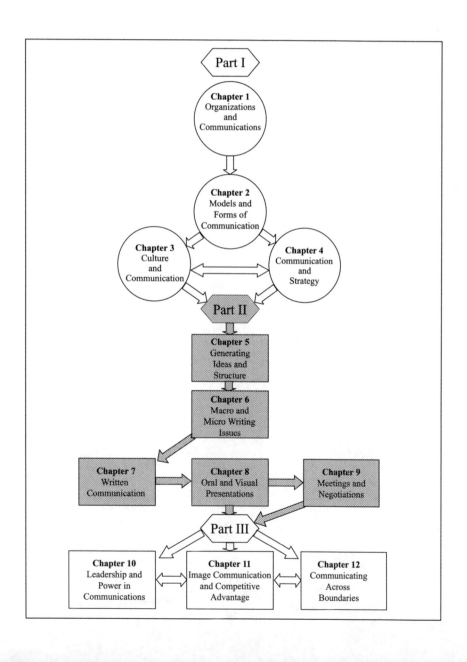

chapter five

Generating ideas and structure

THE CHAPTERS in Part II provide practical help with the dynamics of standard business communications: writing letters, reports, memos, e-mails and press releases, giving oral presentations and conducting meetings and negotiations. We begin with written communication. Do not begin your writing task until you have developed a well-considered communication strategy as described in the previous chapter. Once you have completed your strategy you can move to the pre-writing phase.

Writing is a process. Effective, clear writing comes from clear thinking. Clear writing comes from taking time in the pre-writing phase to plan and structure your ideas. The aim of this chapter is to provide you with some tools for the first steps in writing: generating ideas, finding source materials and structuring or organizing your materials and ideas. These steps are important in producing high-quality written or oral communications. Following the steps outlined in this chapter will help you organize your thoughts to make the most effective use of your writing time.

LEARNING OBJECTIVES

In this chapter we concentrate on the skills needed in the pre-writing phase. By the end of this chapter you will be able to prepare for any writing task by:

- Defining the objective of your writing task

- Using a variety of methods to generate ideas

- Knowing where to look for source material

- Evaluating your source material

- Conducting effective research interviews

- Structuring your ideas into a coherent outline

/e write

Effective writing is as important in your academic work as it is in a business environment and writing skills are transferable to many other areas of your life. In college or university you will be required to do a substantial amount of writing: reports, essays, timetables, notes, presentations and exams. In the business environment you will be called upon to write letters, memos, reports, e-mails, internet material and other specialist items such as contracts, advertising copy, proposals, technical manuals, depending upon your field. The success of all forms of writing depends on the quality of thought and organization that goes into the pre-writing phase of any writing task. Short memos and e-mails will not require the amount of preparation that reports and longer documents need but should still adhere to the principles of a sound communication strategy.

ADVANTAGES OF WRITING

Writing is not always the best channel for your message. Some situations always call for face-to-face communications. Discussing personal problems, dealing with employee dissatisfaction or making someone redundant always require speaking directly to the person involved. In more routine situations writing often has advantages over verbal communications:

- writing provides a permanent record
- written documents can be distributed to more than one person at a time
- writing is private and confidential
- writing can convey a sense of formality
- writing makes it easier for your audience to absorb lengthy arguments or complicated issues
- writing can confirm arrangements made verbally.

Writing is almost always necessary if your message is a complicated presentation of arguments or evidence. Readers may need to refer to or reread the material to understand it. Writing is necessary where a permanent record of your message is required. Information such as confirmations of salary increases, personal data on employees, financial information and legal issues can be kept private in written documents if care is taken to maintain confidentiality. Writing also allows precise details to be recorded which may not be remembered from conversations.

DISADVANTAGES OF WRITING

Writing can be the wrong channel for some messages. If you need to communicate sensitive material you would be better to use a personal interview. If you want immediate feedback or are anxious to know how your message will be received you would be better to deliver it in person. You will get more feedback from the non-verbal cues of your audience than you would from a letter. Disadvantages of writing are:

- writing takes more time than speaking

- feedback/response is slower

- writing creates a permanent record of your message when you may not want one

- the writer has no control over when the message will be read

- writing is less spontaneous than speaking.

Writing is time-consuming. You have to plan your message in more detail, draft it and possibly edit and rewrite. It has to be put in an envelope, addressed and mailed unless it is being sent by fax. In some cases writing can be less time-consuming, however. If you know that a lengthy discussion will follow your face-to-face communication, you may want to avoid it and save time by delivering the message in writing (Jay 1999).

How to approach a writing task

Writing and thinking are linked processes, but thinking in the sense of organizing must always precede writing. Thinking includes good ideas, bad ideas, complete and fragmented information, metaphors and analogies and muddle and mess. The result of your thinking is a conclusion or synthesis of material. Writing involves presenting your audience with the summary or conclusion to your thought processes. You would not want to inflict on your audience the details, false starts, irrelevant ideas and mixed messages that occurred to you as you synthesized your material. Show your audience a clear path either to or from (remember the direct and indirect approach) your conclusion.

Instead of writing down your thoughts as they occur, think of the pre-writing process as a series of steps based on:

1. understanding the question and expectations

2. generating ideas

3. finding source materials

4. structuring your ideas.

Additional steps that involve the actual writing process such as drafting and editing, and producing specific types of writing will be dealt with in subsequent chapters.

Step one: Understanding what is expected

Have you been asked to produce a report or a technical manual? How long is it going to be, i.e., are there page or word limitations? Are you expected to produce a complete analysis, or is your task to write a section of a longer document or a partial analysis? What format is required for the work? If you are uncertain about the right format for a piece of writing, check with people who know or have experience with that type of writing. They may be able to give you an example of a completed document. Knowing the correct format and style is important. Your organization's culture or your area of work such as law or accountancy may dictate the style and even format of specific kinds of documents. The context of your work or the industry in which you work can affect the way you think about the entire project, from how you research it to how you format each page of the finished document.

You must identify the main question in any writing task. The best researched and written report will not be successful if it answers the wrong question. Keep a copy of the question in front of you when you are both researching and writing, and constantly ask yourself, 'Is this relevant?'.

Not all writing tasks are initially framed as questions. In a job situation your supervisor might ask you to compile a report on a particular issue. For example, a marketing analyst might be asked to produce a report on the effectiveness of a particular advertising campaign. Turning the task into a specific question will help clarify the objective: 'What effect has the 30-second television advertisement had on the accessing of and sales from our website of our new mobile phone range?'.

In your communicator strategy you defined your general and specific objectives. Use your general objective to define the central question or problem of your writing task. Once you have defined the general question you can then make a list of subsidiary questions that relate to specific aspects of the main topic. Also important in defining your objective is asking yourself what is the purpose of the writing task. You should define your purpose by using action verbs. Your purpose might be to define or to discuss or compare or analyse a particular topic. In the above example the purpose is to analyse the results of the advertising campaign.

Once you are clear about your objective, have defined the main question and the subsidiary questions and have clarified the purpose of the writing task, you can begin the process of generating your ideas and finding the materials or data you need to support your objective.

Step two: Generating ideas

Assume you are a marketing analyst for a large food processing manufacturer. You have been asked to write a preliminary research report on the potential market for a new line of organic snack foods. You have defined your general objective in terms of the question 'Is there a market for a new line of organic snack foods?'. Your purpose is to analyse the market opportunities. Your specific or secondary questions are:

- Who is the target market for organic snack foods?

- What are the costs and selling prices of the products?

- How many products should be in the range?

- What retailers should stock the product?

- How large is the sales potential?

- Who are the competitors?

Your communication channel is decided for you. It will be a 20–30-page analysis, presenting the outcome of your research and your recommendations. Your audience is the marketing research group which includes your immediate colleagues, your department manager and his superior, the Vice-President of Finance and Marketing and representatives from sales and finance. Your report will be distributed to all concerned parties for review before a meeting is held to discuss your recommendations. You can assess your credibility with your audience fairly easily as they are all known to you. Since you do not know the outcome of your research you cannot predict whether your audience will be receptive to your message or find ways to motivate them until you have collected your research material and decided on your recommendations.

Your next step is the creative phase. Start developing ideas for how you might approach your research. What kinds of information do you need? Where will you get it? What tasks do you need to do first? Begin by spending some time thinking about alternative approaches and generating some new ideas. To stimulate creative thinking use a variety of methods: questioning, idea books, mind-mapping, brainstorming, mindstorming, storytelling and free writing. If your writing task is uncomplicated and is primarily for providing information you can use questioning techniques.

QUESTIONING

One of the simplest and most straightforward places to begin is by taking a journalistic approach to questioning. Journalists' reports answer basic questions: who, what, when, where, why and how? If you need more ideas you could expand on the basic questions, for example, by asking what are the causes or the consequences of an action or how or why something should be done or not done. You could also ask comparative questions. How does one thing relate to or affect another? Is there a relationship between two actions? Should something be done at one time rather than another? Should it be done by one person or a group? Cause and effect questions can stimulate ideas. If we take one course of action how will it affect another? If I recommend one action, what effect will it have on my results? If we reduce staff overheads, what effect will it have on productivity?

Posing a question and then answering it in the form of another question can produce ideas. From the marketing example above, you could ask your first question: 'Who is the target market for organic snack foods?' and then answer it with the second question 'What age, sex, and socio-economic group would buy organic snacks?'. Then you can keep repeating the process until you have a number of secondary questions to answer for each main one.

If you have trouble coming up with questions, turn the process around and ask yourself what answers would interest your audience. What do they want to know? What kinds of recommendations or conclusions might they expect? You can then fashion questions from the potential answers. If your writing task is complex and will take substantial time and effort you would be better to use more creative approaches that allow you to explore ideas and expand the scope of your knowledge about your subject.

IDEA BOOKS

One way to come up with ideas is to keep an idea book. To make an idea book work you must always have a notebook with you and record ideas as they occur. When you are thinking about a particular question or topic your subconscious mind works on it while you are occupied with other things. Often when you are least expecting it, a good idea or solution to your question will occur spontaneously. Note it in your idea book immediately. Jot down any other thoughts that occur to you in relation to the new idea.

Note immediately to what the idea refers and how it might be used – by the time you come to use the idea you may have forgotten the significance of single words or phrases.

Other sources such as television, newspapers, magazines, the internet and conversations can spark an idea for your writing project. Again, be sure to note them on the spot. Note the section of your work to which they belong. Use your idea book when you have a few minutes to spare, standing in queues, waiting at the doctor's surgery or waiting for the bus. Flip through the ideas you already have noted and see if anything occurs to you that you could add to them. Just the practice of reviewing the ideas helps keep them in mind and reminds your subconscious to keep working on them. By quickly reading through your notes, you can often find links between things you had not seen before. Use graphics or doodling if you tend to be visually oriented. The ideas will seem fresher and more memorable when associated with pictures. Generating graphic representations of your ideas is a powerful creative tool which is central to mind-mapping, the next method for generating ideas.

MIND MAPPING

A mind map is a type of hand- or computer-drawn graphic that you can use to generate ideas. Mind mapping was created by Tony Buzan (1995) following his research into note-taking techniques. ('Mind map' is a registered trademark of the Buzan Organization 1990.) Buzan studied the three common techniques for taking notes during a lecture:

- writing a complete transcript

- writing a summary

- writing key words only.

He then tested each of these and found the following results when testing how much was learned or remembered:

Least learned = 1   Most learned = 6

1. Complete transcript given to student

2. Student writes complete transcript

3. Summary given to student

4. Student writes summary

5. Key words given to student

6. Student writes own key words.

In a different experiment he asked a group of people individually to draw single-level mind maps (one-level deep, that is, having only concepts which are directly related to the central idea) around the word 'shoe'. Each person was asked to quickly generate seven related ideas. The startling result was that no two mind maps were even close to being the same. At most there were two words in common between some of the participants. Further studies have shown that the average is one word in common, and anything above two is very unusual. When used in a creative context to generate ideas Buzan found that people never produce the same mind maps for the same topic.

The surprising result was that mind maps can be used in many different ways other than just simple note-taking. With these results and other research Buzan came up with a method that works both for organizing and for generating ideas.

Mind mapping is based on the premise of making the notes or ideas as brief as possible and also as interesting to the eye as possible. To create a mind map you begin by writing or drawing a representation of your central idea and then branch off from it other secondary ideas that relate to the central concept. The structure of the map is similar to tree branches sprouting from a central trunk. You then take each of the secondary ideas and branch off from each of them ideas that relate to the secondary ones. In this way an exponential number of related ideas can quickly be generated with a minimum of time and effort. An important aspect of creating mind maps is to use very bright colours and graphics to enhance the visual memory effect of the ideas.

Mind maps may be either hand- or computer-drawn. The example in Figure 5.1 is a computer-drawn mind map of some of the main concepts in business communications you have been dealing with in this book. Note that

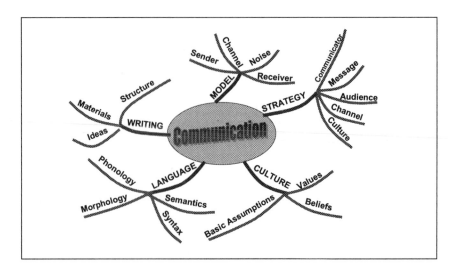

FIGURE 5.1 *Mind map of communications*

the central idea is large to represent the main idea, i.e., communication. Branching off from it are some of the main topics in communication such as language, communication model, culture and communication strategy. Branching off from them are some of the subsidiary components of the secondary topics. It helps recall if you place the words or pictures on the tree branches and make certain that the branches are limited in length to the size of the word. When recalling the map you can visualize which branches are short and which are long and thus have information about the length of the word you are trying to remember.

When using a computer to create your mind map you can easily restructure it, moving words and trees of words around in seconds. This makes the computer mind map even better for quickly creating new ideas and ordering ideas into a meaningful structure. Using the colour system you can instantly highlight different features of a complex mind map. You might want to make the most important concepts appear bright orange or all the 'good' ideas appear in bold underlined type.

Being brief and using single words is the key to a good mind map, but sometimes you need to write sentences of explanation for yourself or others. The computer mind map allows you to do this but to keep the extra information hidden until it is needed. This can also be used for learning information. You should be able to recite the 'comment' information without looking at it. When you can do this you have 'learned' the contents of the mind map and only need the key words to bring it back.

Mind maps work well for note-taking, as they have several advantages over simple summarizing systems:

- You can place each new idea in the right place, regardless of the order of presentation.

- It encourages the reduction of each concept to a single word.

- The resultant mind map can be 'seen' by the eye and retained in your memory more easily because of its structure and visual impact.

A mind map lets you rapidly produce an almost infinite number of ideas and at the same time organize them by placing each idea next to its related ideas. This makes a very powerful tool for creative writing or report writing, where generating the initial ideas and structure is important. It then becomes a relatively easy task to read the mind map and write a sentence or paragraph on each 'key word'.

Mind mapping can be very helpful in the reading phase of any writing project when you are gathering your materials. Instead of simply reading a book try creating a mind map of the book while you read. Begin by drawing your central word or concept and, while reading, add, in the appropriate place, any idea that strikes you as important or interesting. When you have finished reading the book you will have a one-page mind map which summarizes the main themes and concepts of the book. You will probably also have added several ideas which you generated yourself while reading. The act of creating the mind map will have greatly increased how much you absorbed from the book, and when you want to review the topic you simply refer to your mind map. Mind mapping can also be adapted for revising for exams. When you are trying to absorb difficult concepts draw a mind map of the material then try to redraw the mind map from memory several times until you are satisfied that you have retained the material.

Mind maps can also be used in group work or at meetings. A number of people can work together to produce a mind map by following a series of steps:

1. Individual members of the group draw mind maps of what they already know about the subject.

2. One member of the group or the group leader draws a group mind map combining the individual ones, eliminating any overlapping information.

3. Through discussion of the group map, the group decides what needs to be learned and/or which ideas need developing.

4. Individual members construct new mind maps based on the group discussions either addressing the general topic or individual tasks as assigned.

5. The group leader draws a final master map based on the individual contributions.

Mind maps can be used in meetings in a simpler way by having the group leader construct a mind map on a whiteboard during a discussion. This method allows every idea to be recorded and mapped in an appropriate place so that it becomes clear which ideas are workable or most important. By recording everyone's contribution no one feels ignored as all ideas are placed on the central mind map.

Mind maps are powerful intuitive tools for generating ideas. Linear methods tend to draw on the side of the brain that deals with reasoning and logic whereas the visual and spontaneous nature of mind mapping allows you to draw on the creative, more intuitive, side of the brain. When you apply your logical analytic skills to the ideas you have generated intuitively you will often surprise yourself with your own creativity. Other intuitive tools such as brainstorming which we discuss next have similar properties but lack the memory retention benefits of mind mapping.

BRAINSTORMING

Brainstorming is another intuitive method for generating ideas that works well for both individuals and groups. It has some similarities to mind mapping in that it creates links with the topic of interest in an unstructured way.

Brainstorming involves letting your mind wander over the various possible ideas and alternatives that relate to your question. By making random associations with your topic you generate a list of potential ideas or solutions, most of which will be abandoned in favour of the few pertinent and useful ones. Try to be as creative as possible. The most unusual ideas often produce the best result. Some 'off-the-wall' ideas can stimulate other valuable ones. The idea is to generate a long list of possible alternatives.

A brainstorming session has three stages: generating a list of ideas, reducing the list to the most relevant ideas and deciding how to implement them. The following are some key points to remember in a brainstorming session (adapted from Munter 1987):

1. Begin by generating ideas freely. 'Play' with the ideas

2. Note all associations with the topic as they occur

3. Do not attempt to come to any conclusion

4. Avoid negative feedback. Do not censor or criticize any ideas

5. Review the list of ideas and associations

6. Evaluate each alternative's strengths and weaknesses

7. Group related ideas and eliminate irrelevant ones

8. Further reduce the list to those that most closely relate to your objectives

9. Decide which ideas to implement

Brainstorming can be used effectively in groups. Group members can build on each other's ideas. One member can say something that will stimulate a related idea from someone else. The 'no criticism' rule is particularly important for group sessions to keep people from withholding ideas for fear of ridicule. Recall from the 'barriers to communication' section in Chapter Two, the drawbacks of groupthink. One way to avoid groupthink and reduce censorship is for each member to list ideas on a sheet of paper within a stated time frame. The group leader can then record the ideas, taking one idea from each member in turn until all ideas are recorded. When the list is complete, the discussion begins, and it continues until the core ideas are identified.

MINDSTORMING

Mindstorming is a method similar to brainstorming that works equally well for individuals and groups. Two steps are required. Firstly, a problem is constructed in the form of a specific question. For example, if a company wanted to increase its sales by 20 per cent the question might be 'How can we increase our sales by 20 per cent in the next year?' Write the question at the top of a clean page or computer screen and then list the numbers 1–20 down the page. The group must generate a minimum of twenty possible answers. As in brainstorming all ideas no matter how unusual should be recorded. The first ten will be easy to produce. It will get increasingly harder to find more ideas. Generating the last few is the most difficult, though often near the end is when the most creative and potentially powerful ideas come. When the list is complete, review it and highlight the most appealing options, narrowing it down to the two or three that have the most potential. Review and discuss them in depth until one shows itself as the most promising.

In the second step you repeat the process. Reformulate the chosen solution into a question and generate twenty solutions. In the above example, the solution might have been 'Make our product more appealing to the 20–35-year-old market'. It would be rephrased into 'How can we make our products more appealing to the 20–35 age group?' List twenty options, review them and take immediate action on those that you agree or sense will be the most likely to generate results. Mindstorming is as powerful a tool for meeting individual goals and solving problems as it is for businesses.

STORYTELLING AND FREE WRITING

Storytelling and free writing draw on the creative side of the brain much like brainstorming, but work better for a straightforward writing task than a problem-solving task. In free writing, instead of generating a number of single related ideas you simply start writing and write anything even remotely linked to your topic. Start with a clean sheet of paper or blank word-processing document. If you cannot think of anything relevant write whatever you are thinking at the time until you eventually come up with something relevant. Free writing is useful for people who have a difficult time getting started with either writing or gathering material. Once you have begun to write something on your topic it will often lead you into areas that will lend themselves to answering your question or stimulate you to seek out relevant sources.

Storytelling is a form of role playing. You begin by talking aloud about your topic either to yourself or into a tape recorder. Pretend you are having a conversation with a friend who wants to know what you are doing with your time. You explain the project you are working on, trying to be succinct. Do not ramble on. Repeat the process several times until you have a tidy summary of your project or topic and its related ideas. You will then have identified the main ideas and can start developing them.

You now have a number of tools you can use in the pre-writing phase of any project whether for academic work or in business situations. First choose the method or methods that appeal most to you and if you do not get the results you want try some of the others. The effectiveness of any method for generating ideas is related to its compatibility with your own style of working. Often it takes some experimentation to find out which is the most congenial for you.

Step three: Finding source material

Again assume you are creating a marketing analyst's report on organic snack foods. After brainstorming for ideas and mind-mapping the subsidiary questions, begin gathering data. You will need to consult different sources using a variety of data gathering methods: reading trade journals, company reports and financial data; researching other firms in the industry through the internet and business databases; interviewing potential buyers and customers individually and in groups. You will need to interview colleagues in the product development department, the manufacturing plant, the finance department and the marketing department.

You can begin by dividing your information sources into two types: primary or secondary. Primary sources are original sources of data. They are data you gather yourself from the source. Interviews, focus groups, surveys, questionnaires and observation are all primary sources. Secondary sources are those that have already been gathered and synthesized into a readable format before you see them. Books, journals, newspapers, magazines, reports, government documents and most internet data are secondary sources. You can begin with either primary or secondary research, depending on your familiarity with your topic. If you are unsure about how to begin, start with secondary sources. They can save you time by showing you what research has already been done on your subject and give you some idea of the standard kinds of research for your topic.

PRIMARY SOURCES

The most common primary source of data is interviewing. Interviewing can be face-to-face or by telephone, mail or internet. Interviews can be structured or unstructured. Surveys and questionnaires involve structured interviews where each subject gets asked the same questions. In most structured interviews, the subject must choose a response from a set of alternatives. In an unstructured interview the questions are not rigidly prescribed and can be changed, altered or deleted during the interview. Focus groups are a type of group interview where the subjects discuss their views on an issue set by the interviewer.

Interviewing

Face-to-face unstructured interviews can be an excellent source of material. They allow you to get information directly from people who have substantial experience and knowledge of your topic. Although the questions are not rigidly prescribed as in a survey, it is nonetheless important to prepare a list of questions. You need to know in advance what information you want or hope to get from the interviewee. Ensure that the interviewee is informed of the reason for the interview when you initially request an appointment. If you intend to tape-record the interview, ask permission in advance. Immediately after the interview make note of your own thoughts and ideas in response to the information you have gained from the interview.

Before you conduct the interview make certain you know your purpose and have a clear objective. Conduct an audience analysis and decide how you will approach the interview. Interviews have three stages, the opening phase, the question – response phase and the closing phase (see Figure 5.2). The opening phase of an interview includes three steps: rapport, orientation and motivation (Hamilton, Parker and Smith 1982).

The opening minutes of an interview can be the most important. Establishing rapport makes both participants relaxed and willing to talk. Being on time, dressing appropriately and being business-like and well prepared will help. To start the conversation refer to an item of mutual interest such as the weather, a local or national event or a mutual acquaintance.

The orientation step gives the interviewee an overall view of the interview. You might reiterate your name and why you are conducting the interview. If you are representing a company, state your position in that company. State the purpose of the interview and what kind of information is needed and how it will be used. If anonymity is important assure the interviewee of confidentiality. You might also state how long you think the interview will take.

The third step is motivation, or how you will interest the subject in giving you the information you need. Make use of motivation theory to appeal to your subject. If you need specific information that only your subject can provide, you could appeal to their need for recognition by stating your awareness of the fact. Remember to be sincere. The interviewee will sense quickly if you are not and will become suspicious and unco-operative.

The middle or main part of the interview consists of questions and responses. Most interviews for research purposes are to elicit information. You should develop a list of questions and place them in a coherent order to make it easy for your subject to give full responses. You should decide in advance which questions are the most important. In the event that you begin to run out of time you can confine your questions to those you consider essential. You should also limit the number of questions to what you think can be covered in the time available. People speak about one paragraph per minute on average which accounts for about 20 questions per half hour, allowing for some answers to be longer than others.

Each interview should include a mixture of questioning styles. The following are the most common types of questions:

- direct questions

- open-ended questions

- closed questions

- probing questions.

Direct questions are short questions that require simple answers. They can either be answered by 'yes' or 'no' or by a very short response. Examples of direct questions are:

- What are your sales targets for the month?

- Have you finished the report yet?

- What is your best-selling product line?

- Where is head office?

Direct questions elicit very little information and should only be used sparingly in interviews. Their advantage is that they require little time or effort and they limit responses which is helpful if your subject tends to wander from the topic.

Open-ended questions are broad, general questions that allow the interviewee to decide how much information to provide. They give maximum freedom to the interviewee and contribute to a relaxed atmosphere. Open-ended questions should be used at the beginning of the interview to start things off. Open-ended questions can sometimes generate information that it would be difficult to get otherwise. Since they take time to answer, they can provide the interviewer with an opportunity to think about what to ask next. The following are examples of open-ended questions:

- Tell me about your responsibilities as a project manager.

- What do you think about the proposed merger?

- How would you go about creating a new product line?

- What would you do with the money if you won the lottery?

Open-ended questions can be too time-consuming. If the subject is very talkative, there may be a tendency to wander away from the topic. Open-ended questions can also hand control of the interview to the interviewee. If the subject is excessively nervous, it may be better to start with some direct questions until the atmosphere becomes more relaxed.

Closed questions like direct questions call for short answers. However, the answers are limited to the options offered by the interviewer, for example:

- Would you rather design a house, an apartment complex or an office building?

- If you had a choice would you prefer to visit Spain, Italy or France?

- What motivates you more, money or job satisfaction?

- Who would you like to work with on the project – Jason, Sarah or William?

Closed questions save time and allow the interviewer maximum control over both questions and answers. They are easy to interpret and simple to use. They can be frustrating for the interviewees if the options offered do not include their preferred choice.

Probing questions are follow-on questions. They encourage the subject to expand on a previous point or add to an explanation. Use phrases such as 'tell me more about', 'and what did you do next?', 'why' and 'oh, really'. Sometimes your body language is enough to suggest further probing. Raising eyebrows, leaning forward, smiling and nodding can encourage added explanations.

Questions need to be organized based on some criteria (Fig. 5.2). If you want to know about someone's career, for example, you might use a life history approach and ask chronological questions. Begin with childhood, go on to education, early career and major highpoints, up to the present. If you think the subject might be reluctant to talk about early experience, use a reverse chronological approach: begin by asking about the current position and then on to the previous position and so on. If you have several themes to cover, organize them according to their relevance to each other, clustering similar ones together. If some questions are going to be more difficult or sensitive, put them in the middle part or towards the end of the interview. Start out with simple, non-controversial questions until you and the

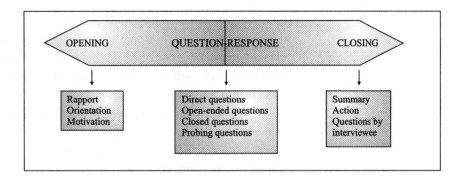

FIGURE 5.2 *Interview structure*

interviewee are relaxed. You can also organize your questions by moving from the general to the specific. Whatever approach you take, it must be well planned and have a rational structure.

The third phase of an interview is the closing. Summarize the interview briefly and if any conclusions were reached, restate them. If it seems appropriate give the interviewee a chance to ask questions. This is particularly good practice in job interviews and performance reviews. If any action is to be taken, reiterate who is to do what. Arrange a time and place for a subsequent interview if necessary. Thank the interviewee for taking time for the interview and for being co-operative.

Surveys and questionnaires

Surveys are used to conduct research with groups, often a large sample of a population. Surveys are normally conducted by using structured questionnaires where all subjects are asked the same set of questions and given the same options for answering. Surveys primarily use closed questions though sometimes they include an open-ended question or comment section where the subjects can add their own views. Political polling uses the survey method to sample large sections of a population chosen randomly from the electoral roll.

Constructing scientifically sound surveys and questionnaires requires specialized skill to gather reliable data. Reliable data give results which would be repeated if the survey were repeated. Be wary of constructing weak or leading questions that would make the results suspect. If you are constructing a questionnaire, plan to spend some time thinking about the meaning of each question and its potential interpretations. Be as precise as possible, asking only one thing per question. Get other people to read the questions and see if they interpret them as you do. Make sure you give clear instructions for completing the questions. Think about the type of answers you will get. Will the data be easy to tabulate? Will it give you the information you require? Are you prepared to accept results that may not accord with your views? Before you begin a major survey, pre-test the questionnaire with a small group. You will be able to see where the flaws might be in your questions and reword any unclear or misinterpreted ones.

If you are mailing your questionnaire, be prepared to get a low response rate. Most people will not bother to respond to mail surveys, particularly if you have not enclosed a postage-paid return envelope. You might add an incentive to encourage people to reply such as entry in a prize draw or you could appeal to their growth needs by emphasizing the importance of the research. Always include a covering letter to explain the nature of the research and how the data will be used.

Focus groups

Focus groups are a tool often used by marketing agencies to determine how consumers might react to a new product or service. In the organic snack example, focus group interviews might help determine whether the product line is viable, how it should be packaged or what consumer group would be interested in purchasing it. Focus groups are usually small – about five to fifteen people – and are normally chosen to represent specific social categories. A product may be tried on several different groups such as middle-aged professionals, young singles, or families with small children. They might also be organized geographically to learn about regional differences in product appeal.

The focus group interviewer, usually called a 'moderator', gets people talking about the subject until the discussion generates its own momentum. The moderator might begin by showing the product or advert, or introducing the topic, providing a short explanation and allowing the group to discuss their reactions to it. In consumer research, competitive products might also be used to stimulate discussion or for comparative purposes. The interview may be video-taped or tape-recorded. The interviewer or an assistant may take notes.

Focus groups are effective for providing a snapshot of consumer preferences. Like other group efforts, they are subject to the disadvantages of groupthink. Focus group results cannot measure precisely the attitudes or behaviour in a general population. They are useful for getting an indication of how pervasive an idea, value or behaviour is in a population and for determining feelings about products, issues and public figures (Bernard 1988).

SECONDARY SOURCES

Secondary sources are used in what is known as 'desk research'. Information is gathered from existing published sources. Reading and note-taking are the standard methods used. Creating summaries of material and paraphrasing as you read can be helpful. Be careful to record the source of all notes and summaries so that you can properly acknowledge your sources in your references section. Remember that secondary sources provide information that has been gathered for a specific purpose which may be different from yours. When using secondary sources keep your objectives in mind and ask yourself if each source is relevant to your purpose.

Use the internet, newspapers, books, periodicals or whatever other sources might be appropriate for your topic. Trade associations, company reports and government publications are useful sources of business data. Secondary data can also be purchased from organizations such as Mintel that compile syndicated reports and market data. Libraries often have CD-ROMs with database summaries of recent research in most subject areas. There are also on-line internet services, some providing data free and others charging for access.

The massive volume of information now available on every subject can be overwhelming. Read selectively. Set boundaries for your topic. Ask yourself what is inside and what is outside the boundaries. Be aware, too, that reading is an excellent procrastination device. There are two steps to ensure that you do not finish a writing project: (i) read yet another book or journal article, (ii) repeat step (i). Make sure you read enough to feel confident that you understand the topic and can answer the most important questions you have identified in your objectives, but leave plenty of time to write and edit.

When you are satisfied that you have enough information from primary and secondary sources, you are ready to start organizing your material. You will probably have far more than you will eventually use. You should first take some time to evaluate your source material.

EVALUATING YOUR SOURCES

If your research task is complex you may have gathered materials from a variety of sources. When synthesizing the material you need to be selective and evaluate your sources to ensure that you use the most relevant and reliable information. You should be particularly careful about material taken from the internet. Establishing the reliability of internet sources is often difficult. Use only internet sites that are very clear about the source of their information or are reliable government, organization or business sources.

The following are some questions that will help you evaluate the quality of your source material (adapted from Bovée and Thill 2000). Note that they refer to both written and oral sources.

1. What was the purpose of the material?

2. Is the material current?

3. How credible is the source?

4. Is the source potentially biased?

5. Where did the source get its information?

6. Can you verify the material independently?

Note that the reliability of statistical sources is particularly difficult to assess. The interpretation of statistics is based on knowing about the record-keeping process and how the data were collected. Unemployment figures, for example, are calculated differently in the UK than in some continental European countries. In the UK, they are calculated on the basis of the number of people on benefits who are actively looking for work. In other countries they are calculated from the number of people of working age who are looking for work. The results would be substantially different. Before you use statistical data always query the underlying assumptions that went into the tabulations.

In the process of collecting your materials, verifying and selecting your strongest sources, you will have generated many ideas and possible ways to approach your writing task. The next and last step is to organize your ideas into a coherent structure.

Step four: Structuring your ideas

Structure your ideas in an outline, a mind map or an idea chart. Which method you choose will depend on your writing task and your preference for working with words or pictures. Each method begins by selecting one main idea and three or four subsidiary or second-level points. Limit the subsidiary points to no more than four. Audiences are not likely to retain more than that from a single communication. If you are not sure about your main and subsidiary ideas, refer to your original communicator objectives.

In our organic snack foods example, the main idea from the general objective is an analysis of the market for a new line of organic snack foods. The subsidiary points are from the specific objectives. Each second-level idea can then be further subdivided according to the relevant number of supporting points needed. Your conclusion or recommendations may be put either at the beginning or end depending on your audience analysis. Use the direct approach if your audience is likely to agree with your conclusions and the indirect if you will have to persuade them.

The simplest structuring method is outlining. List the topics in a linear progression on a sheet of paper or word-processing screen. Indent second- and third-level ideas. Think about which of your subsidiary points is most important and decide whether you want it at the end or the beginning. You may organize the subsidiary ideas chronologically if appropriate or from the simplest to the most complex.

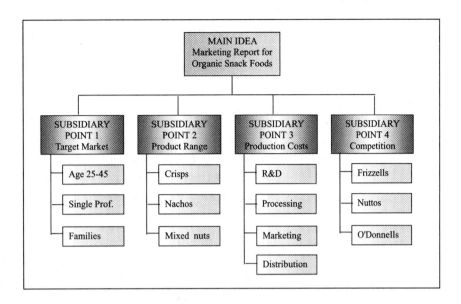

FIGURE 5.3   *Idea chart*

An easy way to represent your structure graphically is to use an idea chart. An idea chart is a hierarchical structure resembling an organization chart. Figure 5.3 illustrates an idea chart for an analysis of the market for organic snack foods. Note the three levels and how the ideas move from the general (main idea) to the specific (subsidiary points) to the details or evidence (third level).

The amount of structuring you will have to do will depend on the length of your project in pages or your time in minutes if you are preparing an oral presentation. If you are doing a ten-page report you can spend two pages on each major point and a page each for the introduction and conclusion. For a one-page letter, allot one idea per paragraph. If you are writing a long document such as a technical manual, book or thesis, you may need to add another level, but try to keep the levels to a maximum of four. Otherwise you may confuse your audience. For more complicated tasks, expand your idea chart horizontally. Each subsidiary idea should correspond to a chapter in your finished work.

You can apply the same structuring principles to a mind map. Start with your main idea in the middle and make branches for each subsidiary idea and continue for each level. Mind maps are particularly effective if you are having trouble sorting which ideas are important and which belong on which level. Mind maps are more flexible than outlines and idea charts. Mind maps stimulate the free flow of ideas. Add colour and pictures to your mind map for emphasis. Mind maps can make it easier to see the relationships between topics and move ideas around trying out different combinations.

Use the method that works best for you and your writing task. Writing without a plan will waste writing time and decrease writing effectiveness. In the next chapters we will be looking at putting the words on the page –

drafting and editing – and applying the precepts of effective writing to specific writing tasks.

References

Bernard, H. Russell (1988) *Research Methods in Cultural Anthropology*, Sage, London.

Bovée, C. and Thill, J. (2000) *Business Communication Today*, Prentice Hall, Upper Saddle River, NJ.

Buzan, T. (1995) *The Mind Map Book*, BBC, London.

Hamilton, C., Parker, C. and Smith, D. (1982) *Communicating for Results*, Wadsworth, Belmont, CA.

Jay, Ross (1999) *The Seven Deadly Skills of Communicating*, International Thomson Business Press, London.

Munter, M. (1987) *Guide to Managerial Communication*, 2nd edn, Prentice Hall, Englewood Cliffs, NJ.

Further reading

Babbie, E. (1982) *Social Research for Consumers*, Wadsworth, Belmont, CA.

Buzan, T. (1991) *Use Both Sides of Your Brain*, Plume Books, New York.

Peterson, R. (2000) *Constructing Effective Questionnaires*, Sage, London.

Pont, T. and Pont, G. (1998) *Interviewing Skills for Managers*, Piatkus Books, London.

Saunders, M., Lewis, P. and Thornhill, A. (2000) *Research Methods for Business Students*, Financial Times/Prentice Hall, Harlow.

chapter six

Macro and micro writing issues

Introduction

WRITING ISSUES can be divided into two levels: macro and micro. Macro issues focus on general tasks such as creating an initial draft of your work and editing or revising it to produce a clear, polished final product. Macro issues affect the document as a whole. Micro issues involve the details of writing: grammar, spelling, sentence and paragraph construction, word choice and referencing (acknowledging your sources).

In Chapter Five we looked at the pre-writing phase and the first steps of a writing project: (1) understanding the question and expectations, (2) generating ideas, (3) finding source materials and (4) structuring your material. The first part of Chapter Six deals with the actual writing: getting your words on to the page or the computer screen. The last sections focus on micro issues that can increase the effectiveness and clarity of your writing.

LEARNING OBJECTIVES

By the end of this chapter you should be able to:

- Produce an initial draft of your writing project
- Edit and write subsequent drafts
- Construct effective sentences and paragraphs
- Use appropriate wording
- Avoid sexist language
- Use standard referencing systems to acknowledge your sources

Macro writing issues: getting it written

CREATING A FIRST DRAFT

Drafting is not the production of perfect prose according to perfectionist ideals. Drafting is the stage when you attempt to get something written – just get the ideas out. Start with a blank page or word-processing document. Look at your idea chart, mind map or outline. Compare it again to your objectives to be certain every topic is relevant. When you are satisfied it suits your purpose, begin by listing all the main ideas and subsidiary and supporting ideas in the form of titles and subtitles. You will then have the skeleton structure of your document.

Do not censor your writing in the first draft. As you learned in the generating ideas section, creativity flourishes in a non-critical environment. Begin with writing what you know and avoid editing. When you reach a difficult patch or need more information to complete a section just make a note in the text and carry on, e.g. 'add example here' or 'more on this later' or 'find a better word'. If you do not note things to change later, you may forget about them.

As you work through each section ideas will occur to you for writing other parts. Note them right away in the relevant section. Instead of starting with whole sentences and paragraphs, you might jot down ideas in point form under the titles and subtitles. Then you can easily go back and construct coherent prose for each cluster of ideas. Getting ideas down quickly helps stimulate follow-on ideas. Starting with point form saves the effort it takes to write whole sentences when you are not certain which ideas will be used in the end.

Look over the sections and pick out the one you are most confident about to get started with prose writing. You do not have to write in a linear way from beginning to end. If your project is long, you may change the order of ideas, delete unworkable ones or add new ones as they occur to you. Since the structure of your material may change it can be a time-saving strategy to leave writing the introduction until you have finished the main body of the work, to avoid having to rewrite.

Continue writing one section at a time in the sequence that is most comfortable for you. When you are confident that you have covered each topic in sufficient detail for your purpose, set the draft aside for a few days if you have time. Any flaws and weaknesses will show up better once you get some distance from it. If you have problems getting your first draft written you may be suffering from writer's block.

WRITER'S BLOCK

Most writers experience writer's block to one degree or another. Writer's block can happen anywhere in the writing process. During a project a writer can get 'stalled', much like a car when it stalls and will not start again. Some writers simply cannot get started. Writer's block is not just a problem in writing long documents like books, reports and manuals. One-page articles, press releases, even letters and e-mails, can trigger writer's block. Writer's block can stem from fear of failure, insecurity, anxiety, overwork or negative experiences with writing in the past. Whatever the causes, writer's block can be avoided or overcome.

If you suffer from writer's block try some of the following strategies to get you writing:

1. Have a structure. Go through the pre-writing steps sequentially until you have a clear plan of action and document structure that you can translate into titles and subtitles or individual paragraph topics.

2. Avoid editing or censoring in the first draft. Do not censor, criticize or edit until you have a full first draft of your document.

3. Begin anywhere. Start in the middle, at the end or with whatever section makes you feel least anxious.

4. Create a writing environment. Always write in the same spot, preferably one that is set aside for the purpose. Play your favourite music in the background, have a pot of tea to sip as you write. Do whatever makes you feel comfortable and relaxed. Repeat the same behaviours each time so they provide cues that tell you to begin writing.

5. Schedule your writing time and tasks. If you write best in the early morning, make that your regular writing time. Scheduling writing sessions at the same time and in the same environment can get you into the habit of writing.

6. End where it is easy to begin again. End each writing session at a point where you know what you want to say next. It will be easier to pick up where you left off the previous session.

7. Remember that writing is a task. Writing is rarely inspiration. Do not wait to be inspired. Writing is simply a set of logical tasks that, when done, accumulate into a finished product, much like decorating a room or building a house.

EDITING AND REDRAFTING

Once you are satisfied that you have a passable first draft, you can begin to edit. Editing can be done on your word processor or on a hard copy of the document. A combination of both is best. Read quickly through your draft on the computer and fix any glaring errors. Do not make any major changes to the structure at this point. Print out your document in hard copy. Reading the material in a different form will give you a different perspective on it. Strengths and weaknesses in structure will become evident and you will get a better sense of its overall style and coherence. While you are reading through, ask yourself the following questions:

- Is the material relevant to my objectives?

- How will my audience react to it?

- How does what I am saying affect my credibility?

- Is the structure logical?

- Does the writing flow well? Is it coherent?

- Is it written in a business-like style?

- Have I used an appropriate style and tone?

- Can I improve my paragraphs, sentences and wording?

Make any necessary editing and adjustments to address the above issues. Do you tend to use the same terms and phrases again and again? In a long document it can be difficult to avoid overuse or repetition. Use a thesaurus to find alternatives. Good grammar and punctuation are essential but you should not edit for them until you have a good revised draft that will not require major changes. Otherwise you may waste time editing material that might not appear in the final draft.

You may have to move large sections of text around or simply rearrange sentences in a paragraph. You may decide you have put too much emphasis on one topic and not enough on another. Structural issues occur at document, paragraph and sentence levels. Paragraph and sentence structure are dealt with later in the second half of the chapter, Micro Writing Issues. The next section deals with the macro issues of document structure, coherence, style and tone.

Structure

Structuring your document is easy if you have followed the steps in generating ideas and structure. Look at your mind map, idea chart, or outline. In any lengthy document you will probably change your outline many times before you settle on the final structure. As you write, you begin to think very deeply about your subject. In the process of writing you should get new insights that may change anything from the whole organization of your work to just a few words. If you are struggling with your material, trying to find a workable structure, just relax and assume it will occur to you as you go. Often when you are well along on your first or second draft, you will have an 'ah-ha' experience. Your ideas will fall into place and the optimum arrangement of your material will be clear. Alternatively, once you begin to focus and concentrate, you will slowly realize what you want to say and how you want to say it.

Organize your document on the simple model of introduction of the main idea, followed by supporting points in paragraphs, and a conclusion. Each paragraph must have one main idea which is stated in the first or topic sentence. Subsequent sentences use details to illustrate the point in the topic sentence. Document structure can be visualized as a series of triangles and squares (Figure 6.1). The top triangle introduces the topic and states the point or argument. The squares represent any number of paragraphs to support that point. The bottom triangle is for summarizing, presenting recommendations, consolidating your argument or emphasizing your main point.

You will have to choose whether to state your conclusion or recommendations in your introduction or your conclusion. As we noted in the section on structuring ideas, your approach should be chosen to accord with your audience analysis. If they are likely to be receptive to your ideas, take the direct approach. If you will have to persuade them to your point of view, use the indirect approach.

When editing for structure, move sections of texts and paragraphs around to see if they work better in a different order. You may find that the whole thing flows better. The fluidity of your text is also related to its coherence.

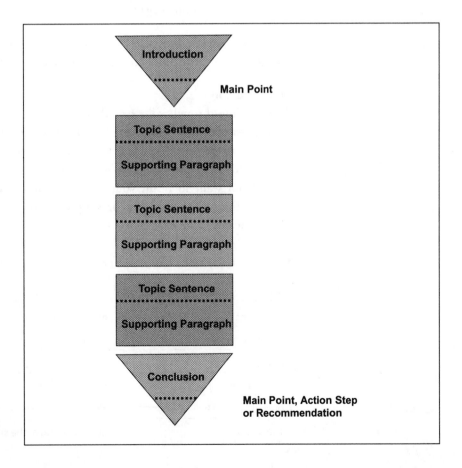

FIGURE 6.1 *Document structure*

Coherence

Good writing flows smoothly from one paragraph or section to the next. It must be internally coherent. Coherence comes partly from the organization of your ideas. You can structure your main points on any number of criteria: most important to least important or vice versa, chronologically, simple to complex, least controversial to most controversial, theoretical to practical, or whatever method suits your material best. As long as there is a logical sequence, your material will be structurally coherent.

Coherence comes also from linking ideas, paragraphs and sentences using transitional words or phrases. Your writing will flow easily if you make effective use of transitions. Table 6.1 gives some examples of transitions and their uses (adapted from Munter 1987).

Create your own transitions by referring to or repeating a term or idea in a previous sentence or using parallel constructions.

> e.g. Writing with vigour and style keeps your audience interested. An interested audience is more likely to remember your message.
> e.g. Culture is about shared beliefs, values and basic assumptions. Organizational culture is about sets of values and beliefs that are specific to one organization.

Your document must also be stylistically coherent. Maintain a consistent style and tone throughout to create a sense of flow and internal coherence.

Style and tone

After reading through your first draft, you may find you have not pitched your message at the appropriate level for your audience. If your text is too technical or too oversimplified, try to raise or lower the tone. Eliminating jargon and using plain English will correct most interpretation problems. You do not want to insult your audience with an overly simple message. Analyses that are too shallow or simply omitted can leave your audience feeling cheated. Pure description is rarely interesting to an audience. In most

TABLE 6.1 *Transitional words and phrases*

When to use	Word or phrase
Add a point	and, also, next, finally, too
Expand on a topic	subsequently, but, similarly, moreover, besides
Contrast	yet, but, however, although, still
Provide an example	for example, thus, for instance
Conclude	therefore, as a result, consequently, finally, then
Time or place	above, below, at the same time, further on, until

business and academic writing, analysis is essential. Check that (i) you have done an appropriate analysis of your topic, and (ii) that the analysis is of sufficient depth to interest your audience.

Written documents have an overall tone or a sub-text that gives off a particular impression. Make sure your sub-text is not complaining, lecturing, pompous or 'know-it-all'. Nor do you want to sound too modest or self-effacing. Strive for a firm, fair and confident tone. You want to appear knowledgeable about your subject area, confident in your material and sincere in your delivery.

Have you used the style of writing that is appropriate for your subject matter and audience? Styles vary depending on the type of message, audience and channel. Informal styles are common with personal conversations, telephone calls, e-mails and letters. The same channels in business can be formal or informal depending on the relationships between the sender and receiver of the message and the context. Reports, theses and legal arguments tend to require a more formal structure and tone. When informality is called for, avoid being too familiar or using too much humour. You risk not being taken seriously and may jeopardize your credibility.

When you have edited for structure, coherence, style and tone, you will have addressed the macro writing issues. The next step to a final draft is attention to detail at the micro level.

Micro writing issues: getting it edited

Micro writing issues deal with the mechanics of writing. Basic mechanics such as grammar, spelling and punctuation you will have learned at school so we do not deal with them here. As a refresher or to check things you are unsure about, have a good dictionary and a standard reference book for English usage close at hand when you are writing. In this section we look at more general ways to improve your writing by paying attention to how you use sentences, phrases and words. Good writing should have the following qualities:

- clarity

- precision

- vigour

- variety and rhythm

- emphasis.

TABLE 6.2 *Pretentious and obsolete language*

Pretentious	Obsolete
Accordingly	Heretofore
Aforementioned	Inasmuch as
Commence	In due course
Indeed	Permit me to say
Furthermore	Please find herein
Obviate	Pursuant to
Utilize	The undersigned

ADD CLARITY

To add clarity, choose clear words and use as few as possible to convey your meaning. The simplest words that say what you want to say are often the best. Most of the common words in English, those which sound natural and direct, are short. They are also among the oldest words in the language. English is rapidly becoming the language of business internationally and plain English is the appropriate style for business communications.

You might occasionally use technical terms and longer words when relevant to the standards of your industry or field. Use technical language when it will help explain something more efficiently. Sometimes unfamiliar, foreign or long words are the only ones that will work. Use them sparingly. For everyday business messages, think clear and simple.

Avoid using out-of-date terminology or pretentious wording. Terms such as those in Table 6.2 make your writing sound stilted, overly formal and dated.

Recall from our discussion on language that words have denotations and connotations. The denotation is the dictionary definition and the connotations are alternative meanings dependent on usage. Always check on the meanings and usages of words with which you are not familiar. Using an alternative word or phrase you found in a thesaurus can sometimes add meanings that obscure your message or say something you do not want to say. Think about the implications of word usage, particularly where key terms are involved. Attention to context and meaning promote clarity and precision.

BE PRECISE AND CONCISE

Precision and brevity add strength to your writing. Every word must serve a communication or stylistic purpose. Be precise in word choice. Do not use a phrase where a word will do or three clauses where one phrase is sufficient. Do not be tempted to include descriptive 'fill' to meet a word length requirement. If you are writing a magazine article that has to be 1000 words, make every word count. If you feel you have to pad your writing you need more ideas, not vacuous sentences. Go back and brainstorm or mind-map for inspiration.

To add precision, avoid vague wording and unnecessary qualifiers. Imprecise adjectives such as 'great', 'major', 'significant' and 'important' should be used sparingly. Instead try to explain precisely what you want to say.

> e.g. Vague: Staff overheads are a significant part of the budget.
> Precise: Staff overheads are 40 per cent of the budget.

Unnecessary qualifiers such as 'very', 'rather' and 'extremely' lack precision. To say something is 'rather difficult' can have less impact than just saying it is 'difficult'. If you need to use a qualifier try to use a more descriptive adjective or phrase.

> e.g. Vague: Our survey response rate was very low.
> Better: Our response rate was lower this year than in 1999.

Some unnecessary qualifiers are repetitive and can be removed without changing the meaning of the sentence. The words 'very' and 'past' in 'very unique' and 'past history' are redundant. Redundant words repeat an idea within a phrase. Also avoid trite expressions. Trite phrases are clichés such as 'when all is said and done' and 'at the end of the day'. If you find a phrase comes very quickly to mind, ask yourself if it might be trite or repetitive. Table 6.3 provides some examples of redundancies and trite phrases that should be avoided. Add your favourite ones to the list.

Do not overuse adjectives and adverbs. Too many simply obscure your message and make your prose cumbersome.

> e.g. Wordy: For the second year in a row sales were off the mark and well below average.
> Better: Sales were below average again this year.
> e.g. Wordy: Costs were growing increasingly larger as the price of oil was rising quickly and steeply.
> Better: Costs increased as the price of oil rose.

Prepositions (in, to, from, on, over, etc.) are necessary but often overused, especially 'of'. Keep your prepositions to no more than four per sentence. If you find yourself using more, break the sentence into two. In the next example the first sentence has six prepositions. The second sentence, which conveys the same message, has only three.

TABLE 6.3 *Redundancies and trite phrases*

Redundant	Trite
Absolute guarantee	All and sundry
Actual truth	At the end of the day
Each and every	At long last
End result	Giant step forward
Ever since	In the near future
Follows after	In all likelihood
Past history	Leaps and bounds
Reason because	Point in time
Refer back	Tired but happy
Repeat again	When all is said and done
Surrounding environment	Window of opportunity

e.g. Wordy: In the middle of the day on the fifth of January, the siege of eleven months came to an end.

Better: After eleven months, the siege ended at mid-day on 5 January.

Try to avoid compound prepositions. Compound prepositions are phrases that can usually be replaced by an appropriate word. Compound prepositions make your writing sound formal and stilted. Table 6.4 lists some compound prepositions to avoid.

ADD VIGOUR

Vigorous prose is forceful prose. To be forceful use action verbs and strong subjects. Try not to overuse weak openings such as 'it is', 'there is' or 'that is'. Your sentences should be more vigorous and precise. For example, the sentence 'It was clear to the manager why the merger was being undertaken' contains 12 words. Compare it with the following sentence: 'The manager knew the reason for the merger'. The first contains 12 words; the second has only 8. Eliminating the impersonal opening reduces the word count by half.

Increase vigour by avoiding long sentences with nested clauses. Look at the following quotation:

To perceive a work in a specifically aesthetic way, that is, as a signifier meaning nothing other than itself, consists not, as is sometimes suggested, of regarding it without relating it to anything other than itself, either emotionally or intellectually, in other words surrendering oneself to the work taken in its irreducible uniqueness, but in picking out its distinctive

TABLE 6.4 *Some compound prepositions to avoid*

Use	Avoid
about	in regard to, with reference to, in relation to, with regard to
although	despite the fact that, notwithstanding the fact that
because	as a result of, due to the fact that, in the event that, for the reason that, in view of the fact that, owing to the fact that
before	in advance of, prior to, previous to
by, under	by means of, by virtue of, in accordance with, on the basis of
if	in the event that
in	in terms of
later	at a later date, after the passage of some time
like	along the lines of, similar to
now, then	as of this date, at the present time, as of this writing, at this time, at that point in time
to	in order to, for the purpose of, so as to, with a view toward
whether	as to whether, the question as to whether
with	accompanied by, in connection with

> *stylistic characteristics by relating it to the works constituting the class of which it is a part, and to these works alone.*
>
> (Bourdieu, Darbel and Schnapper 1991: 40)

What the authors are trying to say in the above passage is that art appreciation is learned. The qualifiers and nested ideas are important to their argument, but do not need to be contained in one sentence. Long-winded, complex, obscure and intimidating prose may be a stylistic device in some genres. For most writing, particularly business prose, it is poor practice. Avoid chains of nested clauses. Try reducing them to short phrases or single words. Overly long sentences should be broken into smaller sentences using transitions, parallel constructions or bullet points if appropriate.

Using active rather than passive verbs adds vigour. Passive verbs tend to produce lengthy and wordy prose. Passive sentences reverse the subject and object positions. Consider the following:

e.g. Passive: The factory was visited by the committee.
    Active: The committee visited the factory.
e.g. Passive: The game was lost by the blue team.
    Active: The blue team lost the game.

Sentences with active verbs tend to be shorter and livelier than passive sentences. Occasionally passive verbs are necessary. In the sentence 'The troops were attacked from the air', the passive construction must be used to convey precise meaning. If you knew the subject of the sentence you could then make it active: 'Helicopters attacked the troops from the air'.

Where possible use personal subjects to add immediacy and interest. Sentences are more lively if people are doing something rather than having an impersonal subject taking action. Using active verbs often means personalizing the subject. To add force and vigour, edit for passive constructions and impersonal openings.

ADD VARIETY AND RHYTHM

Varying sentence and paragraph lengths adds variety and interest. Sentences should be no more than 20 to 25 words in length but can be as short as 2 words. Most sentences fall in the 5- to 15-word length. Use short sentences for dramatic effect. Several short sentences in sequence can sound too clipped and military-like. Too many long sentences together lack vigour. Use medium-length sentences primarily, adding occasional short or longer ones for variety.

Vary the number of sentences per paragraph. Business writing should contain a maximum of six to eight sentences, depending on length. Use occasional short paragraphs of two or three sentences, particularly if your message is informal. Paragraph length is related to the length of your document. If you are sending a short letter or memo, use shorter paragraphs. If you are doing a lengthy report, use some long and some short paragraphs.

To add variety to your paragraphs, when your subject is the same for a series of sentences, use 'stand-in' words. For example, when you are sending a letter of application for a job, you would not want to start every sentence with 'I'. Instead, rephrase to use 'my' or turn sentences around to bury the first person subject within the sentence: 'While training as a legal assistant, I learned property conveyancing'. Too many sentences with the same subject will bore your audience.

Vary word length. Too many very short words make your sentences seem terse. Too many long words can sound pretentious. Strive for a mix. Do not string too many nouns together in one phrase. Avoid noun clusters with three or more lengthy nouns, e.g. 'stockbroker futures committee' or 'consultants business forum division'. In a long document, if you cannot avoid lengthy noun clusters use acronyms where appropriate, e.g. 'SFC' or 'CBFD', to avoid repeating the cluster too many times. Be careful with acronyms. Unless they are really well known, it is best to define acronyms on first mention. Use only one or two at most in any document.

Rhythm is related to flow. Some sequences of sentences or words just sound better than others. Adding variation to words, sentences and paragraphs varies the rhythm of your document and creates fluidity. You should get some sense of what sounds best as you read through your draft. Reading your work aloud or into a tape recorder can help. If something seems to lack fluency as you read through, change the word or sentence order until it flows smoothly.

USE EMPHASIS

Use emphasis to highlight certain points or make important ideas stand out. Subordinate one part of a sentence to highlight another part. In the sentence 'The door was unlocked and they walked straight in' neither idea is emphasized. If written 'Because the door was unlocked, they walked straight in', the emphasis changes to the second part. To add weight to a point, put it at the end of the sentence.

Repetition can add emphasis. If you want to make three strong points in sequence, for example, use a parallel construction for emphasis: 'Designing a product, marketing a product and consuming a product are three distinct processes'. Use repetition only occasionally for a dramatic effect.

Emphasize a point by placing it next to a contrasting idea: for example, 'Unlike the utilities industry, clothing companies face more competition'. Providing a contrasting example adds weight to your point or conclusion. Using bullet points or numerical lists can also make ideas stand out. Setting words or phrases off from the body of your text marks them out as important ideas and adds variety to your document.

AVOID SEXIST LANGUAGE

Just as there is no place for sexism in everyday life, academia or business, there is no excuse for using sexist language in your communications. At the very least, 'politically correct' language shows respect. Show that respect in your writing. Use gender-neutral language as much as possible. For example, all managers are not male. All care-givers are not female. Aside from ethical considerations or simple good manners, sexist language can alienate large segments of your audience, resulting in failed communication. If you find it awkward using 'he/she' or alternating male and female pronouns, reframe your sentences in the plural. Instead of 'When a man is doing a good job, we reward him with bonuses' use 'When employees do a good job, we reward them with bonuses'. Edit for sexist language. Write as a professional: effectively, efficiently and respectfully towards your audience.

ACKNOWLEDGE YOUR SOURCES

Referencing means acknowledging all sources of material which you have used in preparing any document. You must acknowledge your sources. Referencing is essential for two reasons: (1) trying to pass someone else's work off as your own is plagiarism; (2) referencing enables anyone reading your work to see what source material you have used. If they then want to consult the material, your references will provide them with the information they need to find the sources.

Every writer needs to know how to reference properly. In business you will need to reference sources for any reports or articles you may have to write. In university or college you will have to use referencing for all essays, research papers and theses. You must acknowledge all ideas, facts, theories, research and quotations from external sources.

The first step in referencing is noting all relevant data for your sources as you collect them. If you do not note them as you go, you will spend an inordinate amount of time searching for missing references at the end, often when you are under most pressure to meet a deadline. Make detailed notes of your sources as you find them. Include the following for books: author(s), editor(s), title, year of publication, edition, volume number, publisher, place of publication. Note the page numbers for any quotations or notes you have made. For journal articles note the author(s), year of publication, article title, journal title, issue number and page numbers. For electronic materials note the author, date, title, type of medium (CD-ROM, on-line) and date accessed.

The second step in referencing is noting your sources in the body of your text. Start this step as you are writing your first draft. If you have the reference to hand, note it immediately. If you know a reference has to go in a particular spot but do not have the details, put a note to yourself in the text at the appropriate point to fill it in later. Referencing in your text using the Harvard system (see below) means making a short notation at the appropriate point in the body of your text with the author's surname and year of publication. The notation refers the reader to the corresponding full citation (reference) which appears in the references section at the end of your document.

Note the difference between references and bibliographies:

- References are those sources which are referred to in your text.

- Bibliographies cover additional useful sources which are not specifically mentioned in your text.

In some cases you will be asked to provide a list of references and a bibliography. References and bibliographies are listed alphabetically by author's last name.

The third step in referencing is creating an alphabetical list at the end of your document that includes all sources of information you have cited in your text. The next section provides specific examples for referencing different kinds of materials.

The mechanics of referencing

All ideas or quotes should be attributed to their original author. In the text of your writing this is done in a shorthand way by simply providing the original author's name and the date of the publication. A full reference is then given at the end of the document in the list of references. The standard for referencing in business is called the Harvard system. The Harvard system uses the author's name and date of publication within the text, e.g. (Jones and Wilson 1987).

Where quotes are used they must be referenced in full. If significant items of text (more than forty words or two or more sentences) are quoted they should be placed on a separate line, indented and referenced in full at the end of the quotation as shown below. Note in the example below page numbers are included for direct quotations.

> *Tastes in style reflect the times. In earlier centuries, when few people outside the leisured class ever had a chance to read, many respected writers wrote in an elaborate style that we would think much too wordy. Now almost all of us read, but newspapers, radio and television compete with books for our attention, and as a result we tend to favour a simpler kind of writing.*
>
> (Northey and Tepperman 1986: 142)

Full references for books in the Harvard system are given by providing the author's name, date of publication, title, publisher and place of publication. When an item such as a newspaper article has no author, it is cited by its title and listed in the references section by the first significant word of the newspaper's name (e.g. *The Guardian* would be listed alphabetically under 'G'). Note that the title of a book or journal must be highlighted usually by italicizing or, if you are using a typewriter, by underlining. The following examples illustrate how to reference for books, and edited volumes:

Books, single author:
> Mintzberg, H. (1979) *The Structure of Organizations*, Prentice Hall, Englewood Cliffs, NJ.

Books, multiple author:
> Miles, R. and Snow, C. (1978) *Organizational Strategy, Structure and Process*, McGraw-Hill, New York.

Books, edited volume:
> Hargie, O. and Tourish, D. (eds) (2000) *Handbook of Communication Audits for Organizations*, Routledge, London.

Journal, magazine and periodical articles are referenced in a similar way. Details of author(s) and date are given first, followed by the journal article's title, the journal name, volume and/or issue number and the pages on which the article appears. Again, italicizing or underlining is used to distinguish the journal title from the article title.

Journal article:

Pfeffer, J. (1996) When it comes to 'best practices' – why do smart organizations do dumb things? *Organizational Dynamics*, 25, 33–44.

Article in an edited volume:

Chatov, R. (1981) Co-operation between government and business, in *Handbook of Organizational Design*, P. Nystrom and W. Starbuck (eds), pp. 487–502, Oxford University Press: New York.

Newspaper article:

Legge, K. (1987) Labour to cost the 'Keating Factor', *Times on Sunday*, 1 Feb., p. 2.

Government documents:

British Standards Institution (1990) BS5605: 1990 *Recommendations for citing and referencing published material.* Milton Keynes, BSI.

Two references by the same author in the same year:

Note: Use alphabetical notations with the year of publication to match the sequence in which you cited them in the text.

Reichfield, F. (1996a) Learning from customer defections, *Harvard Business Review*, 74, 56–61.

Reichfield, F. (1996b) *The Loyalty Effect*, Harvard Business School Press, Boston.

Internet and electronic sources such as CD-ROM databases must be referenced. Most website material is copyrighted. Any information you derive from a website and quote or paraphrase in your document must be referenced. The following are general guidelines for acknowledging web-based sources:

For individual works

Motorola (1997) *Motorola History and Evolution* [on-line]. Available from http://www.mot.com/General/Facts [Accessed 26 May 1998].

Holland, M. (1996) *Harvard System* [on-line]. Poole, Bournemouth University. Available from http://bournemouth.ac.uk/service-depts/lis/LIS_Pub/harvardsyst.html [Accessed 15 April 1996].

If the electronic publication date is not available, write 'No date'.

CD-ROM sources:

Deere and Company (1999) *Adapting, Transforming and Staying the Same.* [CD-ROM] Deere and Company, Moline, IL.

Referencing must be consistent in style and format. Referencing errors are the most common kinds of mistakes in long documents. When completing your final draft, check the citations in your text against your final reference list to make certain that all entries in the text are on the list and all items on the list are cited in your text.

The finished product

Your final draft should be edited for spelling, grammar, punctuation and consistency of references. Use titles and subtitles to break up long passages of text and make your document more visually appealing. It can help to get someone else to read it at this stage. Everyone benefits from an editor. A well-edited text can take several drafts. After drafting and redrafting you will lose perspective on your writing and be unable to see errors or inconsistencies that will jump out at someone who reads it with 'fresh eyes'. Finally, if you have time, set it aside for a few days and do a final read through before you deliver it.

You can now apply the precepts of good writing to any writing task. Plan your communications strategy, generate your ideas and source materials, structure an outline, draft and edit, paying attention to macro and micro writing issues. In the next chapter we look at how to apply the process to specific types of messages such as letters, memos, reports, e-mails and press releases.

Discussion questions

1. Find a business article in a magazine or newspaper and one on a similar subject in an academic or technical journal or trade magazine. Compare the style and tone of the two articles. How is emphasis used? Does one have more or less vigour or clarity? Note the use of referencing. What audience are they targeting?

2. Conduct an audit of your writing habits. When do you produce your best work? What kind of a writing environment do you find most congenial? Do you feel more comfortable with a linear mode of writing where you can start at the beginning and work systematically to the end or would you rather start with the conclusion or the middle? Do you have problems with writer's block? What strategies would help you overcome it?

3. Look at a sample of your written work. Read through it, identifying any weaknesses related to micro issues. Do you overuse passive verbs or

impersonal openings? Are your sentences, paragraphs and word lengths varied? Do you have favourite trite or pretentious phrases? Is your style ponderous or stilted? When you have identified the problems, make a table with two columns. On the left list the problems you identified and on the right how you will correct them.

References

Bourdieu, P., Darbel, A. and Schnapper, D. (1991) *The Love of Art: European Art Museums and their Public*, Polity Press, Cambridge.

Munter, M. (1987) *Guide to Managerial Communication*, 2nd edn, Englewood Cliffs, NJ: Prentice Hall.

Northey, M. and Tepperman, L. (1986) *Making Sense in the Social Sciences*, Oxford University Press, Toronto.

Further reading

Burchfield, R. (1998) *The New Fowler's Modern English Usage*, revised edn, Oxford University Press, Oxford.

Ewing, D. W. (1979) *Writing for Results in Business, Government, the Sciences and the Professions*, 2nd edn, John Wiley, New York.

Gallagher, K., McClelland, B. and Swales, C. (1998) *Business Skills: An Active Learning Approach*, Blackwell Business, Oxford.

Jay, R. (1999) *The Seven Deadly Skills of Communicating*, International Thomson Business Press, London.

Lanham, R. (1981) *Revising Business Prose*, Scribner's, New York.

Li, X. and Crane, N. (1996) *Electronic Styles: A Handbook for Citing Electronic Information*, 2nd edn, Information Today, Medford, NJ.

Strunk, W. and White, E. B. (1979) *The Elements of Style*, 3rd edn, Macmillan, New York.

chapter seven

Written communication

Introduction

BUSINESS WRITING has accepted formats and conventions for the most common forms of documents: letters, memos, reports and e-mails. The principles of effective communication you have learned in the last three chapters can be applied equally to all forms of organizational communication. Organizational communications can be either internal or external. External communications represent the image of the organization to the outside world. Internal communications tend to reproduce and affirm a company's style and organizational culture. This chapter deals with the principal forms of both internal and external business communications.

The widespread use of electronic communication and the globalization of business practices have changed modern business communications in the last few decades. Wording and sentence structure are simpler and more direct. Writing styles are more relaxed and informal, yet the basic formats for standard documents remain relatively unchanged.

The decision to use a particular type of document is related to the purpose of your writing. Your objective and strategy will determine your choice of communication channel and media. If you choose written communication you will have to decide on a format appropriate to your message. Whether you choose to use an e-mail, memo, letter or report will depend on the context and your desired outcome.

LEARNING OBJECTIVES

By the end of this chapter you will be able to:

- Compose business letters: good news, bad news, persuasive, informative
- Write effective memos: internal and external

- Produce business reports in various formats

- Compose other documents: e-mails, press releases

Strategies for effective letters

Business letters can serve a number of purposes. Generally they are either initial letters or replies to letters about goods, services or information. You might be writing to inquire about a defective purchase or to get a job. As a manager you may have to write reference letters for employees, deal with consumer complaints, negotiate with suppliers and chase unpaid invoices. Most typical are letters written to:

- buy or sell products and services

- recruit, make redundant, discipline or reward employees

- discuss or negotiate terms of agreements

- answer or make requests for information

- pay for or demand payment for goods or services

- make a complaint or reply to complaints

- confirm details of oral communications.

Whatever the purpose of the letter it will in most cases fall into one of the following categories: good news, bad news, persuasive, informative.

GOOD NEWS LETTERS

Writing a good news letter (Figure 7.1) is one of the easiest and most pleasant of writing tasks. Because your audience is eager to hear what you have to say you should be direct and state the good news or main idea at the beginning. For example, if you are writing to tell a job applicant that she has been successful you should state the good news in the first sentence: 'Dear Ms Jefferies: Our recruitment committee met this afternoon and decided unanimously to hire you for the position of office manager.' Avoid using dated and formal expressions like 'we are pleased to advise you' or 'it is our pleasure to inform you'. Refer to the list of pretentious words and outdated phrases in Chapter Six.

The body of the letter should provide the details. You may have to include some negative information with the goods news. If so, always provide the good news first and bury the negative information in the body of the letter. Remember from the audience memory curve, your reader will always remember most the first and last thing you say and least, the middle of your communication. In the recruitment example above, you may have to offer the job at a lower salary than the applicant was anticipating. In that case you would state the negative information later in the letter when you provide other interesting details about the job. Negative information or bad news is always softened if it is preceded and followed by positives.

Good news letters might also be written to accept an offer to purchase goods or services, to provide a positive recommendation for an employee, to reward an employee for special service or achievement or to resolve a complaint to a customer's satisfaction. In all of these cases your tone should be friendly, warm and direct yet professional.

Close a good news letter on a positive note to retain the overall tone of the letter.

Commercial Bank Corporation
2134 Market Way, London NW2
Tel: 0208 869734 Fax: 0208 869804

15 October 2000

Mr. Derek Watson
45 Emery Close
Leicester LE1 5N6

Dear Mr Watson

Your application for a car loan has been approved. As a new customer we welcome you to Commercial Bank and are certain you will be pleased with our Customer First service commitment.

Enclosed are two copies of the loan document. The amortisation period, monthly payments and interest rate (APR) for your loan are stated in the agreement. Note the terms and conditions and check that all the details are as agreed in our telephone conversation yesterday. Please sign both copies of the loan agreement, retain one copy for your records and return one copy to me as soon as possible. You will receive a banker's cheque for the full amount of your loan within three working days of our receipt of the signed loan agreement.

When we receive your signed agreement your name will be eligible for entry into our new customer draw for a £1000 pound cash back on your loan. If you have any queries or concerns contact me immediately on 0208 869545.

Yours sincerely

Jacob Hunter
Senior Loans Officer

Encs.

FIGURE 7.1 *Good news letter*

BAD NEWS LETTERS

Bad news letters are difficult to write and take more thought and planning. Your objective should be to convey the bad news while retaining some goodwill. Taking an indirect approach to bad news is good diplomatic practice. Begin with a positive statement but if that is not possible begin with a neutral statement. Bad news such as rejection of a job applicant, redundancy (note: a redundancy letter usually follows a personal interview), requests for payment, refusal of credit, inability to meet a request or perform a service, etc., should be softened initially by a positive or neutral opening sentence. You might tell a job applicant that the hiring committee had given serious consideration to the applicant's qualifications which were of a high quality before stating the bad news.

When you are planning your strategy for a bad news letter (Figure 7.2), note the following points:

1. Use an indirect approach.

2. Bury the bad news in the middle of the message.

3. Try to retain the goodwill of your audience.

4. Use a tone that suggests your message is firm and final.

5. Retain your credibility by appearing sincere, reasonable and fair.

The best way to meet these objectives is by giving the receiver something positive. Your tone should convey respect rather than be accusing. If you are refusing a customer's claim, avoid the use of 'you' in an accusing way. Rather, use the third person impersonal and passive constructions. Bad news messages are one constructive use of impersonal subjects and passive verbs. Rather than saying 'you abused the appliance' state 'the appliance appears to have been subject to some misuse'. That way you are not directly accusing the customer. Also avoid strong negative words like 'no' and 'refuse'. Rather, say 'we are unable to meet your request'.

After you have opened your bad news message with a buffer sentence or two provide the reasons or explanation for your actions. Next give the bad news, concisely and firmly. If you can, place the bad news in the middle of a sentence where it will have less impact. Emphasize any positive aspects of the situation. If possible state how the decision will benefit the receiver. Try to close the letter with a positive tone or with a forward-looking statement such as 'Please resubmit your application when we have our next hiring round in March'. In closing do not use any words that imply apology or regret and avoid all reference to the bad news.

Paragon Press
58 Industrial Way
Becksted, Hampshire HA4 5K9
Tel: 01254 782498 Fax: 01254 782691

13 October 2000

Ms Denise Thelton
45 Harris Close
Guildford
Surrey SU19 4M8

Dear Ms Thelton

RE: Editorial Assistant, Paperback Division

Thank you for attending the interview for editorial assistant in our paperback division.

Your qualifications and experience met and in most areas exceeded our requirements for the position. The hiring committee had a very difficult task to decide between several highly qualified applicants. We regret, however, that we are unable to hire you at this time.

We do anticipate two openings in the editorial department of our magazine division in the new year. We urge you to apply and will notify you when the positions become available.

Thank you for taking an interest in Paragon Press and I hope we will see you again in the new year.

Yours sincerely

Margaret Delmer
Human Resources Officer

FIGURE 7.2 *Bad news letter*

PERSUASIVE LETTERS

Persuasive letters (Figure 7.3) are written to convince your audience they should take action on your requests. Persuasive letters aim to change, even if in a small way, the attitudes, beliefs or actions of your audience. They may take the form of sales letters, requests for funding, asking for favours, co-operation or resources, or simply persuading the receiver to see a situation from your perspective.

Use the following strategies to write persuasive messages:

- Structure your message with a logical progression of arguments and evidence.

- Use audience analysis and motivation theory to appeal to your audience.

- Use personal openings; address your audience by name, if possible.

- Use active constructions and vivid language.

- Enhance your credibility without compromising your sincerity.

- Attract attention to your message with striking images or unusual text.

- Be ethical.

In most cases persuasive letters have to overcome initial resistance from the receiver. Audience analysis is extremely important in writing persuasive letters. You need to know your audience, assess your credibility for that audience and try to ascertain where the resistance to your objective might originate.

The most effective approach for persuasive letters is indirect. Because you are trying to persuade, you need to construct a convincing argument before you make your request. You will see this approach in sales letters you get through the post. They sometimes start with a question to get your attention such as 'Would you like to save £100 on your home insurance?' or they might

---

Fresh Foods Inc.
Unit 5, Harston Way
London NE9 5BN
Tel: 0207 543623 Fax: 0217 542691

23 September 2000

Mr. Simon Pearson
PBX Consulting
Harlow Road
London, NW5 2VC

Dear Mr. Pearson:

As you know we are a specialized catering firm who provide high quality organic meals for a small number of customers. We are proud of the quality of our food and level of service and strive to maintain them at all times.

Your firm is one of our most valued customers and as such we give your orders priority whenever we can. We use fresh, organic and highly specialized ingredients in our dishes that often take time to source. With that in mind and our growth in sales, we find it necessary to request a minimum of two weeks notice on orders for over ten people.

Of course, if you have an emergency we will try our best to meet your needs but would appreciate having your orders in advance wherever possible. As an incentive we are offering our best customers a 10% discount on all orders that are placed 30 days in advance.

We value your business and are committed to meeting your needs by maintaining our high standards of quality and service.

Yours sincerely,

Alyson Morrison,
Catering Manager

FIGURE 7.3 *Persuasive letter*

begin with a sympathetic question to show they understand your problems, 'Are you tired of waiting months or even years for proper medical treatment?'. A charity requesting donations might begin with a scenario of an individual whose life has been changed by the help the charity provides.

After an attention-getting opening you should expand on the theme of the opening in greater detail. Draw attention to the benefits that your audience may accrue from complying with your request. Provide details of the request followed by evidence to back up your position. Draw attention to any enclosures. End the letter by suggesting action to be taken by the audience and/or restating the potential benefits of complying.

INFORMATIVE LETTERS

Informative letters (Figure 7.4) are primarily used when requesting routine information or providing information in response to a query. The direct

Salisbury Insurance Adjusters
5th Floor, Hardy Johnson Building
Goodall Road, Leeds YK5 7TM
Tel: 01820 8428 Fax: 01820 8436

15 June 2000

Mr. David Barton
Sunlife Insurance
45 Powell Avenue
Leeds, YK3 3BU

Dear Mr. Barton:

Reference letter for Thomas Jacobs

Mr. Jacobs was employed by this firm from January, 1996 to September, 1999.

He joined initially as an insurance clerk in our adjustments department and within six months had progressed to junior adjuster. When he left in 1999 to take up another position in the insurance industry he had just received accreditation from the Insurance Adjusters Association.

Mr. Jacobs always performed his responsibilities with great care and attention to detail. He consistently demonstrated good judgement and fairness in assessing claims. He had very high standards and managed to maintain them sometimes under intense pressure. The only weakness he had was an occasional tendency to take on too many responsibilities.

His duties often involved working with teams of adjusters and he proved to be very amenable to teamwork. He showed leadership qualities when required and could be counted on to put in extra time when necessary.

I highly recommend Mr. Jacobs and I am certain you will find him a very valuable employee.

Yours truly,

Anil Gupta,
Claims Manager

FIGURE 7.4 *Informative letter*

approach is most effective for informative letters. The reader should know from the beginning the purpose of the letter, e.g. 'Dear Mr Calder: Your query about our upcoming sales conference was passed to me by the Marketing Manager'. In this case the reader knows immediately that you will be providing information about a specific request. Unlike bad news and persuasive letters, there is less need to buffer the information or persuade the audience of your credibility before stating the purpose of the letter.

If you are requesting information use a polite, impersonal tone that is not demanding. Write with the assumption that the receiver will respond positively to your request. After you have stated what you want, justify your request or explain its importance to you. If appropriate state the possible benefit to your audience of responding, such as potential sales, new client, contribution to research, etc.

If your request is complex, break it down into an itemized list. Make sure the audience knows what you want to happen next. If follow-up action needs to be taken state it clearly but without sounding demanding. Close with a polite restating of the request and provide details such as addresses and phone numbers that will make it easy for the receiver to comply with your request. Indicate if there is a deadline or time frame to receive a response. Finally, show appreciation for the receiver's efforts to provide the information you need.

LETTER FORMATS

The basic structure of a letter includes a heading, date, sender's and recipient's addresses, salutation, body text, closing/signature and enclosure notation. Other optional elements are subject or attention lines, confidentiality notations, copy references and information about the means of delivery (by fax, courier, recorded post).

The most commonly used letter formats are full block and modified block. Examples of both styles are provided in the above letters. Figures 7.1 and 7.2 are full block style and Figures 7.3 and 7.4 are modified block. Full block style means that all elements of the letter begin at the left margin and there is no punctuation other than in the body text of the letter. In modified block format everything but the date and the closing are at the left margin and punctuation is used in the address, salutation and closing.

The full block format is now the most widely used in business communications. The format you use will depend upon the style used in your business context. Many organizations adopt a format that is used consistently in all correspondence that goes out on company letterhead. Whichever style you use the important point is to be consistent and not mix styles within a single letter. Most word processing software contains templates for different letter formats.

Letters should be kept to one page in length if possible. Business people are busy and will often only read the opening paragraphs of a letter to see if it is worth their while to read the whole thing. If you keep your message short, it will be read right through. If it is too long, you risk having part of it ignored.

FORM LETTERS

Computer programs for word processing and database management make it relatively simple to send letters to a large number of people with little effort. If you own a small business and want to send a standardized letter to your 500 customers, for example, to inform them of a new offer or a change of address, use mailmerge techniques. Most businesses retain large databases of customer or supplier information: names, addresses, account numbers, purchases, accounts receivable and payable. The simplest way to reach a large audience is by designing a pro forma letter in word processing and merging it with database information. Instructions for mailmerge operations will be in the help files or tutorials that accompany software programs.

When sending standardized letters, mailmerge programs personalize each letter by addressing them individually from the information you have on file. Most have samples of letters already constructed that you can simply amend to suit your message. Make sure to print the letters on good quality paper with a professional letterhead.

Sign the letters individually if you have time and there are a manageable number. If not you can put your signature on the letter electronically. Sign your name on a blank sheet of paper in blue ink. Using a scanner, scan it into your computer as a file and import it into the form letter, placing it appropriately above your typed name. When the letters print out they will have your signature appearing in blue to stand out from the black print of the text. If you use good equipment, it can be difficult to tell the scanned signature from an original.

Writing reports

Businesses rely on reports for making decisions, providing information and solving problems. They may take the form of research reports, sales forecasts, activity reports such as quarterly financial reports, position papers, guidelines, operating reports, trouble-shooting and planning. Reports can be generated for internal or external business audiences. Reports may be oral or written but are primarily factual accounts that communicate objectively about some aspect of business.

Reports can vary in length from a few pages to several volumes, depending on the complexity of the topic. Because they often present a large amount of complex information they need to be organized and planned with care. Begin with determining your general and specific objectives. Do a detailed audience analysis, paying attention to culture and context. Develop a message strategy and begin to generate ideas. Gather your source material, and create a structure for your finished report. Draft, edit and redraft.

All reports have the following elements: title page, cover letter (for external) or cover memo (for internal), abstract or executive summary, table of contents, introduction, body text (which includes detailed development and support of your ideas), conclusions, recommendations, appendices, exhibits, and references or bibliography. Research indicates that managers will most likely read only the abstract/summary, introduction and conclusion whereas technical people will probably focus on the body text. Few readers examine the appendices or exhibits.

EXECUTIVE SUMMARY

The executive summary of a business or technical report is a short synopsis of the report's findings. If the report is an academic or scientific paper it is likely to be summarized in an abstract which is usually less than one page, normally one or two paragraphs at most. An executive summary may be several pages long itself, depending on the complexity of the report. It should contain a short overview of the report's contents and state its important findings. The summary might be distributed to a wider audience than the actual report itself so it must be self-contained and not rely on the report to be understood.

The executive summary is a 'mini' version of the report itself intended for readers who lack the time or the interest to read the complete version. Because decisions may be made based on the executive summary, it needs to contain all essential information including findings, supporting data and graphics where appropriate. The length of the summary depends on the length of the report. If the report is less than 10 pages in length, a short summary in the letter or memo of transmittal may be sufficient. If it is over 30 pages it will require a fuller executive summary. If it falls in between 10 and 30 pages a decision will have to be made based on the complexity of the material and the standards and conventions of your organization.

BODY OF THE REPORT

As in any written communication you need to decide the objectives and purpose of your report and frame it in terms of a problem or questions.

Because it may include a large amount of detailed technical or financial information, or present complicated arguments, the composition of a formal report is fairly standardized. The basic formula of introduction, body of the report, conclusions, recommendations and references provides the framework but there are some additional elements you need to consider if your report is to be well developed, comprehensive, logical and clear. The tone of your report should be unemotional, objective, factual and impersonal.

Use the introduction of the report to do the following (Bovée and Thill 2000):

1. State the purpose and objectives of the report.

2. Outline the contents and organization.

3. Set the tone and style of the report.

4. Motivate your audience to read the text of the report.

5. Establish your credibility.

The length of your introduction depends on the length of the report. It could extend to several pages if your report is very long. You need to establish your credibility and the authorization for the report in your introduction. State who requested or authorized the study, why it was done, for whom and by whom. These are the terms of reference for the report. Make clear the scope of the report and its limitations – what it includes and what it excludes. Give some background or historical conditions leading to the report and explain the sources for the material in the report such as surveys, records, interviews and other reports. Briefly outline the organization of the report.

The body of the report contains the details and findings and should be divided into sections or chapters if it is very long. Each section should have headings and sub-headings at various levels. There should be a logical progression of ideas, building complex arguments clearly and factually. It is here that you provide the 'proof', the support for your conclusions and the argument that shows how you came to those conclusions. Restrict the detail in the body of your report to that which is needed to make your case. Put any extraneous and lengthy supporting documents into appendices. Use tables, charts and figures to add clarity, not simply to repeat what you have already said in the text.

CONCLUSIONS AND RECOMMENDATIONS

When you have finished presenting the findings, your audience will be anticipating your conclusions and recommendations. Conclusions are the answers to the questions that led to the report. Recommendations are your opinions about what action should be taken in light of the conclusions. In a short report they may be included in the body of the report but in most cases you will use a separate concluding section or chapter. Here you provide an analysis of what the findings mean and present the implications. If there are a number of conclusions and/or recommendations you may want to present them in a list format.

Make sure you do not present any new findings in the conclusion section. All findings should appear in the body of the report. If the purpose of your report was to lead to action, you should outline in your recommendations what action should be taken, who should do it and when it should be done. It is important to be firm and clear about your conclusions and recommendations if you want your report to be an effective impetus for action.

After the conclusion and recommendation section come the supporting materials – appendices, exhibits, and references or bibliography. Be certain to provide detailed references to give credit to all of your sources of information. Besides being an ethical and legal requirement, acknowledging your sources adds authority and credibility to your report.

REPORT PRESENTATION

Professional-looking reports also increase your credibility. Take some time to plan how your report should look. Make sure you consistently format the text, headings and sub-headings. Do not use too many different fonts or styles and colours of graphs and tables. They can distract the reader from your message and weaken the authority of your report.

Keep the following points in mind when constructing your report (Pearsall and Cunningham 1982):

- Use good-quality paper of a heavier weight than standard photocopy paper.

- If multiple copies are required, reproduce on good-quality paper on a laser printer or have them professionally reproduced.

- Use a minimum of one-inch margins. If the report is to be bound use a two-inch left margin.

- Enclose your graphics in boxes for more effect.

- Use bullet points for random lists and numbers if the order is important.

- Use simple fonts with a clear, business-like typeface.

Always present your report with a letter or memo of transmittal. Use a memo if the report is internal and a letter if it is external. Depending on the

Standard Report Format

Cover Letter or Memo:	To, from, title of report, authorization for report, Short statement of scope of report (Optional)
Title Page:	Title of report, author, date, receiver's name
Executive Summary:	Preview contents and organization
Table of Contents:	Number chapters or sections
Introduction:	Generate interest, build credibility, state purpose, Provide background or context
Conclusions or Recommendations:	State here if using direct approach
Body of Report:	Build arguments and provide evidence and support Use numbering for sections or headings and sub-headings. Add visual material - tables, figures
Conclusions or Recommendations:	State here if using indirect approach
Appendices and Exhibits:	Samples of questionnaires, tables, forms Additional supporting data, charts, graphs
References:	List of sources used
Bibliographies:	Additional recommended sources.

FIGURE 7.5
Organization and structure of reports

context and findings of the report you can use either a direct or indirect approach. The basic function of the transmittal letter is to convey the report to its readers. You might want to point out particular aspects of the report that warrant special attention. You can also use it as an opportunity to thank people and organizations that have helped you with the report.

Memos

Memos are the major form of internal business communication. Primarily used for routine communications about day-to-day business matters, they are useful for communicating to a number of people at the same time. Memos are less private than letters. They are effective for confirming oral discussions, outlining company policies and procedures, arranging meetings, providing agendas and transmitting general information that is primarily impersonal. Managers often use them to make internal announcements to all staff about changes in policies or announcements that affect the whole workforce. They may be transmitted individually, sent over an internal 'intranet' or posted on company notice boards.

Memos are designed to communicate in concise and informal terms to people who are busy and want information they can absorb at a glance. Memos may be in hard-copy or electronic form. Many organizations have pre-printed memo forms or their own company format. Whether or not you are using forms make sure your memos have the following information:

Date:	Today's date – day, month, year
To:	Receiver's name or a distribution list
From:	Sender's name and job title or department if appropriate
Subject:	Subject heading should be neither too general nor too specific.
(Body text)	Sender's message. Be concise and provide only the details needed to meet your communication objective.
(Signature)	Sign or initial the memo depending upon the level of formality in the organization and the intended audience.

Electronic mail

E-mail is similar to memos and may actually take the form of memos transmitted electronically. E-mail formats vary depending on your software but most incorporate the basic information of a memo: date, sender, receiver, subject line, body text and signature or initials. E-mail is less formal than a memo and can be used to send very short messages of a few words only, which would not be feasible using paper memos. E-mails conveying important information are usually followed up by hard copies personally signed by the sender. If transmitting confidential material by e-mail you must ensure that the receiver has exclusive access to your message and that the system is secure. Most highly sensitive material should probably not be transmitted by e-mail unless you are very certain of the security arrangements.

E-mail has its own system of etiquette and conventions. E-mail is an instant message system and as such people expect quick responses to e-mail queries. If you are an e-mail user, check your mail regularly to avoid your correspondents getting frustrated by your lack of response. Compose and edit e-mails off-line to save costs. Do not send large attachments or files without prior notice to the recipient. Do not add too many attachments to one e-mail. E-mail is cheap and easy to use and people tend to overuse it, adding to the workloads of already busy people. Avoid adding to information overload by sending junk mail and trivial requests and responses.

Change the subject line when replying to an e-mail, if appropriate. Make certain when you reply to an e-mail that was sent to multiple recipients that you are not replying to all recipients unless appropriate. Simply using the reply button when the message was originally sent to multiple recipients will result in your reply going to all concerned, sometimes causing you and the readers embarrassment.

Most large companies now maintain 'intranet' systems – internal electronic mailing and information centres to which employees have varying amounts of access. The most common types of intranet information are company phone and e-mail directories, company policies and newsletters, job openings and information that would be of interest to employees in general. Other data such as company records, accounting systems, personnel records, customer orders and suppliers would have restricted access available only to those directly working in the relevant area.

One of the important effects of the growth in e-mail is the parallel growth in egalitarianism. In most e-mail systems, anybody can send mail to almost anyone else. Employees and customers can have access to the top managers in an organization. People can make their views known simply, impersonally and immediately. Top management teams are much more aware of the problems and concerns of employees and customers in their organization. The distribution of information electronically has also contributed to better informed individuals and opportunities for direct contact with influential people. One of the main benefits of electronic communication has been the growth in an egalitarian, free-access 'open-door' style of management.

Facsimile messages

'Fax' messages are a quick and cheap method of transmitting documents. External letters are rapidly becoming replaced by fax. Faxes are also used internally in organizations to transmit documents between departments and divisions. The only method of document transmission that is perhaps faster is e-mail attachment. However, documents that have not been generated on a computer are easier to send by fax. Fax also provides an instant paper copy.

Faxing has its disadvantages. Fax machines can send only one document at a time so queuing can be a problem. Fax machines are relatively expensive so that each office normally has only one. People have to be taught how to operate fax machines, though they require little more training than operating a photocopier.

Composing faxes is similar to composing memos. Include the name of the sender, the receiver, the date and the subject of the fax. Ensure that there is a fax number for both receiver and sender. Add the receiver's department and phone number if the fax is to go to a central receiving area. Short faxes can include the message on the cover page. If longer than one page, use a cover page and indicate on it how many pages are being sent so the receiver will know the entire message has been received.

Press releases

Public relations is a key aspect of modern business communications. The media – newspapers, television, radio, the internet and magazines – are all

Commercial Bank Corporation
2134 Market Way, London NW2
Tel: 0208 869734 Fax: 0208 869804

4 February 2001

PRESS RELEASE

FOR PUBLICATION 5 FEBRUARY 2001 AT 1400

Commercial Bank Corporation announces the appointment of Richard Salston as Chief Executive Officer effective immediately. Mr. Salston has been with the Commercial Bank since 1987, most recently in the position of Vice Chairman of Financial Services. He replaces Sir Colin Watkins who is retiring after 35 years of service with the Bank, the last five as Chief Executive Officer.

Commercial Bank has recently acquired a majority holding in Credit Bank of America which will also come under the direction of Mr. Salston.

The Bank is at the forefront of new developments in consumer banking services. Commercial Bank has just launched its internet banking service and will be introducing new electronic initiatives in consumer investment services over the next year.

We welcome Mr. Salston in his new post as Chief Executive Officer of Commercial Bank.

For further information, please contact Debra Saunders, Director of Public Relations. Tel: 0208 8669740 or at D.Saunders@cbcorp.com.

FIGURE 7.6 *Sample press release*

important tools organizations use to convey their desired public image. (We look in detail at corporate image and public relations in Chapter Eleven.) Media attention can be positive or negative. Your organization may give out information to the media which then translate it into their terms for public consumption. Because the media are seen as objective, the public will more readily accept their 'version' than the company's own public relations materials. It is thus important that great care is taken in the production of press releases.

Press releases should contain the following basic information: the organization's name and/or logo, the date the release was issued and the date and time it is to be published, if different, the purpose of the release and supporting information, notes to editors, if required, and contact details of the author or sender. Press releases should support the objectives or mission of the organization and be well timed to have maximum impact. Press releases, when positive, can be an important source of free publicity and need to be carefully written and edited. They must also be relevant to the target audience and newsworthy. Items of interest to specialist trade magazines may not be of interest to the general public. What is of interest to local people may not be relevant for the national press.

Other document formats

Other specialist documents you might encounter are notices, circulars, newsletters, in-house journals, forms, brochures and advertising material. Each has its standards and conventions which vary from business to business. The best way to learn to compose specialist materials is by using previous samples as guides. Computer software programs for publishing also have sample documents for designing more complicated documents such as newsletters, brochures and advertising material which require good-quality graphics and unusual text formats.

Whatever kind of document you are creating, whether you are writing for an internal or external audience, the most important marker of success is how well you adhere to the principles of good writing. If you put thought and care into constructing your communication strategy, following the steps to effective writing, and presenting your results professionally, you will increase your chances of meeting your objectives.

1. As the human resources officer for your firm you have just had an employment review interview with an employee whose performance is far below standard. At the meeting you set out the problems: late and undone work, missing time, and argumentative relationships with office mates who have complained. Compose a letter to the employee to confirm what you have discussed in the meeting and to state what action must be taken.

2. Compose an e-mail to the head of a large food chain to complain of sub-standard customer service at your local branch.

3. As public relations officer for a large packaging company, you have been asked to send out a press release to the national press, informing them that due to falling demand, the company will be making 300 employees redundant within a month. How would you structure your message?

References

Bovée, C. and Thill, J. (2000) *Business Communication Today*, Prentice Hall, Upper Saddle River, NJ.

Pearsall, T. and Cunningham, D. (1994) *How to Write for the World of Work*, Harcourt Brace, Fort Worth, TX.

Further reading

Locke, L., Spirduso, W. and Silverman, S. (1987) *Proposals that Work*, Sage, London.

Nickson, D. and Siddons, S. (1996) *Business Communications*, Butterworth Heinemann, Oxford.

Taylor, S. (1998) *Communication for Business: A Practical Approach*, Addison-Wesley, Harlow.

chapter eight

Oral and visual presentations

Introduction

ORAL PRESENTATIONS differ from written communications in that they require your physical presence before an audience. In both the academic and business worlds you may be required to give presentations from time to time. Because you are exposing yourself and your work to an audience whose attention is fixed solely on you, giving a presentation can be an anxiety-producing experience. Giving successful presentations is a learned skill which takes time and practice to acquire. The more often you do it, the easier it becomes.

Whether you are a beginner or an experienced presenter, the key to reducing anxiety and presenting in a relaxed manner is thorough preparation. Thorough preparation means using the techniques you have learned for effective writing and for developing a communication strategy that gives you confidence.

In addition, successful presentations require attention to a range of skills related to the delivery of your prepared material. You need to know how to make effective use of visual aids and present yourself according to norms of appearance and posture. Other techniques such as handling questions in a professional manner and being flexible enough to adjust your presentation in response to audience feedback are also valuable professional presentation skills.

LEARNING OBJECTIVES

By the end of this chapter you should be able to:

- Plan and prepare for oral presentations
- Match your material to your audience's needs
- Use appropriate audio and visual aids

- Use a variety of techniques as memory aids for presenting
- Recognize and respond to audience feedback

Planning and preparing your presentation

You are already familiar with the steps for producing successful written work. You can now apply those steps to preparing for a presentation:

- pre-writing

- writing

- adapting to presentation format

- compare material with time allowed

- review audience analysis.

In the pre-writing phase you should have decided on your objective and purpose as part of your communicator strategy, developed your initial audience strategy, given initial consideration to message strategy, generated some ideas, and created a structure for your material. At this point the process is not locked in. In fact, you will most likely need to change some of your early ideas and strategies based on what you do in later steps. Figure 8.1

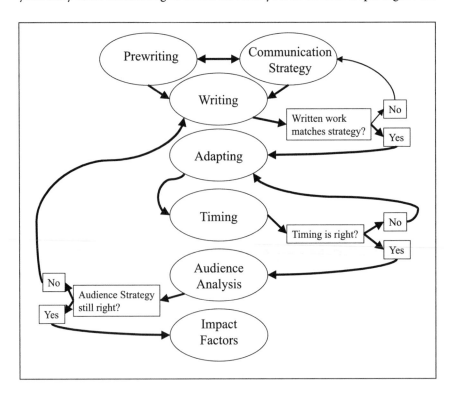

FIGURE 8.1 *Planning and preparation for presentations*

shows the entire process as an iterative one in which early steps are rethought and, if necessary, changed based on later steps. Do not skip these initial steps. The pre-writing phase prepares you for the substantive content phase – writing the presentation.

Write out the content of your presentation. Sometimes you will be generating your presentation from material such as a report that is already written. In fact, the material may have been written by someone else in the organization, and your job is to present it. If so, you will only need to make sure that the material you have to present is in an order that makes sense in terms of your message strategy. The structure and strategies for a written report may be different from those best suited to getting the results you want from an oral presentation of the material to a specific audience. There may be certain parts of the report you will want to emphasize or over-communicate. Your audience for the presentation might also be different from the wider audience for the report.

If you are working from a pre-written document, take the time to examine carefully the structure and issues before you begin adapting that material into presentation format. If, on the other hand, you are writing specifically for a particular presentation, you can structure the document in the same way as you intend to present it. This method – while not always an option – reinforces the material, the linkages and the flow of the material in your mind and makes the presentation easier to remember.

In the writing phase you should have applied the principles of good writing from the macro and micro writing issues of the previous chapter. Remember to pay attention to transitions, to move your presentation seamlessly from topic to topic. You need to be concerned with emphasis and structure. Your audience will only have your words and possibly your overhead transparencies to organize the material for them. Pay attention to grammar and style. We write differently than we speak. Writing out your presentation is more effective if you can write it the way you might say it.

Once you have completed the writing or your review of what has already been written, the next step is to adapt your material into a form that is appropriate for oral presentations. Before you begin to put the presentation together you should explicitly answer the following questions (some of which will be familiar from your communication strategy audience analysis):

- What are the key points you want to get across to your audience?

- How much time have you got to make them?

- Who is your audience?

- What is your audience size?

- What does your audience know about your subject?

As noted, you may be giving a presentation from a piece of written work such as a report or research paper or you could be writing the material in its original form for a specific presentation. In the second case you need only include the material you will be presenting. If you are converting the material from a report or essay, you need to pay particular attention to the first question – what key points you want to get across to your audience. Formal reports and papers tend to include much background and supporting information that would not be of interest to an audience or would take too much time to provide. Go through your written work highlighting key points, subsidiary points, examples and conclusions or arguments you want to communicate.

When you have streamlined and adapted your material, compare it with the time you have available for your presentation. If you have too much material you will have to reduce it even further. Marking the key points in order of importance will make it easier for you to eliminate the less important ideas or keep them as a back-up in case you run out of material. It may take several sessions of reducing, trying it out, reducing it further, trying that out, and so on until you get it about right (Figure 8.1). If you have worked with your material as we have recommended and you know your topic well enough, you will be able to be a bit flexible in terms of skipping minor points or adding more detail and other material as you speak if you find you are running ahead of or behind schedule during your actual talk – and with thorough preparation you will have the confidence to be able to do just that.

Audience analysis is extremely important for presentations which is why we recommend that you review your audience strategy once you have prepared some of your material for the talk. To avoid talking down to the audience or over their heads you need to know the level of information your audience has in your subject area. For example, if you are presenting a financial report to an audience of accounting and finance experts you can employ specialist terms common to financial analysts with confidence that you will be understood. If your audience is a mixture of finance and human resources people, however, you would not be able to use technical financial terms without explaining them.

Once you have composed your presentation, and completed your audience analysis, you should have a good idea how the audience is likely to respond to what you have prepared. Is it still suitable? Should you include more or less detail? Are key points over-communicated sufficiently? Is your conclusion strong enough to make an impact? These considerations can be dealt with in more detail once you have actually prepared your material.

Knowing the size of your audience is particularly important as it will affect your style of delivery. With a very large group you will need a microphone and a more formal style whereas with a small group your own voice should suffice and your style can be less formal. Does the material you have prepared reflect these considerations? Does your strategy fit with the material you have prepared (Figure 8.1)?

Having completed the pre-writing steps including developing your communication strategy, adapting the material to presentation format, reducing it further to fit the presentation time, and reviewing your audience analysis, you can consider impact factors – how you will create the best impression through your presentation.

Implement for impact

There are five basic factors that will affect the overall impression you give to an audience when you are presenting:

1. structure and content

2. style of delivery

3. appearance and posture

4. use of visual aids

5. question handling.

STRUCTURE AND CONTENT

All presentations, like all written communications, should have a beginning, a middle and an end. This simple advice is even more important for oral presentations. Recall from the communication strategy chapter that your audience remembers most what is said at the beginning and the end:

- at the beginning you should say what you are about to say

- in the middle you should say it

- at the end you should tell the audience what you have just said.

If you have adhered to the steps for effective writing you should have a well-organized and edited written paper from which to structure your presentation. Your opening, or introduction, should include an outline of what will be covered in your presentation and its structure. It should also put the content of the talk into some context. This is particularly important for an audience who do not have much knowledge of your subject area. You will also want to begin with something that will catch your audience's attention. It can be a new fact, startling discovery, or new way of looking at something the audience usually takes for granted, an interesting anecdote or a core issue or problem. The beginning is your most important opportunity to generate interest in your talk. Finally, your opening should include the objectives of your presentation (e.g. to inform, to persuade, or to amuse).

The main body of your presentation should develop logically. Points should be made clearly and 'signposted' by phrases such as 'What I have just described illustrates...' or 'From this it is clear that...'. When changing subjects and moving on to make new points, linkages should be clear. The audience should be made aware that the presenter has finished talking about subject 'A' and is now talking about subject 'B', for example, 'I have just made the point that..., now let us move on to...'.

When closing a presentation, your main points should be briefly summarized, i.e. 'tell the audience what you have told them'. It is important that you finish your presentation cleanly, rather than drift off to an indefinite end. This should be done with a concluding sentence or two, related to the objectives you stated at the beginning. For example, 'This morning I discussed..., which clearly shows that...'. A good way to end may be to link your ending to your opening so that a mental loop is set up that pulls the audience's attention back to the beginning of the presentation. You can refer them back to the problem you have now solved, or to the new information.

If you began your talk with a memorable opening or 'attention grabber' you can refer to it. For example, here is the opening sentence of a presentation about industrial relations in a Canadian coal mine: 'It was dark, snowing and bitterly cold and 130 people were trying to keep warm near a remote stretch of railway track in the Canadian Rockies – they were there to stop a train from entering a coal mine'. This opening is interesting and dramatic and raises the question: 'Why were these people trying to stop a train in the middle of the night in the middle of "nowhere"?'. After giving your presentation on the state of industrial relations at the mine and what might be done to change it, you could end by referring to the opening. You might say, 'If we change our industrial relations practices our employees will not have to resort to industrial action. They will not have to try to resolve their problems by stopping coal trains from entering the mine.'

DELIVERY

No matter how good the structure and content of your talk, the way you put it across to your audience will have the greatest impact on the impression you will make. Preparation, again, is important.

Do you have enough material? Most people speak at about 130 words a minute. Find out how fast you talk and use this a basis for estimating how long your presentation should last when it is delivered. Most word processing packages have a 'word count' function that will automatically count the words in your written material. Simply divide your word count by your speaking rate and you will have a good idea how long your presentation will last. For example, if you speak at about 130 words per minute and your presentation contains about 3250 words then you have enough material for about 25 minutes not counting questions.

You should rehearse your presentation either by simply speaking it aloud and timing it or by recording it on audio or video tape. It can also be very helpful if you can rehearse in front of a friend, colleague or family member and ask for feedback. If it is a particularly important presentation you may want to form a small group within your department to hear the presentation and give feedback and to give you the chance to rehearse in front of a live (if small) audience.

You need to decide in advance what method you will use to remember your material. There are a number of techniques commonly used, some more effective than others:

- prompt cards with key words for topics and subtopics

- mind-map or idea structure

- overhead transparencies with or without prompt cards

- word-for-word script

- memorization.

The least desirable alternatives are reading word-for-word from a prepared script and relying on memory. Unless you have a very animated speaking style and inject some interesting additional material, reading your presentation will sound stilted and monotonous, and your audience will lose attention quickly. While reading you maintain little eye contact with the audience and therefore get little feedback. Relying on memory alone is very risky unless you are extremely familiar with the material and have presented it many times in the past. Memorized presentations can also sound very monotonous.

The recommended method is using overhead transparencies, slides or a computer-based display showing key points with accompanying notes or prompt cards. Visual aids (see below) will help your audience grasp your points and will serve to jog your memory about related examples or explanatory material. If you know your material very well you can manage with a simple outline or mind map of primary and secondary ideas and fill in the details from memory. If using prompt cards or cue cards make sure they are attached in one of the upper corners to avoid dropping one or getting them in the wrong order during your presentation. Use a ring or string for ease of turning. Even with the precaution of attaching the cards in some way, it is still a good idea to number them. If you do drop them and the ring opens, you can then take the few seconds necessary to put them back in order and proceed with the presentation. Knowing they are in the right order will give you more confidence.

As you are presenting *to* an audience, look *at* the audience. Do not look at the floor, the ceiling, the back wall, or, importantly, the overhead projector screen. Look at the audience and vary your gaze, moving your eyes around the room to take in the whole audience. You may find that some people pay more attention than others to what you have to say. As you speak you notice by their body language that they are interested – tilting the head, taking notes, nodding slightly in agreement as you speak, making eye contact with you, and so on. If you are nervous about speaking, focus on those people in the audience who demonstrably want to hear what you have to say. This will increase your confidence. You will know that they are paying attention, that what you are saying is important, and that you are doing well.

Speak clearly, varying the pace and rhythm of your speech, to maintain the interest of your audience. Remember to use language appropriate to your audience. This is particularly important when presenting technical material to 'non-technical' people. At the writing stage when you were considering your message strategy and audience analysis, you will have translated any jargon or technical language for the audience if they are not specialists.

Your delivery style is related to the pitch and volume of your voice and the speed and rhythm of your speech. Vary the pitch of your voice. If you have a very high or very low-pitched voice practise varying it by taping your presentation on a tape recorder. You may need to do several versions, modifying your voice to emphasize key points, until you get the right variations in pitch. Lower voices are generally perceived to be more authoritative so if your voice is naturally higher-pitched, you may want to work at developing a lower-pitched voice to give more authority to your presentations. Former prime minister Margaret Thatcher is said to have taken voice lessons partly to accomplish precisely that effect.

Voice volume should match the size of the room and the audience. Make certain your voice is loud enough that every member of the audience can hear clearly. If you are uncertain, experiment in the presentation room in advance with a friend standing at different points in the room to check your volume level. If it is a large room or one that has bad acoustics, you may have to use a microphone. If so, you will want to practise using it before you give your talk. You should also vary the volume of your voice to emphasize key points.

Inexperienced presenters often tend to speak too quickly. Nervousness makes them rush through the presentation without pausing, causing the audience to miss much of what was said. Make use of pauses between sections of the presentation or when moving from one major point to the next. You can also use a pause to make eye contact with your audience but make certain that the pause is at an appropriate break in your material. Vary the rhythm of your speech. A monotonous tone makes the audience lose interest. Increase your speed a little on the less important parts and slow down for emphasis when you are making key points.

If you have a time limit for your talk, make sure that you stick to it. Do not go on for too long and try not to stop too early. If you speak faster than you practised, you will also discover that you have run out of prepared material. You will be tempted at that point to improvise. Improvisation is not usually a good idea. You may have finished early, but you have come to the conclusion and – hopefully – made your point. Rambling on will dilute your well-constructed message. Rather, take questions or end as if you had filled the allotted time.

Choose whether you are going to sit or stand depending on the room and audience size. Make your choice before you speak. If the audience exceeds 15 or 20 it is probably best to stand. If you are giving your presentation standing up, move around a little to help keep your audience interested. Use appropriate gestures to help illustrate what you are saying. Whichever you choose, try to appear comfortable and natural, even if you are feeling nervous.

Nearly everyone feels nervous when doing presentations. Practising your presentation beforehand helps considerably. Giving effective presentations is a learned skill which you can acquire by actually doing it as often as you can. Remember that the audience is generally on your side and wants to see you do well. Mistakes you make that you think are enormous are likely to be barely noticed by an audience. If you do make a major mistake or lose track of what you are saying, as everybody does at some time, stop. Look at your notes, get your bearings, take a deep breath to relax, and carry on. Nobody expects perfection.

APPEARANCE AND POSTURE

Research suggests that the impact made in a presentation is probably based more on appearance and posture than the content of what we say. Non-verbal cues have as much as four or five times the effect of actual words when we make a presentation. This translates into the following estimates:

50 per cent of the impact you make is based on appearance
40 per cent on your confidence
10 per cent on what you actually say.

To appear confident, relaxed and in control does mean that a disproportionately high amount of effort is needed in preparing, writing and rehearsing than on mere grooming. The impact is the result of rigorous preparation.

Compromises will sometimes have to be made with your values and style, and those of the organization you represent or the values of the audience you will be addressing. Generally it best to play safe and merge with your surroundings. For business it is usually safest to dress as a television newscaster might – appear timeless, classless and unobtrusive. You do not want your appearance to overwhelm what you are saying or draw attention away from it. Based on your audience analysis, your clothing must be appropriate.

Standing or sitting well creates a feeling of confidence in the speaker. The audience will want to see someone who is confident, authoritative and knowledgeable. Put your feet slightly apart. Look comfortably ahead but maintain eye contact with the audience. Stand with good posture. However, do not exaggerate or strike too rigid a posture. You will feel stiff and uncomfortable and your audience will sense it.

If sitting, choose a chair in which the seat and back form a right angle. Sit upright, which conveys an impression of alertness. If you have an uncomfortable or unsuitable chair sit forward on the seat, leaning very slightly forward.

Appropriate posture, neither too rigid nor too relaxed, and a well-groomed appearance signal that you are interested, enthusiastic and able to speak authoritatively on your subject.

VISUAL AIDS

Visual aids help convey ideas and information in a way which is more easily understood and absorbed by an audience. There are a number of visual aids available to presenters. These include overhead transparencies, whiteboards, flip charts, slides, video tapes, films, maps, models and computer-based displays. It is important to remember that visual aids exist to support the spoken component of the presentation and should only be used when they add to what is said.

Effective visual aids should do one or more of the following (Nickson and Siddons 1996):

- introduce a topic

- link complex ideas

- define terms

- summarize key points

- compare information

- help the audience visualize abstract concepts (charts, diagrams)

- help the audience remember what you have said (colour, humour, eye-catching images)

- represent reality (photographs, maps, plans)

- reinforce important information

- inspire (slogans, mission statements, quotes).

Work out in advance exactly what you want from a particular visual aid. Think about other ways of presenting the same information. Instead of tables of figures, perhaps you could use a graph. Make it as simple and as bold as possible. Too much information on one slide or transparency makes it difficult for the audience to read. Figure 8.2 shows a typical slide or overhead transparency (OHT). Try to make your images as interesting as possible. Figure 8.3 shows another OHT slide but this time utilizing an image.

Practise using the visual aids you have chosen beforehand, so that you know what you are doing during the presentation. Good presenters make the transition from one OHT to another during a presentation look natural and easy – that is because they have practised. A presentation must be choreographed to get that seamless flow. OHTs need to be placed on and taken off the projector at the right time for effect.

Know how to use the OHT projector. Ahead of the presentation you should make sure you can turn it on and off without fuss and learn how to bring a new projection bulb into position or to replace one if it should burn out during your presentation. It is generally best to turn off the overhead or slide projector when you are not actively using it. When drawing the audience's attention to a particular point on an OHT, point on the

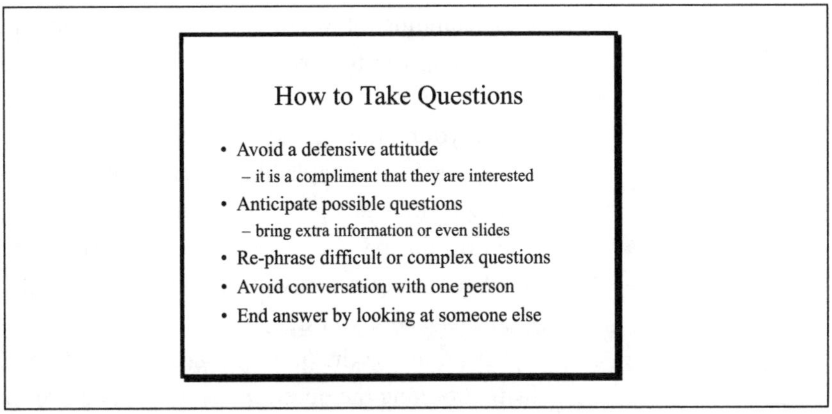

How to Take Questions

- Avoid a defensive attitude
  - it is a compliment that they are interested
- Anticipate possible questions
  - bring extra information or even slides
- Re-phrase difficult or complex questions
- Avoid conversation with one person
- End answer by looking at someone else

FIGURE 8.2 *Example of OHT*

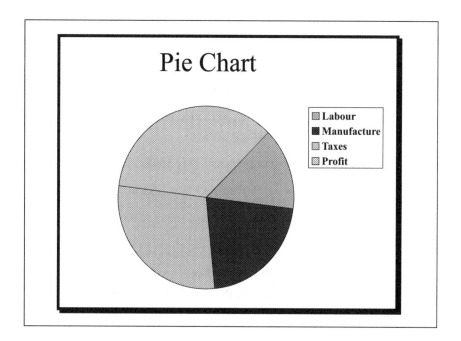

FIGURE 8.3 *Sample of chart on OHT*

transparency itself and not on the screen. Even then it is best to simply lay a pen or pencil on the OHT so that any nervousness is not exaggerated by the projector. Even if you are calm a pencil held in the magnifying light of the projector as you point to a line on your OHT will look like it is shaking. Your audience will see the shaking pencil, assume you are nervous and will become uncomfortable. You will see from their body language that they are ill at ease and that will make you nervous – and then the pencil will really begin to shake! It is best to just lay the pencil on the OHT where it will be firmly in place.

QUESTION HANDLING

Here your audience has an opportunity to participate, developing their understanding of what you have said, and, indirectly, testing you. Your presentation is not over yet! It is important that you know what you are talking about.

Let your audience know at the beginning when you want to receive questions. Some people like to field questions during the presentation, others at the end. It is up to you – it is your presentation. If someone asks a question during your presentation and you are not ready to answer it, tell them so and that you will come back to that point at the end of the talk – then make sure you do.

Set limits for the questioning session before you begin to take questions. State how long the question session will be and that you will permit only one or two questions per person. Limiting the number of questions one person can pose helps to prevent getting into a heated exchange with a member of the audience or having one person monopolize the question time.

When someone does ask you a question ensure that you fully understand it. If you do not, ask them to repeat or explain it further, then answer it clearly and succinctly. If you think some of the audience did not hear the question, repeat it clearly before answering. If you cannot answer the question, it is usually safer to say so than to try to bluff or waffle your way through, particularly when you are presenting to an audience with some knowledge of the subject.

When the end of the question period approaches, prepare the audience by saying that you will take one more question. When you have answered the last question you might quickly summarize your argument in a sentence or two and close.

Occasionally it might happen that there are no questions. In that case you might prepare a few questions in advance. State that you will start the questioning with the question you most often get in conjunction with the topic. Another strategy to head off the situation is to have a friend in the audience who has agreed in advance to start off the questioning if none are forthcoming. As a last resort you might close by saying that you know the most interesting questions are always asked after the formal question period so you will be available after the session for informal questions.

Feedback

In Chapter Two we looked at the importance of non-verbal communication. It is important to remember that the non-verbal has a greater impact than the content in oral presentations. Much of the feedback you receive when giving a presentation comes from non-verbal signals. You need to be aware of the feedback you are getting from your audience during your presentation.

Check for the non-verbal behaviour of your audience. Do they seem interested and alert? Are they yawning and looking out of the window? Be flexible and adjust your presentation if you get the impression that your audience has lost interest. You may have to pause and ask a question to find out if what you are saying has been understood or if it is covering familiar ground. Alternatively the audience may not be able to hear you clearly or you may be speaking too quickly. If you can adjust your performance in response to audience feedback you can turn a potentially bad presentation into an effective one.

All communications – especially oral presentations – rely on feedback to provide cues and to help improve performance. In this section we discuss feedback in general: how to give it, and how to benefit from it.

How many times have you heard phrases such as, '*Brilliant!*', '*Great presentation!*', '*Next time try to improve!*', '*Good report, direct and to the point with sufficient detail!*'? Each phrase is an attempt by one person to give feedback to another. We require feedback in order to gauge whether we are doing well or poorly and even if we are on the right track at all. Feedback is a positive process.

PRINCIPLES OF FEEDBACK

Accept people as they are. The goal of feedback is not to change people but their behaviour. Indeed if people are reasonably well adjusted their personality will be such that feedback would not change them in any event. The goal of feedback is to improve performance. That is, feedback is for changing specific behaviours. If the feedback is accurate and the recipient is perceptive, it will help define more accurately the effect on others, which will lead to improved performance.

Feedback needs to be constructive and given in a spirit of helpfulness, not to 'score points' or embarrass. The following points for giving and receiving feedback are presented as guidelines.

GIVING FEEDBACK

1. Be descriptive, not interpretative. Report the facts, not what you think is meant by them.

2. Focus on specific behaviours rather than generalities which are less helpful.

3. Be sincerely helpful. Check your motives. Are you providing feedback to be helpful, or to be superior? Negative feedback should be directed at the goals of the communication, not at the speaker.

4. Keep feedback impersonal. Say, 'the conclusion will have more impact if...', rather than 'You messed up the conclusion'.

5. Use appropriate timing. Decide when would be the most helpful time to provide feedback. The closer to the event, the more helpful it is.

6. Make change possible, not demanded. Usually this is done by sincerely suggesting change, not demanding change, and directing feedback towards what can be changed. If something cannot be changed, there is no positive result to be gained from mentioning it.

Feedback is an integral part of any communication system. Knowing what constitutes feedback, how and when to give feedback, and then using feedback to improve your performance will improve your oral communication skills and effectiveness.

Presentation checklist

Rehearsal of your presentation is the only way to check that you have managed to get everything right. You will be much more confident doing the presentation when you have already practised it several times in advance.

These notes are a guide to help you give more effective presentations. You should, as you get more experience, try doing things in different ways and develop your own style of presentation.

Below is a checklist for preparing presentations giving the main criteria which you should consider for your presentation.

STRUCTURE

- Does your opening catch the audience's attention?
- Does your opening contain an outline, set the context and state your objectives?
- Are the main points you want to make set out clearly?
- Do your main points follow each other logically and link together well?
- Are your points well 'signposted'?
- Do your main points need support from visual aids?
- When closing do you sum up the main points?
- Is your conclusion strong?
- Have you tied your closing to your opening?

DELIVERY

- Do you know your topic very well?
- Are you going to speak from cards, notes or OHTs?
- Are you going to sit or stand?
- Is the language appropriate for your audience?
- Have you practised using your visual aids?
- Can you operate the equipment?

APPEARANCE AND POSTURE

- Are you dressed to meet your audience's values or expectations?
- Have you practised your speaking posture (standing or sitting)?
- Are you groomed in a way that is appropriate for your audience's expectations?

VISUAL AIDS

- Are your visual aids simple, interesting and easy to read?
- Do they fit well with your talk and add to your presentation?
- Do they have a standard format and colour?
- Are they legible from the back of the room?

QUESTION HANDLING

- Have you advised your audience when you will take questions?
- Do you know your topic deeply enough?
- Have you anticipated and prepared for any likely questions?
- Have you practised answering questions?
- Do you have plans about how to end the question time?
- Have you prepared a very short summary to use after questions to restate your main point and objective?

Discussion questions

1. Discuss the importance of audience strategy for oral presentations.

2. How might the presentation of a scientific environmental impact report have to change if it were presented to a group of people from a local community?

3. How would you change your presentation depending upon whether you were (1) giving a speech to an outside audience or (2) making a presentation to your department?

4. How would you handle a question when you do not know the answer?

5. Former American President Woodrow Wilson is reported to have said, 'if you want me to talk for ten minutes I'll come next week. If you want me to talk for an hour I'll come tonight.' What did he mean by this?

References

Nickson, D. and Siddons, S. (1996) *Business Communications*, Butterworth Heinemann, Oxford.

Further reading

Applebaum, R. and Anatol, K. (1982) *Effective Oral Communication for Business and the Professions*, Science Research Associates, Chicago.

Bailey, E. (1999) *Writing and Speaking at Work*, Prentice Hall, Paramun, NJ.

Jay, R. (1999) *The Seven Deadly Skills of Communicating*, International Thomson Business Press, London.

Morreale, S. and Bovée, C. (1998) *Excellence in Public Speaking*, Harcourt Brace, Fort Worth, TX.

Nierenberg, G. I. and Calero, H. H. (1975) *How to Read a Person like a Book*, Pocket Books, New York.

chapter (nine

Meetings and negotiations

Introduction

THIS CHAPTER deals with two related aspects of communication in groups: meetings and negotiations. Meetings are a common group activity in business, involving large amounts of time and labour. They often have a negative reputation for being unproductive or a waste of time. Unproductive meetings are due to a lack of planning, structure and leadership. Whether they are formal or informal, with two or twenty participants, there are strategies for making meetings productive and efficient.

Meetings can have a variety of purposes but almost all meetings involve negotiations to one degree or another. The art of negotiation is one of the most powerful skills you can acquire, not just for business, but in all areas of your life. Whether you are aware of it or not, you are constantly negotiating. When you make a purchase, you are negotiating a sale. When you are deciding among friends what to do on a Saturday night, you are negotiating. When you make choices about any aspect of your daily activity or behaviour from among a variety of options, you are negotiating. In business, when one company is merging with another, buying out a company or forging a strategic alliance, negotiations are needed to work out the details and agreements. In politics, the peace processes in Northern Ireland and the Middle East involve very complex and high-stakes negotiations that affect the lives of millions of people. In the second half of this chapter we will look at successful negotiations, the primary aim of which is a positive (win–win) outcome for all parties.

LEARNING OBJECTIVES

After completing this chapter you will be able to:

• Identify the purposes and types of meetings

- Prepare a meeting agenda
- Plan and lead a formal meeting
- Prepare and distribute meeting minutes
- Demonstrate an understanding of negotiations

Effective meetings

Meetings have many advantages and disadvantages. One of the main benefits of meetings is the ability of a group of people to generate more ideas and solutions to problems than could a single individual. Having a diverse group involved in making decisions at meetings means even more ideas get generated than could be expected from a more homogeneous group. Research into diversity (Cox and Blake 1991) suggests that diversity can be a competitive advantage for companies. Additionally, if a group makes a decision, the members of the group are more likely to be committed to seeing it carried out.

Meetings are a social process that we will consider at two levels:

- richness of communication

- social complexity of the process.

The social aspect of meetings is important as it allows face-to-face contact with team members and colleagues, particularly if they are not in daily contact with each other. Face-to-face contact is a rich form of verbal and non-verbal communication. In meetings people not only hear the words, but see the body language. They see who is sitting next to whom, and who is consulting whom. All of these cues are part of the socio-cultural context of meetings. Thinking about that context can lead to better management of meetings.

Meetings lacking firm leadership can fail easily. Decision-making can be needlessly prolonged which can be a disadvantage when a quick solution is important. Meetings can be repetitive and monotonous if the same ground is gone over too often or if one or two participants are allowed to dominate the discussion. They can get bogged down in trivial items of business, dragging on for hours, creating monotony and frustration. They can become forums for playing out interpersonal politics. Some of these negative meeting outcomes can be directly related to the sociological context in which meetings occur.

Meetings are a socially complex organizational decision process. A meeting is not a singular event within an organization. Rather, it is an event – a decision process – embedded within a stream of organizational events.

Precisely because meetings are a decision process, they tend to fit what Cohen, March and Olsen (1972) have labelled the 'garbage can' model of organizational decision-making. The garbage can model recognizes that a number of things are going on in organizations before meetings are held to make routine (or otherwise) decisions. They cite four distinct but related organizational themes relevant to how decisions are made:

1. Problems – represent an issue for which a solution is sought. Of course there can be problems with no solutions and problems for which no solution is even sought.

2. Choices – are potential solutions to problems. There can be several solutions to the same problem or several problems that can be fixed with the same solution. Also, people can have a good idea (a solution) but no problem they can solve with it.

3. Participants – are the people in the organization, some of whom are at the meeting. Participants have different values, cultures, perhaps come from different departments and therefore may not recognize some issues as problems and may not recognize some solutions. They might also have problems (personal, psychological, power-relationship, etc.) for which the organization cannot – or would not – provide solutions even if it had them.

4. Choice opportunities – are occasions, such as a meeting, when an organization makes decisions.

What occurs in organizations (research and experience bears this out) is that all four themes percolate and flow about and get communicated and move around. Personnel are transferred or quit and others are brought in. The metaphor of the garbage bin was chosen because an organization is like one big container full of the four streams getting stirred about rather like refuse in a bin. The only time a solution to a problem is chosen is when the problem, the solution and the right participants meet at a specific contingent moment or choice opportunity.

The result of all this is that when a meeting is called to handle even routine business problems it is a bit like fishing around in a garbage can for dinner. What happens as result in most meetings is that:

- choices are made without actually solving the problems

- no choice is made so problems continue

- solutions may be proposed when there is no problem to solve

- or, when things are going well, some choices will be made that actually solve some problems.

The point of the garbage can model as we have described it in the context of meetings is that meetings are social processes and not discrete events set apart from everything else that goes on in organizations. Meetings do work well when participants, but especially the leader, understand that more is going on in a meeting than merely a group of individuals making rational decisions to solve objective problems.

A meeting consumes a large amount of resources not just in the actual time set for the meeting but in planning, in participants' travelling time and expenses and in follow-up activities. You must be certain before committing to holding a meeting that it is the appropriate channel to meet your objective. Like any communication exercise, a successful meeting depends on good planning and a well-thought-out communication strategy with a clear objective and purpose.

Meetings may be formal or informal. The degree of formality is linked to the amount of structure, organization and documentation involved. Informal meetings are usually spontaneous and small, without a printed agenda, and have little record-keeping and no structured leadership. Formal meetings require scheduling, notification, the circulation of an agenda, leadership by a chairperson, recording of minutes and follow-up. Formal meetings must also have a quorum which is the minimum number of participants present to make the meeting valid. The purpose of the meeting often dictates the degree of formality required.

PURPOSE OF MEETINGS

Meetings can fulfil a range of purposes of which the most common are:

- to inform
- to advise
- to make decisions
- to solve problems
- to plan
- to consult
- to motivate.

An informative meeting might be held to make employees aware of new procedures or changes in company policy or to brief managers on new situations or the day's or week's priorities. Advisory meetings are used to solicit information such as expert technical or legal advice, or to hear opinions, for example, from the organization's departments on how a new strategy or policy might affect them. Decision-making meetings often follow advisory ones, so that a firm decision can be made on the basis of the advice given. Decision-making meetings may be held at any level of the organization depending upon its culture and the degree of involvement normally expected from employees.

Problem-solving meetings and planning meetings are the most creative. Brainstorming, mind mapping and other idea-generating techniques are often used to find the most effective solutions or develop a comprehensive plan of action. Consultative meetings allow people to air their opinions. Consultative meetings are used by politicians and planning committees to hear the views of their constituents on proposed developments or to reappraise unsatisfactory ones. The government often sets up a commission to investigate an issue, a large part of which is usually a series of consultative meetings around the country.

Motivational meetings are aimed at generating interest in or enthusiasm for a project or idea. They also create a feeling of involvement and can stimulate commitment to teamwork projects. Companies may hold motivational meetings to advise employees on how well they are doing, and to encourage them to continue to produce at a high level. Sales meetings are often very motivational with awards and plaudits for those employees with the best sales record.

Types of business meetings range from general board meetings to small work- group meetings. Companies are required to hold Annual General Meetings and Statutory Board Meetings which are at the very formal end of the scale. Managers may meet with other managers and section heads. Managers meet with their subordinates and employees. There are departmental meetings, committee meetings, meetings of task forces, work projects, audit meetings, review meetings, annual, quarterly, monthly, weekly, daily meetings, etc.

MEETING LEADERSHIP

The effectiveness of any meeting is in large part the responsibility of the meeting leader. The meeting leader or chairperson has a number of duties. To conduct a successful meeting, an effective meeting leader should:

- generate the agenda and make sure it is followed

- facilitate and stimulate the discussion

- pace the meeting

- summarize the discussion and recommendations

- circulate the minutes.

Choosing the right participants for the meeting is an important consideration. Make sure all participants can contribute and choose good decision-makers and problem-solvers. Where possible, be aware of the kinds of issues with which participants might be dealing in their departments or divisions – it is important to be aware of any 'hidden agendas' people might bring to the meeting. Other than at a large informational meeting, the number of participants should be kept to a maximum of twelve, preferably fewer. Too many participants can make for lengthy discussions. Make sure the key people with the necessary information for the agenda items are invited.

Choosing the right location is just as important. Check that details like ventilation, light, heating, acoustics and refreshments are satisfactory. Seating arrangements should also be planned – where people sit symbolically communicates meaning to participants. The person sitting next to the chairperson, for example, is perceived to have more power than other participants. Do you want people at a number of small tables or around one large table or perhaps a table for the meeting leaders and rows of chairs facing? The purpose of the meeting and numbers attending will determine which physical arrangement will work best.

If you are chairing a meeting it is your responsibility to stimulate discussion and debate. All those attending should be brought into the discussion. Ideally the leader should guide the meeting so that there is a free flow of debate with no individual dominating and no extensive discussions between two participants. As time runs out for each agenda item:

- stop the discussion

- summarize the debate on that item

- move on to the next item.

Where action is to be taken on an item, state who is to be responsible for it and note the person's name or initials on the agenda beside the item. To avoid misunderstandings, at the end of the meeting summarize the discussion and actions to be taken and clearly identify the time by which action should be taken. This will avoid misunderstandings. After the meeting, make certain that the minutes are circulated to all participants.

MEETING DOCUMENTATION

All formal and some informal meetings require documentation. The two basic meeting documents are an agenda and minutes. In some cases a separate notice may be provided with the time, place and date details or those on the agenda may be considered sufficient notice. An agenda is a list of topics to be dealt with at the meeting. It should begin with the notice details setting out the time, place, date and type of meeting. It may also include a list of participants but more usually they appear in the minutes. The topics to be discussed constitute the main body of the agenda.

In a formal meeting, items on the agenda are considered either ordinary or special business. At the beginning of the agenda come ordinary business items: apologies for absence, minutes of previous meetings, and matters arising from previous meetings. After the ordinary business items, any reports to be submitted are presented. Next the special business items are discussed in order of their presentation on the agenda. Two more ordinary business items are placed at the end of a meeting: any other business and the date of next meeting (Figure 9.1).

The meeting leader may have a special agenda, the chair's agenda. It includes detailed information on agenda items and helps make certain all subsidiary issues are covered. To facilitate the pace of the meeting the chair's agenda may have time limits allocated to each item of business. Sufficient blank space should be left on the right-hand side of the chair's agenda to allow for notes to be taken.

Meeting minutes are generated from all formal meetings and some informal ones. The secretary or a nominated person records the minutes which can range from word-for-word accounts to summary minutes or simply recording resolutions. Verbatim minutes are seldom used in business.

Fresh Foods Inc.

The monthly meeting of the purchasing and production staff will be held in the Main Office on Tuesday, 14 October 2000 at 9:00 a.m.

AGENDA

1. Apologies for absence
2. Minutes of last meeting
3. Matters arising
4. Production Manager's Report
5. Purchasing Manager's Report
6. Kitchen expansion proposal
7. Computer ordering system
8. Service staff uniforms
9. Any other business
10. Date of next meeting

D. Farold
Secretary

FIGURE 9.1 *Meeting agenda*

More common are short summaries of the discussions on each agenda item and the resolutions or recommendations.

Minutes must be accurate and objective. They should begin with the date, place and time of the meeting followed by a list of those present with the meeting leader's name first. They should be written in the past tense using the third person: 'It was decided unanimously that new white jackets would be purchased for service staff'. At the end of the minutes include a space for the chairperson's signature and date of the signature which will be filled in at the next meeting. Figure 9.2 is an example of meeting minutes prepared from the above agenda.

Make certain all minutes are distributed as soon as possible after the meeting so corrections can be noted while the details are still fresh in everyone's memory. The minutes must be circulated to those who were invited, but did not attend.

Win–win negotiations

Negotiation is everywhere. From governments' dealings with terrorists, to attempts at preventing or stopping violent conflicts, to industrial relations, to business mergers and acquisitions, dealing with suppliers and customers, career path development in the workplace, to students' discussions with tutors regarding submission of coursework, negotiation is an important element in all our lives. While some negotiations have much greater impact on our everyday lives than others, it is still the case that we live in a world where we are all involved in negotiations to some degree or another.

Some people negotiate better than others. The better negotiators tend to create better circumstances for themselves or their organizations. The alternative to negotiation is conflict – whether at national or individual levels. A key element of the emerging global business culture (as with the international community generally) is that negotiation is preferable to conflict.

Businesses need to be able to negotiate effectively. So, too, do individuals. In this section we explore:

- the nature of negotiations

- preparation for negotiations

- the negotiation climate

- the need for common ground

- elements of persuasive communication.

Fresh Foods Inc.

The monthly meeting of the purchasing and production staff was held in the Main Office on Tuesday, 14 October 2000 at 9:00 a.m.

Present: B. Kubica, Chair   F. Delaney
           H. Norfield   J. Peters
           B. Blackley   E. Martin
           A. Hassan   B. McDonnell

AGENDA   **ACTION**

1. Apologies for absence

    All members present.

2. Minutes of last meeting

    The minutes were amended to correct an error in last month's purchasing budget from £9352 to £9532 after which the chair approved and signed the minutes.

3. Matters arising

    No matters arising.

4. Production Manager's Report

    H. Norfield reported a 10% increase in the number of meals produced in September with a 4% increase in costs due to requests for special meals for diabetic and kosher customers.

5. Purchasing Manager's Report

    A. Hassan reported on a new supplier for organic chicken and duck and an increase in prices from Healthwise Greens for salad and garnish ingredients.

6. Kitchen expansion proposal   HN

    It was agreed that the kitchen expansion would be postponed until February when business would be slower. H. Norfield to obtain three quotes by 15 Jan.

7. Computer ordering system   EM

    Several staff members reported problems with entries in the system not taking multiples of items. E. Martin to contact PBX Computer Systems by 20 October.

8. Service staff uniforms   BM

    It was decided unanimously that new white jackets would be purchased for service staff. B. McDonnell to contact suppliers week of 21 Oct.

9. Any other business

    No other business.

10. Date of next meeting   AH

    Date of next meeting was tentatively set for 15 Nov. A. Hassan to confirm.

D. Farold

Sec.

Signed: _____   Date: _____

FIGURE 9.2 *Meeting minutes*

NATURE OF NEGOTIATIONS

Negotiation can be defined as a social process of interaction and communication between people with the purpose of obtaining a lasting agreement based on some common interests for the purpose of achieving goals and avoiding conflict.

Negotiation is a social process (Kramer and Messick 1995). While admittedly individual characteristics affect negotiations, it still remains the case that negotiation – like communication – must occur between people. Negotiation is social interaction. Through that social interaction people exchange information. They communicate. The communication is designed to generate agreement between people who not only have some things in common, but who generally have diverging interests.

In our definition of negotiation we focus on process. In other words, negotiation is not a single event. Negotiation has an element of continuity that is often misunderstood when we view high-profile negotiations such as those concerning the Middle East. Particular negotiation sessions are reported in the press as discrete events, but each session is part of a continuing set of negotiations occurring over time.

There are also one-off negotiations between organizations or persons who, once they have completed their negotiations, may never meet again. The elements, models, strategies and tactics described in this chapter will be useful in those situations as well.

Our definition also emphasizes agreement. Seeking agreement is central to defining or labelling a communication process as a negotiation as opposed to some other form of communication. Without the goal of reaching agreement there is no negotiation. Negotiations can be for gain, to avoid or limit conflict or even to prevent loss of something already held, but in all of these cases the goal is to arrive at some form of agreement.

That agreement generally can only be reached if there is some common ground. We will discuss common ground in more detail below, but, for now, common ground can be seen as characteristics that parties are perceived to hold in common. They might share a history or a culture. They might share a desire to live peacefully, or they might share some future ideal or situation that they can create together such as a joint business venture. In other words, common ground is not just what people have in common but what they could become together or what they might create together.

To that end, the agreement has to be lasting. Negotiators agree – 'rather no deal, than one that breaks down'. The test of negotiation success is whether or not the agreement breaks down. To a large extent the degree to which a settlement is lasting depends on the goodwill of the parties to the negotiation and upon the sharing of any value created by the agreement in a way that is perceived to be fair. An enlightened negotiator will not agree to a settlement with which the other party will become dissatisfied. Good negotiators – no matter how good the deal is for their side – will insist on an equitable deal (even if that means taking less in the short term) for the sole purpose of ensuring that the deal lasts. Not only is this cost-effective (negotiations are costly), but it is also best for long-term relationships and generally results in a better deal for both parties over time.

The goodwill of parties to a negotiation is evidenced by their willingness to compromise. The inability to compromise leads to stalled negotiations. Flexibility is necessary on both sides, particularly with regard to seeking out alternatives. Often those alternatives can be generated from focusing on common ground but this must be done with a frank discussion of differences, too.

There are several forms of negotiation-like activity which contain some or all of the elements of negotiation according to our definition:

- bargaining

- collective bargaining

- mediation

- arbitration

- lobbying

- talks.

'Bargaining' is often used interchangeably with 'negotiation' though often bargaining is used to refer to discussions solely with regard to money. For example, as a seller you might wish to get the highest price you can for your goods or services. As a buyer you want to pay as little as possible. When buyer and seller get together to arrive at a price, they are bargaining. This is basically the same as negotiation. The only difference is that negotiation may be related to more issues than merely the price of the product or service. Indeed, bargaining in its pure sense is relatively rare in business. Generally, firms do not bargain merely for the lowest price, they negotiate for the lowest price while building a relationship with the seller that may last longer than a one-off transaction. In this text we use negotiation in this broader sense.

Collective bargaining is slightly different. It refers to situations – usually related to labour relations – wherein an agent or group negotiates on behalf of a larger group. Often the agreement has to be ratified by either the company's directors or the rank-and-file union members.

'Mediation' refers to a negotiation process that uses a third or neutral party to reach agreements. Generally the neutral party has no decision-making power and, by virtue of being neutral, has no conflict of interest with either of the other parties. The mediator's role is more that of a facilitator who can move between the parties, ease communication and solve problems between them. The final agreement between the parties remains, however, with the parties themselves. Ideally, mediation will set the negotiation climate (discussed below) so that direct negotiation between the parties can resume without the help of a mediator.

Similar to mediation, arbitration relies on third-party intervention. In this case, however, the arbitrator does have final decision-making power. By using arbitration, both parties relinquish their right to reach an agreement but instead rely on the arbitrator to do it for them. Both parties present their points of view and their information to the arbitrator (sometimes in a quasi-courtroom context) who makes a decision that is binding on both parties. Arbitration is often used in industrial disputes between a labour union and the company. When such is the case, the collective agreement usually describes precisely what issues go to arbitration and under what conditions.

Lobbying is a form of negotiation whereby one party attempts to pressure the other into acceding. Lobbying can be relatively formal but is usually informal and may take place 'behind the scenes' either as a pre-negotiation event or during the negotiation event. Often key decision-makers are targets of lobbying efforts. Sometimes other groups that can pressure one of the parties in the negotiations is itself lobbied in order to bring pressure to bear from another direction.

Talks tend to be relatively informal meetings during which parties that expect to negotiate seriously at a later time begin to collect information and to explore each other's points of view. This may be a time for testing the other party in terms of flexibility or need for a negotiated agreement. If the talks seem to suggest that a negotiated agreement is likely, then negotiations may be planned. To begin negotiations without first engaging in talks is in some cases not particularly productive. On the other hand, if talks suggest that an agreement is possible, then negotiators often tend to be more flexible and positive than they otherwise might have been.

There are, therefore, several forms of agreement-seeking processes, but for our purposes here we will refer solely to negotiations.

Negotiations can be classified into different types depending upon variables such as objectives, time and timing, nature of the parties and their relationship with each other, and potential or actual conflict. In other words, there are many ways to categorize negotiations. Nevertheless, negotiators (and those researching negotiations) find it useful to know what kind of negotiations or negotiating context with which they are dealing. For our purposes here we will classify negotiations based on outcome, though there are clearly other variables that could be used. There are three main types of outcome-based negotiations:

- integrative

- distributive

- destructive.

Integrative negotiations have a goal of 'win–win' (Table 9.1). Winning is not as simple a concept as it might appear. Each party does not necessarily get equal amounts of money, for example. It could be that although the other party gets a larger share of the profit in a negotiated joint venture, you might think you are the winner because, as a result of that joint venture, you gain valuable knowledge, experience and technology. In this kind of 'win–win' negotiation, conflict or disagreement is perceived to be more costly (in whatever terms) than agreement and compromise. Costs and benefits are equalized between the parties. This is precisely the kind of negotiation that occurs every day in organizations: managers negotiate with each other over budgets, workers negotiate with managers over benefits and remuneration, buyers negotiate with suppliers. In all these cases an integrative negotiation is sought in order to enhance, build or maintain a valuable relationship.

Distributive negotiations are characterized by 'win–lose' (Table 9.1). Here parties to the negotiation are out to win regardless of the outcome for others. One party has to lose in distributive negotiations. The process is competitive, offensive, manipulative and aggressive. Examples are most court cases and short-term business negotiations where the parties do not particularly care if they deal with each other again.

Destructive negotiations are processes in which one or both parties seek to 'win' even at such cost that they 'lose' though they, technically, may have won. In this situation it is 'lose–lose'. There was a danger of precisely this kind of outcome in the petrol price protests in the UK. Fuel lobbyists who had been successful initially with protests and blockades as part of their negotiation tactics were forced to pull back from a repeat performance because to push on would have meant, not only losing days of work for themselves (and thereby jeopardizing their businesses even more), but also risking losing popular support and undermining their cause. To have persisted would have resulted in lose–lose. Winner's curse (Kagel and Levin 1986) is a further example of how destructive negotiation occurs. In winner's curse situations one party over-values what it desires from the

TABLE 9.1 *Outcome-based negotiations*

	Firm "1" Wins	Firm "1" loses
Firm "2" wins	Integrative win–win	Distributive win–lose
Firm "2" loses	Distributive lose–win	Destructive lose–lose

negotiation (or at auction for example) to such an extent that it 'wins' what it seeks but at too high a price and at the expense of the other party to the negotiations. Similarly, sometimes individuals or groups will seek to 'hurt' the other party to prove a point and win at any cost, only to inflict self-damage in the process.

Generally, integrative negotiations are the ideal. However, sometimes negotiators realize that a distributive outcome is all that is available. In all events, if negotiations are to be successful, negotiating teams must prepare carefully.

PREPARING FOR NEGOTIATIONS

There are seven steps in preparing to negotiate:

1. setting objectives and goals

2. analysing the situation

3. identifying the issues

4. analysing negotiators

5. considering legal implications

6. financial preparation

7. tactics.

The first step is to set your objectives and goals. As with communication strategy for other kinds of communication, you must be clear about your objectives. Intangible goals will most likely exist as well especially if you are engaged in integrative negotiations. Maintaining or building a relationship is often one of those goals which though difficult to measure is critical if one expects negotiations or a relationship to continue over time. Other outcomes are more easily measured. Every negotiator will have both an 'aspiration' base and a 'real' base for measurable outcomes. For example, if a buyer and seller are negotiating over the price of a car, both will have an aspiration base as well as a real base. Where these overlap is the contract or negotiation zone which is depicted in Figure 9.3.

The negotiation zone represents the range of prices within which agreement will be reached. Remember this concept applies equally to all goals in negotiation, not merely monetary issues. It is also interesting to note that as the negotiation approaches the buyer's real base there will be pressure to close the deal. Similarly as the seller's real base is approached pressure for closure will mount. These pressures help bring the negotiation to a successful conclusion.

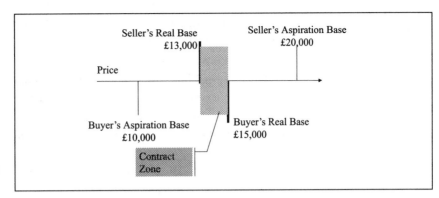

FIGURE 9.3 *Negotiation zone*

When preparing for negotiations, communicator and audience analysis are important; i.e. analyse yourself and the other party to the negotiations as completely as possible. You need to know, for example, whether both sides want integrative or distributive negotiations. Do you both want to build a relationship? What alternatives exist for both parties if negotiations fail? Is there real or potential conflict? What is the least that each party will accept?

The next step is to identify the issues. The issues are the relevant topics that will be discussed at the negotiating table and can be any topic over which there could be disagreement. Issues for both sides should be identified and if possible ranked. Table 9.2 (adapted from Spoelstra and Pienaar 1999) provides a simple example.

Clearly, knowing (or making an estimate about) the relative priorities of issues in the negotiations is important. It helps agenda planning as well as with strategy. For example, if you suspect that service is very important to the customer but relatively unimportant to you, you can make concessions on service early in the negotiations. This gives the customer a feeling of real progress which may make it easier for them to concede more on price which is your number one priority.

TABLE 9.2 *Issue ranking in negotiations*

Issue	Importance of issue:	
	To customer	To us
Price	3	1
Delivery	4	2
Terms of payment	2	3
Contracting out	5	4
Product design changes	6	5
Service	1	6
Warranties	7	7

Just as you must identify the issues, identifying the negotiators as much as you can is important. What can you find out about their personalities? What are their needs and objectives individually and as role players in the other organization? What are your opponents' financial needs, value system, history of negotiation, and performance? The more you know about the other party to the negotiations and the individuals who will be representing the other party, the better you will be able to pursue your own negotiation strategies.

Step five is to consider any legal implications. Ensure that the persons with whom you are dealing can sign on behalf of their party. You must also ensure that any contracts or agreements signed are valid under the law of the country in which the deal is made.

The next step in negotiation is to consider the financial implications. Negotiations are expensive and represent a strategic investment. To that end they should be evaluated not only in terms of results but also in terms of the costs to generate those results. You should also consider the financial implications of no agreement. What will it cost you and your organization over the short, medium or long term if you do not get an agreement? These considerations will help you make decisions about how flexible you can be, how much time you can spend before getting to an agreement, and the frequency with which you are prepared to negotiate.

The final step in negotiation preparation is consideration of tactics. Like all forms of communication, presentation (how you come across, your image and your organization's image) is vitally important, just as are the practicalities of negotiating. You need to consider:

- where the meeting will be held

- room layout

- who will be on your negotiating team

- items and presentation of the agenda

- how to define the issues

- how much time is available

- the negotiating climate

- anticipated common ground.

LOCALE

The home side has the advantage. That is just as true in negotiations as it is in football, baseball, cricket or ice hockey. When negotiators are working out of their home office, or even when they are in their home city or country, depending upon the level of the negotiations, they have a distinct advantage. Consider the example of negotiators who are working in their home city. Unlike the other party, they have access to their offices and secretarial and other organizational support. If they need information quickly, it can be called in and if necessary delivered to the negotiations venue. They also have the additional advantage of being able to convene to favourite coffee shops or back to the office to work out strategies. Negotiations are very demanding and tired negotiators in their home city can go back to their homes where they are more comfortable. Of course, the opposite is true for the visiting negotiations team. While modern communications technology means they can likely get information quickly (e.g. by mobile phones connected to laptop computers), they do not have the advantage of organizational support at hand. Nice as hotels can be, they are not home. Rooms and beds are different, food is different, and there is not the emotional and other support available.

As for the venue itself, the room layout needs careful consideration. What is the shape of the table? Is it appropriate? Where are windows located and will one party or the other have to look into the glare of sunlight coming in, which puts them at a disadvantage in terms of perhaps having to squint or not being able to see body language. If there are bright windows try to make sure that your back is to the windows if possible. If there are curtains and you are facing windows, have them closed. Are there 'breakout' rooms available so that negotiating teams can confer in private? Will there be refreshments available? These are some of the things to which you will need to pay attention.

NEGOTIATING TEAM

Your negotiating team is very important. You will need to know them very well. What are their strengths and weaknesses? Who is the expert in each of the functional areas that may come up in the negotiations? Do you have someone that can be charged with the responsibility of making contextual notes such as impressions about contentious issues, comments and notes on body language, observed tensions in the other negotiation party? Who on your team is likely to become stressed or is already under stress of work or personal problems?

Ensure that everyone on the team has a definite role to play and knows that role. Negotiating teams need to be as small as possible while still providing the needed expertise but without numbering too many or too few compared to the other negotiating party. Everyone on your team should be aware of the negotiating goals and debriefings should occur after every session.

ISSUES AND TIME AVAILABILITY

The issues about which you are negotiating have already been mentioned but need to be highlighted again in this context. Like communication strategy, your negotiating strategy must start with your goals. Everyone on the team has to be 'on side' and informed.

How much time is available for concluding the negotiations one way or the other is key information. Negotiations are expensive and the longer they carry on the more likely negotiators are to move from their original positions. This might not necessarily be a problem if agreement is essential and there is wide flexibility in terms of the outcome, but if there is narrow variation from a position available, then faster negotiations are better. Sometimes, the perspective you hold on the outcome may change as you get into the negotiations. It may necessitate changing the time horizon for an outcome. In other words, try to re-assess as you go through the negotiations. An emergent negotiating strategy – rather than being tied to the original plan – may prove very fruitful.

NEGOTIATION CLIMATE

Climate refers to the mood or tone of the negotiations. Parties to a negotiation can, for example, feel cool towards each other (especially if there has been conflict) or warm towards each other. Either way, it is important to try to de-personalize the negotiations and to conduct them in a climate that is professional. A business-like climate tends to lead to agreement.

Strive to create a climate that is cordial, collaborative and professional. The location should be free from noise and distractions so that negotiators can focus on the business at hand. Make sure the entire negotiating team pays attention to cultural norms of good behaviour and etiquette: handshakes, eye contact, non-threatening behaviour and non-contentious 'ice-breaking' behaviour (Blundel 1998).

NEGOTIATING FOR COMMON GROUND

Regardless of the goal of the negotiations, there must be some common ground upon which to build agreement. Common ground does not necessarily have to be what people already have in common but may be what the parties could build or achieve together.

Key to negotiating for common ground is a series of questions that negotiators should ask at the beginning of the negotiations:

- Why are we here?

- On what do we already agree?

- What issues are keeping us apart?

- When shall we deal with those issues?

By asking these important questions negotiators can find common ground upon which to build an agreement. Common ground, according to Spoelstra and Pienaar (1999), is the joint effort of parties to seek positive outcomes, to minimize loss and to commit themselves to continuing relations.

There is much to think about in negotiations. Good preparation before negotiations begin can go a long way towards generating a successful negotiation outcome. Negotiation is much like other forms of business communications. It is a social communication process that must be founded upon communication strategy and good communication skills in a world understood and interpreted through culturally defined symbols.

Discussion questions

1. What are the purposes and types of meetings?

2. What are the implications of the 'garbage can' model of decision-making for a meeting at your place of work or study?

3. What kinds of non-verbal communication might be important during negotiating sessions?

4. Why is negotiation on your 'home field' an advantage?

References

Blundel, R. (1998) *Effective Business Communication: Principles and Practice for the Information Age*, Prentice Hall, London.

Cohen, M., March, J. and Olsen, J. (1972) A garbage can model of organizational choice, *Administrative Science Quarterly*, 17, 1–25.

Cox, T. and Blake, S. (1991) Managing cultural diversity: implications for organizational competitiveness, *Academy of Management Executive*, August, 45–56.

Kagel, J. H. and Levin, D. (1986) The winner's curse and public information in common value auctions, *American Economic Review*, 76, 894–920.

Kramer, R. M. and Messick, D. M. (1995) *Negotiation as a Social Process*, Sage, London.

Spoelstra, M. and Pienaar, W. (1999) *Negotiation: Theories, Strategies and Skills*, Juta, Kenwyn, South Africa.

Further reading

Doyle, M. and Straus, D. (1993) *How to Make Meetings Work: The New Interaction Method*, Berkley Books, New York.

Murnighan, J. (1991) *The Dynamics of Bargaining Games*, Prentice Hall, Englewood Cliffs, NJ.

Neale, M. and Bazerman, M. (1991) *Cognition and Negotiator Rationality*, Free Press, New York.

Pruit, D. (1981) *Negotiation Behavior*, Academic Press, New York.

Raiffa, H. (1982) *The Art and Science of Negotiation*, Belknap, Cambridge, MA.

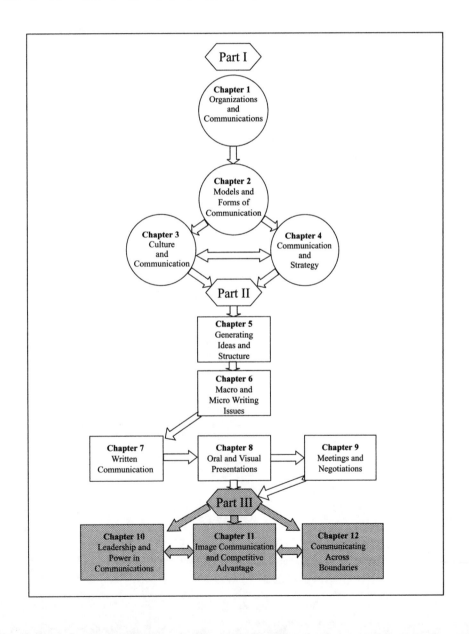

PART III

STRATEGIC COMMUNICATIONS FOR THE CORPORATION

chapter ten

Leadership and power in communications

Introduction

AS WE saw in the last chapter on meetings and negotiations, leadership and power relations are important in business communications. In this chapter we will explore some elements of leadership with particular regard to effective group leadership and how leaders manage cultures for communication. Clearly there are power implications in leadership, but, in addition, there are ethical implications that must be considered by those in leadership positions who have the power to manipulate symbols.

LEARNING OBJECTIVES

By the end of this chapter you should be able to:

- Define leadership
- Identify the differences between managers and leaders
- Explain trait and role theories of leadership
- Describe the three main leadership styles
- Discuss the relationship between leadership and communications
- Identify and briefly describe the five types of power
- Explain four types of political behaviour in organizations
- Discuss the importance of ethics in communications

Leadership and communications

Organizations, teams, meetings and negotiations all require leaders. Amongst all the other things that business leaders must do, they are responsible for communications in their organizations. Chairpersons are responsible for effective meetings and negotiation team leaders are responsible for the results of the negotiations. Leaders and leadership are important, therefore, to communications that get results.

Usually when we think about leaders we think about individuals with certain properties. This is a valid way to think about leadership. **Leadership** is also a process. A definition of leadership must incorporate both elements (Jago 1982). Leadership, then, is a process of non-coercive influence that shapes a group's or an organization's goals, motivates people's behaviour towards the attainment of those goals, and helps define organizational culture. Leadership is also a property or set of characteristics perceived to be held by leaders. A **leader**, by extension, is someone who can influence the behaviours of others without resorting to force, but a leader could also be someone whom others accept as a leader (Griffin 1997).

It is clear from the above definitions that leadership is closely related to management, but they are different. Leaders do engage in managing and managers can be leaders, but a manager is not necessarily a leader. Table 10.1

TABLE 10.1 *Leadership and Management (adapted from Kotter 1990)*

Activity	*Leadership*	*Management*
Creating an Agenda	*Establishing direction.* Developing a vision of the future and strategies for producing the changes needed to achieve that vision.	*Planning and budgeting.* Establishing detailed steps and timetables for acheiving needed results; allocating resources to make those results happen.
Developing a Human Network for Acheiving the Agenda	*Alligning people.* Communicating the direction to all those whose co-operation may be needed to influence the creation of teams and coalitions that understand the vision and strategies and accept their validity.	*Organizing and staffing.* Establishing a structure for accomplishing plans, staffing, delegating responsibility and authority, providing policies and procedures to guide people, and creating systems to monitor implentation..
Executing Plans	*Motivating and inspiring.* Energizing people to overcome political, bureacratic, and resource barriers to change by satisfying basic human needs.	*Controlling and problem solving.* Monitoring results in detail, identifying deviations, and then planning and organizing to solve problems.
Outcomes	*Procedures change*, often to a dramatic degree, and has the potential to produce useful change.	*Produces a degree of predictability and order*, and has the potential consistently to produce major results expected by various stakeholders.

sets out the differences between management and leadership along four dimensions.

Leaders and managers are both needed by organizations. They play important roles in the communication process. We focus specifically on leadership in this chapter. Communication is key to leadership effectiveness. Managers need to be effective communicators too, but management can partly rely on bureaucracy and organizational structures to communicate many of their messages. Effective leadership, however, is required especially for those contexts when bureaucracy and structure on their own do not work well enough. Those contexts are situations of change, new markets, complex or dynamic environments and entrepreneurship. As we shall see, there is a direct relationship between leadership and communications.

There are two central theories of leadership:

- trait theory

- role theory.

Trait theory suggests that there are certain qualities or traits that people have that make them good leaders. Implicitly, or perhaps even explicitly, many of us believe that there are certain traits that are important for leadership (Kirkpatrick and Locke 1991). Similarly, researchers once thought that such individual traits as assertiveness, above-average height, extensive vocabulary, intelligence, physical attractiveness, self-confidence and other similar attributes correlated with effective leadership (Bass 1990).

After over seven decades of research, however, trait theory has not stood up to empirical research. For every sample of leaders studied who possessed a common trait, a long list of exceptions was also identified, to the point that the list of potential traits grew so long that it became of little value in practical terms. There are also many alternative explanations for even those traits that did seem to correlate with leadership. For example, many leaders were found to be relatively assertive and to have good communication skills. The question then arose as to whether these traits were what made these people leaders or whether these traits were displayed as a result of being a leader. As far back as the early 1970s one researcher wrote (Davis 1972: 3):

Research has produced such a variegated list of traits presumably to describe leadership that for all practical purposes it describes nothing. Fifty years of study have failed to produce one personality trait or set of qualities that can be used to discriminate between leaders and non-leaders.

Ironically, although researchers have long given up on the attempt to correlate traits with leadership, many people still select leaders (for public positions as well as for promotion in organizations) based on the perception that in-born traits produce leaders. They may vote for the tallest or most attractive candidate or the one who is most assertive. The point is:

good leaders are not born, they are trained.

Just about anyone can become a leader if they are willing to spend the time to study and to train themselves in leadership skills – especially communications. The **role theory** of leadership suggests that there are certain roles that must be performed within a group or organization for successful results and that those who perform those roles are the leaders. In essence you become a leader by acting as a leader. For the most part leadership roles involve communication. As can be seen in Table 10.1, creating a shared vision, aligning, motivating and inspiring people are some key leadership roles and all rely on communication skills.

Other theories of leadership can be clustered into a role theory of management. Even situational models of leadership that assume leadership behaviours must change from context to context are, in essence, role theories of leadership. Leadership is a complex and exhaustively researched topic. There are a dozen or so major theories of leadership and while this is not the place to go into them all, leadership is important in meetings, negotiations and general organizational communication. In fact, often leaders are leaders because they are the best communicators.

Particular styles of leadership are recognizable. To be a skilled leader, you should know what style of leader you are. Once again, communication is important for portraying your leadership style. You are perceived to be a particular style of leader by the verbal and non-verbal messages you send out day-in and day-out. The three main leadership styles are:

- authoritarian

- democratic

- *laissez-faire.*

Authoritarian leaders tend to determine the roles of team members, tasks, procedures and policies. They often personally praise or criticize individuals' contributions. Authoritarian leaders tend to lead efficient groups, teams or organizations but followers seem to exhibit more hostility and there is more evidence of dissatisfaction and conflict.

Democratic leaders tend to communicate alternatives, but allow or guide the group or team to make policy decisions, task and procedural rules, and to determine roles for themselves. These types of leaders try to facilitate or encourage discussion within groups including appraisal of team efforts. Groups led by democratic leaders are those that exhibit greater levels of motivation, initiative and creativity. These leaders tend to achieve greater levels of commitment from team members. They also tend to communicate better internally.

Laissez-faire leaders tend simply to supply information or input when it is requested of the team. They do not directly take part in team discussions and allow the group to determine roles and set policy, tasks and procedures. This type of leadership style tends to work best for groups of highly motivated professionals who perform many of the needed leadership roles for themselves and can, therefore, be left pretty much alone to get on with it.

Ideally, good leaders can change styles depending upon the feedback they receive from the environment. In deciding which style is best in a particular context or for a particular purpose, consider which style you are most comfortable with, as well as the needs and expectations and goals of the organization or group.

Choosing the wrong leadership style can result in time-wasting, ineffective solutions, misdirection, unhappy or de-motivated employees or team members, and can cause resistance to change. If you are a leader and you want results, you need to communicate the correct style for the situation.

Power and leadership

Power is the ability to affect others' behaviours (Griffin 1997). People can hold power without actually having to use it. Indeed, power can be most effective if it is not used. A manager, for example, can threaten to withhold promotion of a junior manager who is not productive. From the junior manager's point of view, it is enough that the manager has that power. To understand leadership and organizational communications, it is important to understand power in organizations. The powerful are often the most able to make their interpretations of events, and even of reality, prevail. We behave, understand and interpret much of what happens in organizations through our understanding that some people are more powerful than others.

In organizational settings there are five types of power:

- legitimate

- reward

- coercive

- referent

- expert.

Legitimate power is power individuals hold by virtue of their position in the management hierarchy. Managers, for example, have subordinates over whom they have the power to direct that work be done, set work standards, reprimand or even to make redundant. Legitimate power is authority that comes from bureaucracy or from traditional cultural assumptions about the right to rule. While managers can exercise authority, they are in so doing not necessarily leading – though they may be commanding (Kahn and Kram 1994).

Reward power is the power to grant or to withhold valued rewards. Promotion, praise, recognition, salary rises, monetary bonuses, responsibilities, attractive job postings, etc., are all examples of some of the kinds of rewards that can be given or taken away by those holding reward power. Someone can hold reward power by virtue of role or position in the organizational hierarchy, but that is not necessarily leadership. Managers can offer these kinds of rewards in a well-structured bureaucracy. If, however, employees value things other than those rewards structured into their jobs such as informal rewards of gratitude, praise and recognition, for example, then the person who can give those is exercising a type of leadership power.

Coercive power is the power to force compliance by means of physical, psychological, economic or emotional threat. In modern organizations coercive power is relatively limited though it is still not uncommon for managers to coerce employees through threat of economic hardship. For example, managers can threaten redundancy if performance demands are not met. The more managers have to rely on coercive power, however, the more likely there will be a backlash in poor employee morale, resentment, hostility and conflict. Such managers are also less likely to be perceived as leaders and will, therefore, be ineffective in a leadership role.

Referent power is based on charisma, imitation, loyalty or identification with a leader. This kind of power is less concrete than the types of power listed above. Team members may identify in some way with the leader, and it is usually leaders rather than managers that have referent power. Leaders who can inspire enthusiasm and loyalty have some relatively intangible attractiveness to followers.

Expert power comes from knowledge, information or expertise in some area. Scientists, engineers, knowledgeable managers and those with specific information that is valued generally or at specific moments in time are those with expert power. There is a quasi-economy of information related to expert power. The fewer the number of people with the information, and the more important the information, the greater the expert power that a holder of such information will have. People who effectively perform the roles of both leader and manager often hold expert power.

The above examples make the point argued by Giddens (1984) that power is not a resource, but is exercised through resources. This has important implications for communicating power in organizations. Powerful people have access to resources and while they do not necessarily have to exercise their power through those resources, they do have to communicate that they could. If that communication is subtle or implicit rather than explicit, it is, perhaps even more powerful. Giddens also refers to what he calls the 'dialectic of control'. This is simply that subordinates have some resources at their disposal for influencing their superiors. No one in an organization is powerless, though clearly some have more resources and more power than others.

Your relative power in an organization affects your credibility in a communication situation (presentation, meeting, negotiations, submitting a proposal). As part of your communicator strategy you might want to examine your power base. Do you have expert power and therefore have high initial credibility or is your power based on your role or position in the hierarchy? Do you hold reward power? If you are a customer writing to the president of a company you certainly have the power to reward that company with continued patronage. Can you use that power to enhance your credibility and thereby get better results from your communication? Clearly, then, the kind of power you hold has a direct impact on your communications. Similarly, what kind of power do the people at an important meeting have? If you have to address them or submit a proposal, how will their power relative to yours affect how your presentation is received? Power is highly consequential for your communications, and for your ability to be an effective leader.

Political behaviour in organizations

Political behaviour refers to actions and activities for the specific purpose of acquiring, developing and using power and other resources in order to obtain preferred outcomes (Pfeffer 1981).

People engage in politics at all levels of the organizational hierarchy. They can direct their behaviour upwards, downwards or horizontally within an organization. In other words, managers may engage in political behaviour with their subordinates or with other managers and subordinates who, in turn, may direct their political behaviours at their managers and colleagues. People engage in political behaviour in order to further their own ends, to protect themselves from others or just to improve their position in a formal or informal organizational structure.

Political behaviour is a form of communication. It is often difficult to study because it is a fairly sensitive topic within organizations. Research suggests that politics influences hiring, salary and promotion decisions at work and that upper levels of management engage in politics to a greater degree than lower levels in the organizational hierarchy. The research also suggests that people generally perceive politics as bad, unfair, unhealthy for the organization and irrational, but that successful executives have to be good politicians (Gandz and Murray 1980).

Researchers have identified four types of political behaviour (Beeman and Sharkey 1987):

- inducement

- persuasion

- creation of an obligation

- coercion.

Inducement occurs when a person offers to give another something in return for that individual's support. For example, a manager in HRM who is on a promotions panel might say to a colleague in marketing that they will look favourably on their upcoming application for promotion if that person agrees to support the HRM department manager's new appraisal system in an upcoming meeting.

Persuasion is another form of political behaviour. We discussed persuasive letters and much of what was said there applies here as well. In essence, persuasion relies on either emotion or logic (or both) depending upon the context to persuade others to see things your way.

The third tactic is the creation of an obligation. 'I'll scratch your back, if you'll scratch mine' is a common saying that sums up this tactic. Managers may support others' proposals at a meeting, for example, not because they necessarily care about the outcome, but because they see it as an opportunity to create a debt that they can 'call in' when they need support at some future time. All such 'gifts' carry obligations for future reciprocity. People use this seemingly universal cultural norm to their political or positional advantage within organizations. Being 'owed' favours is a situation that provides power.

Finally, coercion is the use of physical, psychological or other force to get one's way. This is the least attractive of types of political behaviour and amounts to bullying. It is also less subtle, tends to work not nearly as well as other forms of political behaviour – especially at higher levels in organizations – and tends to create hostility, conflict and retaliation.

Political behaviour is widespread, has always existed and in some ways is desirable. Persuasion – even though it relies on communication skills that not everyone has – is an attractive way to address issues and decision-making in organizations. Political behaviour can be destructive, however, and needs to be managed.

As a manager, be aware that all actions are symbolic and therefore are interpreted by others. Often a manager's actions may not be politically motivated, but others interpret those actions as such nonetheless. Like all communications, people need to attempt to control the interpretations put on their actions. Keep an 'ear to the ground' and attempt to get feedback so that you can learn how others perceive your actions. Of course, if people are engaging in political behaviour, it should be no surprise that others pick up on that behaviour. To avoid charges of political behaviour, avoid behaving politically and using power in a way that may be perceived as negative or unnecessarily aggressive.

Managers can reduce the likelihood of excessive political behaviour by providing subordinates with autonomy, responsibility, challenge and feedback (Griffin 1997). Any disagreements or conflicts in an organization should be brought out into the open and discussed. Once they have surfaced, such disagreements will be difficult to manipulate with political behaviour because everyone will interpret actions in the context of the now open disagreement. This makes people's 'backroom' work, or lobbying, much less effective and therefore much less likely to occur. Indeed, as a general rule managers should avoid behind-the-scenes political behaviour as a standard method of operating. There is a place for lobbying in organizations but it loses its effectiveness if engaged in continually. The result is that once a person develops a reputation for engaging in covert political behaviour people will tend to use that as the dominant interpretative template for assessing that person's general behaviour, even those behaviours that are not politically motivated (Murray and Gandz 1980).

Other things managers can do to inhibit destructive political behaviour in organizations include communicating clearly to the organization the standards and policies and processes for promotion, performance evaluation, access to resources, and organizational rewards. By having clear policies, the need for people to ingratiate themselves to power holders or to engage in political behaviours to procure promotion or resources is reduced.

In modern organizations it is no longer sufficient merely to be technically competent. All organizations are political arenas. You can enhance your ability to get better results for yourself, your department and your organization by using good communication skills to pursue the following tactics in a positive way:

- build relationships

- expand your network

- under-communicate the negative

- over-communicate the positive.

Relationship building relies on your ability to communicate effectively with others. In building relationships – a positive activity in any event – you are also building your power base. Make the time to talk to other managers and colleagues in order to build relationships and also to persuade them of your points of view – something you do as part of any friendship. Become part of the informal communications network. This is important not only so that you are in position to receive information and to persuade people of your points of view, but also because most key decisions are not made in formal meetings in most organizations, but rather are made in the hallways and corridors by networks of managers who reach agreement amongst themselves. Relationship networks are founded and maintained by communications and good interpersonal relations of respect, trust and sincerely communicating to others that you want to work with them, not exploit them (Vredenburgh and Maurer 1984).

Once you have built some relationships and become part of a network you will need to expand it. Use your current network to build snowball relations. For example, if you know Janice in accounting, and you want to add Mary to your network, and you know that Mary and Janice are friends, you can use your relationship with Janice to make contact with Mary either by having Janice introduce you or by introducing yourself citing your mutual friendship with Janice (whichever method is best, given the norms in your organization). New alliances and larger networks are positive. As new managers are hired be one of the first to welcome them into the organization. Not only is this a friendly thing to do, but it also increases the size of your network.

As part of a network, you will have control over precisely what information you choose to put into the network. You will want to limit the negative information relating to your department or responsibilities. Obviously we are not talking about withholding information from superiors who request specific information – and, of course, lying is not an option. What we are saying is that you want to under-communicate anything negative if it is for communication through the informal network. As you get higher in an organization (not-for-profit and public-sector organizations are no different in this regard) the political behaviour becomes more intense. Given that managers will not want to provide 'ammunition' (i.e. negative information or bad news) to political rivals, it is best to under-communicate the negative. It is also good practice to under-communicate your power. Power is best used quietly. When departmental or personal power is made explicit (e.g. saying in a meeting that since you are the most powerful, your point of view must win) that power is diminished. Everyone in the organization will know which are the most powerful departments, coalitions and individuals. You do not need to make it explicit.

Over-communicate the positive. You will want to fill the informal network with your success and that of your department. When your department demonstrates its expertise in handling a difficult situation, that information should be over-communicated. Similarly, make sure people know if staff under your supervision are successful, win awards, are promoted or are positively singled out in some way. This is part of the reward for those employees, it enhances your position as a good leader and it is yet more positive news to add to the positive image you over-communicate to the organization. It is also a good idea to ensure that your department's and your personal preferences are over-communicated. If you do not ask, you will not get what you want. Be forthright. Explicit solutions, projects, proposals and programmes are generally given much more consideration.

Effective, positive political behaviour relies on good communication skills. Realize, too, that political behaviour does exist and will always exist. Managers cannot control it by issuing commands against it. Neither should managers ignore it. Political behaviour must be controlled. Political behaviour is not totally negative for the organization or for individuals. Political behaviour is communication. People will use it to advance themselves and their causes. As discussed above, in many situations it plays a very useful role (Lenway and Rehbein 1991). For example, a manager may be able to use his or her power and influence to ensure that hiring practices do not discriminate on grounds of ethnicity, religion, age or disability. It is hard to argue against the use of political behaviour to achieve such ends that might not be achievable in other ways.

Ethics and the manipulation of symbols

Power and politics raises ethical issues. Is it right to use power and engage in political activity in organizations? If so, in what situations? Such questions are part of an even larger question. Is it ethical to use knowledge and skills in communication that enable a person to get his or her way when others do not possess similar knowledge and skills? In order to understand the answer to such questions we need to think about ethics and ethical communications.

Ethics refers to principles of right or wrong conduct. Ethics tells us when our behaviour or others' is moral or immoral. Unethical persons are those who behave in a way that can be characterized as selfish and unscrupulous. Ethical people are often characterized as trustworthy, fair and impartial.

Ethics must play a key role in communications. Not only is it right to communicate ethically, to not do so can be very damaging. Beech-Nut advertised that its apple juice was 100 per cent pure. When the CEO found out that the company was putting additives into the juice, he made sure that future juice production was 100 per cent as advertised but tried in the meantime to cover up the facts. Beech-Nut kept selling the old stocks, hoping to use them all up before anyone found out about the false advertising. Of course, the company was found out, and as a result paid millions of dollars in fines. The company's reputation suffered badly and the CEO was sent to jail (*Business Week* 1988).

Unethical communications are not always as obvious as false advertising and cover-up. Words can be used in unethical ways. As discussed in earlier chapters, language is a symbolic system with symbolically loaded words. By using certain words in certain ways, good communicators can influence others, shape expectations and change behaviours. By using communication strategies, good communicators can generate powerful messages that get action. Such knowledge and skills are powerful. The use of power requires some ethical underpinning or there is a danger that the power to communicate can be abused.

Ethical communication should be the goal of every good communicator. In ethical communications messages contain relevant information, are truthful (as much as can be assured by sincere efforts to ensure truthfulness), and are not deceptive. This does not mean, however, that one should not use the audience memory curve, for example, so that the most important information is placed where people will pay attention to it. What is key in ethical communications is that you are accurate and sincere.

Avoid language that discriminates, exaggerates beyond norms of emphasis, and manipulates people's emotions. Ensure that opinions are stated as such and not given a gloss of factuality that is not deserved. Be honest with customers, suppliers, colleagues, co-workers, managers and subordinates. Try to avoid in your communications making others look either better or worse than they are. You can still over-communicate some information and under-communicate other information while holding true to norms of good ethical communication. The following points are especially noteworthy:

- act in good faith

- respect confidentiality

- avoid sexist language

- avoid discriminatory language.

Ethical choices are not as easy to make in practice as they might seem to be from a list of 'dos and don'ts'. Often there are ethical dilemmas that involve having to choose between alternatives that are not clearly either ethical or unethical. How do you make ethical choices?

One place to begin is with law. If writing misleading or false information is illegal then there is no dilemma. The choice is simple. You obey the law and do not write misleading or false information. It is not often that clear-cut, however. If your intent is honest, then what you write is ethical even if it turns out ex post to have been incorrect. If, on the other hand, your intent is to mislead or manipulate people, then the message is unethical even if what you have said is 'true'.

One test is to examine your communication and your intentions to ensure that, on balance, your decisions provide the greatest good for the greatest number of people (Bovée and Thill 2000). You might also consider if you would like to be treated by others in the way that you are considering. This is a 'golden rule' prescribed in many religious doctrines and sums up Rawls's (1971) *Theory of Justice*. Rawls's ethical philosophy is based on what he calls 'the original position'. The original position is a hypothetical scenario where you imagine that you and a group of others must make the laws for humankind. The laws you make will last for ever. But before you can make the laws you lose all self-awareness other than the idea that you must make humankind's rules. In other words, before you and the group make rules to live by, it is as if you put a bag over your heads and in the process lost all knowledge of who you are. The people in your group do not know if they are male or female, rich or poor, disabled or fit, born into aristocracy or born into the working class, healthy or sickly. They are unaware of any religious affiliation so they could be Muslim, Roman Catholic, Buddhist, Shintoist, Hindu, Sikh, Jewish or Protestant or members of some other religious group. They do not know if they are from an industrialized or a developing country. Given the lack of self-awareness what kinds of rule for society would such a group write? The answer is obvious. The rules would be fair and just for all.

Ethical communications can develop from just such a perspective (though there are are other ethical philosophies too). Make your communications decisions on how the the subject of your communications would like to be treated. Would you like to be subject to that kind of communication? Would you make the same decision if a loved one were the subject of your communications plans for others? We do not present any answers here. In fact, there are very few real answers in the field of ethics. Ethical issues are difficult, but progress can be made and you can behave more ethically if you think deeply about the issues.

Increasingly companies are writing codes of ethics to which they hold their managers and employees. These policies often help employees decide if their communications and other behaviours are ethical.

There are still grey areas which relate to decision-making. For example, unethical communication is not limited to telling lies or exaggerating claims. It may be that a communication is unethical because you have omitted important information. While it is true that messages you send cannot contain all the information you have available (some might be confidential) it is important to include enough information so that you are not with-holding information unnecessarily. You can never include complete informa-tion but enough has to be included so that you are not misleading an audience. Indeed, deciding how much information to include and for whom is probably one of the toughest ethical decisions you will make on a regular basis in business.

There are other ethics issues related to communications too. Is it ethical to advertise to children? In the UK such advertising is carefully regulated, whereas in some other countries advertising to children is banned entirely. Can advertisers use any images to sell their products? Benetton's advertising has been very controversial for using images of war and disease to promote its products. Clearly sexual images and innuendoes often work in advertising, but is it ethical to portray people in advertising in a manner that some find offensive? These are difficult ethical questions that are not all covered by legislation and rely, therefore, on corporate and personal ethics for control.

New technology has brought with it new ethical considerations in communications. Computers are used to retouch photographs or even to produce photographs and videos that seem real but have been totally computer-generated. What are the ethical implications of using such images to communicate messages when the images are total fabrications? Additionally, computer technologies allow us very easily to create visual displays of numerical information that can mislead audiences.

Here are two simple graphs (Figures 10.1 and 10.2) that were generated using the same data. Such a display could easily mislead an audience into thinking that we were doing a lot better than our competitors.

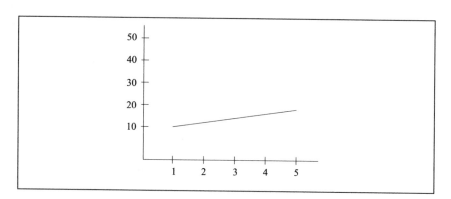

FIGURE 10.1 *Our competitor's growth*

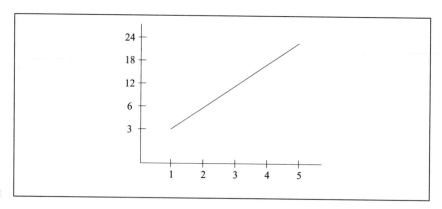

FIGURE 10.2 *Our growth*

Finally, numbers can be misleading. What are the ethics of providing numerical data that, while true, mislead? For example, what do you make of the statistics in Table 10.2? You may be thinking that Barrie has a lot of crime and that Atikokan has a whole lot less crime. But what information is missing? If you said 'population' then you are right. The information presented is misleading because population figures are not included in crime rate. If we assume for purposes of this example that 1 in 1000 people are burglars, then a town twice as large would be expected to have twice as many burglaries and therefore twice as many such crimes per minute. Look at the data if population is included in number of crimes (Table 10.3).

Using the more complete data from Table 10.3 we can see that Orillia shows higher crime rates than Barrie which is exactly the opposite of the data presented in Table 10.2. Would it be ethical for the Orillia Tourism and Business Development Authority to use the data from Table 10.2 to attract new business to their city claiming lower crime rates than their rival town of Barrie? Both sets of data are 'true'.

In conclusion, developing and learning communication skills and how to manipulate the symbols with which we communicate can be very empowering and valuable. Managers and especially leaders involved in change processes rely on communication skills to lead and to exercise power. Everyone in an organization has power and at least some resources through which to exercise their power. With that power comes the responsibility to behave ethically. Ethical decision-making is a core component of effective and professional business communications.

TABLE 10.2 *Crime rates in Ontario towns*

City	One crime every
Barrie	7.87 minutes
Orillia	12.43 minutes
Elliot Lake	83.02 minutes
Atikokan	176.65 minutes

TABLE 10.3 *Crime rates per capita in Ontario towns*

City population	Number of crimes	Population	Crimes per 1000
Barrie	70,547	659,617	106.95
Orilla	41,692	344,566	121.00
Elliot Lake	6,238	108,539	57.47
Atikokan	2,896	51,040	56.73

1. What are the ways leaders might use communication capabilities differently than managers?

2. Describe how leaders might use communications of various kinds to build their leadership image.

3. There are five types of power. To which types is communication particularly relevant?

4. How do you build a power base using communications in organizations?

5. Is it ethical to advertise to children? If so, are there limits to what you can do? If not, is it ethical to advertise to adults in a way that is also appealing to children?

References

Bass, B. M. (1990) *Bass & Stogdill's Handbook of Leadership: Theory, Research, and Managerial Applications*, 3rd edn, Free Press, Riverside, NJ.

Beeman, D. and Sharkey, T. (1987) The use and abuse of corporate power, *Business Horizons*, March–April, 26–30.

Bovée, C. and Thill, J. (2000) *Business Communication Today*, Prentice Hall, Upper Saddle River, NJ.

Business Week (1988) What led Beech-Nut down the road to disgrace, *Business Week*, 22 February, 124–128.

Davis, K. (1972) *Human Behavior at Work*, McGraw-Hill, New York.

Gandz, J. and Murray, V. (1980) The experience of workplace politics, *Academy of Management Journal*, June, 237–251.

Giddens, A. (1984) *The Constitution of Society*, University of California Press, Berkeley.

Griffin, R. W. (1997) *Fundamentals of Management: Core Concepts and Applications*, Houghton Mifflin, New York.

Jago, A. (1982) Leadership: perspective in theory and research, *Management Science*, March, 315–336.

Kahn, W. and Kram, K. (1994) Authority at work: internal models and their organizational consequences, *Academy of Management Review*, 19(1), 17–50.

Kirkpatrick, S. and Locke, E. (1991) Leadership: do traits matter? *Academy of Management Executive*, May, 48–60.

Kotter, J. (1990) *A Force for Change: How Leadership Differs from Management*, Free Press, New York.

Lenway, S. and Rehbein, K. (1991) Leaders, followers, and free riders: an empirical test of variation in corporate political involvement, *Academy of Management Journal*, December, 893–905.

Murray, V. and Gandz, J. (1980) Games executives play: politics at work, *Business Horizons*, December, 11–13.

Pfeffer, J. (1981) *Power in Organizations*, Pitman, Marshfield, MA.

Rawls, J. ([1971] 1999) *Theory of Justice*, Belknap Press, Cambridge, MA.

Vredenburgh, D. and Maurer, J. (1984) A process framework of organizational politics, *Human Relations*, 37, 47–66.

Further reading

Bass, B. (1990) *Bass & Stogdill's Handbook of Leadership: Theory, Research, and Managerial Applications*, 3rd edn, Free Press, Riverside, NJ.

Kotter, J. (1990) *A Force for Change: How Leadership Differs from Management*, Free Press, New York.

Pfeffer, J. (1981) *Power in Organizations*, Pitman, Marshfield, MA.

Rawls, J. ([1971] 1999) *Theory of Justice*, Belknap Press, Cambridge, MA.

chapter eleven

Image communication and competitive advantage

Introduction

ORGANIZATIONS COMMUNICATE what they sell or do and who they are through advertising and public relations communications. Advertising is linked to public relations and both functions tend to affect and reinforce each other. Public relations and advertising are key communication elements of modern organizations because they link the organization in many ways not only with customers but with wider publics and stakeholders as well. In this chapter we examine some of the elements of advertising and public relations and relate them to business communications.

The more effective are those business and organizational communications, both internally and externally, the greater the benefit for the organization. In the final section of this chapter we discuss how effective organizational communications can be a core source of competitive advantage.

LEARNING OBJECTIVES

After studying this chapter you should be able to:

- Demonstrate an awareness of the wider social and economic issues surrounding advertising
- Describe the steps in developing effective advertising
- Identify the characteristics of key advertising channels and styles
- Describe the importance and role of building corporate reputation and brand image
- Describe the relationship between brand image, reputation, superior organizational communications and competitive advantage

Advertising

Advertising refers to communications that effectively and efficiently provide persuasive messages about products or services for potential consumers or buyers of those products/services. At a superficial level, advertising is merely the promotion of goods and services. Advertising communicates, however, much more. Advertising messages are also about deep cultural assumptions, social values and beliefs, economics and information, and they represent societies' most serious concerns: gender roles, relationships, stereotyping, power and influence, business in society, the move from traditional cultural ways, the meaning of youth and old age, environmentalism, corporate ethics and many other values (Leiss, Kline and Jhally 1997).

There continues to be considerable debate about advertising and its effects. At one extreme there are those who claim that advertising has a negative effect on society because it promotes materialism and encourages the misuse of society's resources. At the other extreme are those who claim that advertising is invaluable to the efficiency and effectiveness of a free-market economy. Both of these perspectives assume that advertising actually works. Yet there is another perspective that questions whether advertising works at all. Driver and Foxall (1984) state that advertising does not establish long-term purchasing patterns. The research suggests that advertising does not work on personal mental processes to create attitudes that determine behaviour, but, nonetheless it is recognized that the aggregate effect of advertising is great (Driver and Foxall 1984). In other words, while we have no scientific certainty that advertising works, it is so pervasive, such a large component of our modern economic and social worlds, and so taken for granted as being effective and important, that its impact is nonetheless considerable.

There is little doubt that, while research has not yet enabled the impact of advertising to be settled one way or another, advertising is so prevalent in modern society that it needs to be better understood. By understanding advertising (which is a core element of business and marketing communications), how it works and how it functions, managers and consumers are in a better position to respond to, make informed choices about, and use advertising.

ADVERTISING: PROS AND CONS

Advertising is currently thought of as central to all business and marketing communications. It may seem rather odd, therefore, to ask at the beginning of the 21st century why we even have advertising, but the answer to that question invokes a polarized debate. First we will examine the arguments that advertising has negative effects. We then consider the positive perspectives of advertising.

Advertising has been criticized because of claims that it:

- creates demand

- creates false needs

- distorts information

- creates false role models and promotes stereotypes

- increases costs of goods and services

- distorts market production

- exercises too much power over media content.

The first of the major critiques of advertising is that it actually works to create demand for goods and services. This obviously can be seen as a positive effect of advertising from another point of view (e.g. from a marketing perspective), so why is it construed as negative? John Kenneth Galbraith (1958, 1967) considers advertising partly from the perspective of economic growth theory which proposes that goods and services are generated to satisfy consumer needs. From this perspective consumers are seen as setting levels of demand which control how much is produced of what good or service and which, in turn, impacts resource use, environmental degradation, employment and so on. This view is called 'consumer sovereignty'. The consumer as the setter and arbiter of demand is, from this perspective, the most important decision maker in the economy.

Galbraith proposes that advertising turns this relationship between consumer and production on its head. Through advertising, organizations operating in their own interests create demand through brand and product marketing. In other words, rather than merely responding to demand, demand is created. This results in economic distortion and increased environmental degradation and creates distortions in society's uses of its resources. The market, therefore, should not be left on its own to decide about resource allocation precisely because advertising distorts consumer demand, making consumer sovereignty a fiction. This is a core argument in regulating advertising on other than ethical or morality grounds.

The basis of Galbraith's argument is that advertising succeeds in creating demand – but does it? To do so, there must be a mechanism to accomplish such an outcome. Technology is usually cited as just such a mechanism. Subliminal advertising is often thought to be a powerful technology for directing people to behave in ways that they would not otherwise. Subliminal messages are received at a level beneath the threshold of consciousness. These would be messages that are transmitted with insufficient intensity or duration to produce a conscious response or to register in the conscious mind. **Subliminal advertising** is the insertion into a film, television programme, or other audio or visual media, of a 'subliminal' message which exerts subconscious influences on purchasing behaviour. This is what Key (1976: 2) calls 'secret technology [that] modifies behaviour invisibly, channels basic value systems and manages human motives'. There is no evidence, however, that subliminal tactics actually motivate people to make choices they otherwise would not have made. In other words, there is just no evidence that subliminal advertising works.

Technology is, however, key to advertising. Radio, cinema and television all appeal to mass markets that do not need any particular literacy or critical thinking skills to receive messages that are often delivered attractively and repetitively. It may be that such mass media tend, by their very nature (e.g. the passivity of television watching as opposed to the active engagement of reading), to inhibit critical thinking about the messages being delivered. These mass media may, therefore, provide an ideal vehicle for manipulative, demand-creating advertising.

Some authors have speculated that it is not technology per se that is the mechanism for creating demand. Rather, it is the modern form of advertising as a referent of socio-economic and prestige status that creates demand. No longer do adverts merely provide information about products. Instead, many adverts suggest that products and services provide consumer self-definition or instant gratification of wishes and desires – products can make us instantly attractive, help us find that perfect partner, allow us to make a social statement about our status, provide an entrance into a world of special people, cure us of sickness, make us fit, help us move up in the perfect career. A criticism of advertisements is that they replace 'real' people with carefully constructed categories or images of people in unreal situations (Leiss, Kline and Jhally 1997) and thereby turn people and their self-images into caricatures or even commodities exchangeable in the marketplace.

A related criticism is that advertising creates false needs (Marcuse 1964). It seems that from this perspective, 'true' needs are those basic needs of security, food, shelter and so on, but who is to say what are 'true' and what 'false' needs? Proponents of this perspective argue that people are trapped or manipulated by advertising to the extent that they are, in effect, prevented from exercising true choice and therefore cannot make thoughtful decisions about what are their true needs. Part of that manipulation comes from the creation of media events. The modern world (both in product advertising and in politics) is replete with carefully stage-managed events designed to enhance product (and political) images. In a sense what are being created are false images simply by virtue of being events that are carefully constructed to convey highly compressed, value-loaded 'brand' images. In this way information is distorted to fit a desired-event image.

Role models as opposed to 'real' people are the participants or even the stars of such events. Their involvement in such value-loaded, carefully constructed events means that those values tend to accrue to the role model who in turn helps to construct the values being generated and transmitted by the event in a mutually reinforcing spiral. The result is the social construction of false or harmful and sometimes negative role models. Often, people do try to emulate their role models. But the role model is not the real person. It is a carefully constructed role image. Critics claim that such false role models – which, many believe, are negative or stereotyped images, for example, of women and their 'proper' role – set up false expectations which can only be met through the products or services advertised. The result is that social values are distorted to the pursuit of materialism.

This links directly to Galbraith's (1958, 1967) point that the creation of demand then leads to market production distortions. Society's resource usage is re-prioritized to meet those created needs, leaving fewer resources or lower priorities for 'more important' social needs than for satisfying individual, materialistic, and largely unarticulated and possibly false needs.

There is also another related economic criticism of advertising. It is claimed that advertising directly results in increased costs of goods and services. Advertising is clearly a business expense that must be met by purchasers of the products and services, so, on the surface, this seems a plausible argument. In 1988, advertising expenditures were estimated at US$109.65 billion a year (*Advertising Age* 1989) which would have to be met by consumers as part of the selling price of products. The question is, is it really necessary to engage in expensive advertising when simple product information on the product or its packaging in the marketplace would provide information to consumers enabling them to make informed choices? If that is the case then advertising must do more than merely provide product information.

One key function of advertising is to develop brand loyalty and other barriers to market entry against competitors. For example, if a soap product is advertised nationally at great expense, it would be very difficult for a new producer to compete nationally unless that firm were willing to invest similar amounts in advertising which, without instantly generating similar levels of sales, would put them at a competitive disadvantage since their advertising costs would be a much higher percentage of the selling price of the product than their competitor's. In effect, it is possible for a manufacturer who is less efficient (in terms of utilizing society's resources) to prevent more efficient producers from entering a market by virtue of their advertising expenditures. They have 'deep pockets'. Such barriers to entry may promote trends toward oligopolistic concentration and an economy dominated by the biggest corporations. In an extremely expensive advertising marketplace – only the major firms can compete.

Deep-pocketed corporations have other advantages too. Given that there are, effectively, limitations to the number of outlets for advertising and on people's ability to absorb information, once an advertiser has control (e.g. through contract) over an advertising outlet, there is effectively no other comparable outlet unless of course one bids up the price. For example, in 1983 the final episode of the CBS series *M*A*S*H* in the US drew what was then the largest audience in television history for a single programme. The episode had an estimated 125 million viewers. The going rate for a 30-second commercial was US$450,000 which was US$50,000 more than that paid for a 30-second advertisement during the Super Bowl football game the month before. Clearly, there were very few spots available and at great price. This meant that consumers could only receive information about products of companies that had huge advertising budgets. This amounts to information distortion in the marketplace based solely on the economic clout of advertisers.

Given that advertisers are willing to pay such amounts of money to advertise on certain kinds of programmes, it seems reasonable to expect that they would want to exercise power over media content. For example, in 1991 NBC reported losses of US$5 million as a result of cancelled advertising and production costs when advertisers did not want to advertise on a particular programme. While there is little evidence to suggest that advertisers can explicitly manipulate programming, the amount of money involved would suggest that television (and other media) producers would most likely consider the economic implications of their programming decisions. As advertising and promotion capital becomes concentrated, so too do the interests that shape media content.

Of course, advertising has its defenders. Those who see the positive elements of advertising suggest that it:

- enables economies of scale and therefore lowers prices

- encourages organizations to discover consumer needs

- reduces the power of large corporations

- provides information upon which rational consumers can make informed choices.

In order to be able to produce goods at the lowest possible price, companies require large sales volumes. Bulk purchasing enables lower unit costs, and there are often fixed costs of production and organization that translate into lower unit costs when spread over larger quantities sold. This is

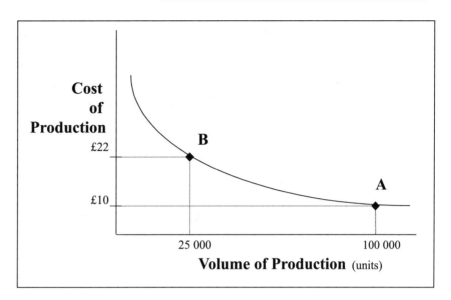

FIGURE 11.1 *Economies of scale*

the concept of economies of scale. Figure 11.1 represents how increased volumes translate into lower production costs. Lower production costs enable firms to be cost leaders in their industry which further enables them to prevent other firms from effectively competing against them. Clearly the company with the lowest production costs can undercut competitors to gain or protect market share and/or drive other competitors out of business. As demonstrated in Figure 11.1, firm A has a cost advantage over firm B. Firm A can produce its 100 000 units at an average cost of £10 per unit whereas firm B has an average cost of £22 per unit to produce its 25,000 units. As long as firm A can keep its production volumes and market share high, firm B will never be able to meet firm A's costs of production. In order to maintain its high volumes and market share versus firm B, firm A must, however, ensure that it can sell what it produces. To that end, firms usually must engage in advertising to generate high sales volumes to support high production volumes that enable economies of scale.

Proponents of advertising suggest that because advertising is available, companies and other organizations find it worthwhile to engage in attempting to discover consumers' needs. If there were no way to communicate a product or service that fulfils an unmet consumer need, then there would be no value in research and development of those products or services. This is the differentiation strategy point of view. Unlike economies of scale whereby a company attempts to be the cost leader and thereby enjoy a competitive advantage in the marketplace, companies that produce products that are customized or differentiated in some way, not for mass markets but for niche markets, pursue those strategies as their preferred way, or perhaps the only way, of competing in an industry. Competing in niche markets means that there must be mechanisms – such as advertising – that enable the company to tell its target market that higher-quality, customized or differentiated products exist to meet their specific needs. In this way, advertising of niche products helps to reduce the power of large corporations that may have a stranglehold on mass-market, standardized products through economies of scale and therefore the economic resources to protect their market position.

Those defending advertising claim that it plays a key role in modern free-market economies because it provides information upon which rational consumers can make informed choices. There is so much information constantly bombarding consumers and so many products from which to choose that a consumer could not possibly understand and know which products would best fulfil unmet needs. Recognized brands, for example, provide a short cut for consumers who want to make a choice. A brand is by definition known for its qualities and so consumers can make a choice about whether to purchase or not based on those known qualities. For example, there are many fast-food, hamburger restaurants, but because McDonald's has a powerful brand image consumers can trust their decision and will know within a narrow range of variance what quality of food, hygiene and service they will receive. Further, they can do so without engaging in expensive and time-consuming research into fast-food restaurants in every major city to which they might travel. Consumers would be hard-pressed to make a choice without having the brand information with which to make their choice.

Advertising also provides information about products and services that do not have a high level of brand recognition. It is not feasible for a consumer to have to find and then learn about all products. A rational consumer wants and needs to be able to base decisions on concise, comprehensive information that is packaged and presented in an effective way. Advertising, therefore, permits the consumer to move reliably and quickly from need to need-fulfilment. Only through advertising is there the means and the motivation for effective information exchange from producer to consumer.

Finally, it is argued that the existence of advertising enables innovation and improvements in the social, spiritual (religious groups advertise) and material quality of life. It is only with a mechanism for advising consumers of innovative, higher-quality, new or better products and services that it makes sense for innovation to occur at all. With advertising, producers have a way to communicate their innovations to consumers. Charities, aid organizations and governments too rely on advertising to get their messages to the public. Without advertising, the consumer and society as a whole would be worse off.

In summary, we have considered the information exchange functions of advertising, and some of its possible negative and beneficial effects on society. Both sides of the debate have the same core argument – advertising is an effective way of persuading and/or informing groups (if not specific individuals and their thought processes) about products and services. Both sides also posit that advertising is the basis of modern free-market capitalist economies. Indeed, it would be hard to imagine our present economic system functioning without advertising. Whether that means society should continue with or needs to change the present system is beyond the scope of consideration in this text. Here, because advertising communicates more than mere product information, we have noted some consequential issues for critical thought. We now move on to discuss the practicalities of advertising for your organization.

Advertising that works

Our definition of advertising at the beginning of this chapter suggests that advertising should be effective and efficient and should target the right consumers/buyers. The first step towards advertising that works is careful consideration of the advertising process using communication strategy. Communication strategy, you will recall, involves four elements or nested strategies: communicator, audience, message and channel. You will need to consider each of these very carefully in developing advertising that works. Specifically, we will explore:

- learning about your customers and competitors

- making the decision to advertise

- choosing the right channel for advertising

- assessing the effectiveness of your advertising.

KNOW YOUR CUSTOMERS AND COMPETITORS

The starting point is learning about your customers and competitors, which should be done in conjunction with your audience strategy. You need to know your customer for two reasons:

1. it will enable you to decide if your product/service fulfils their needs;

2. it will enable you to target your persuasive message effectively and efficiently.

One way of getting to know more about your customers is through market research. Careful and accurate market research is essential to any business. Market research is usually undertaken by outside agencies who are experts. They can often save an organization a considerable amount of time and money because of their experience and resources. Before engaging a market research firm, it is important that you examine what you already know about yourself, your customers and your competitors.

The following are some questions you might ask to gain insight into your customers and competitors:

Current customers

- Who are our customers now? (What are their generic characteristics, e.g. socio-economic status, age, what newspapers do they read, etc.?)

- Where are our existing customers (geographically)?

- How do we currently communicate with our existing customers?

- Why do they choose our products/services? (What is our competitive advantage?)

Potential customers

- Who are our potential customers?

- Where are our potential customers?

- How can we communicate effectively with them?

- What are the product/service values and competitive advantages we need to have in order to appeal to them?

Competitors

- Who are our competitors?

- Are our products/services noticeably different from theirs?

- What are their strengths and weaknesses in the marketplace?

- Do they advertise? If so, how much do they spend and on what?

- What messages are they communicating?

Answering the above questions will help you decide how much you know about your customers (audience strategy), yourself (part of communicator strategy) and your competitors. If you and your organization can answer the above questions in considerable depth then you probably would not benefit from extra marketing research. If, however, your organization cannot answer these questions in sufficient depth to provide insight into your customers and marketplace, then you might want to consider marketing research.

Marketing research can be done through marketing research agencies, but many organizations do their own. There are generally two types of marketing research that can be done: desk research and field research, roughly equivalent to using primary and secondary sources which we discussed in Chapter Five.

Desk research relies on existing archival or published information. Many sources are readily available. Trade and professional magazines often publish surveys and reports specific to particular markets or market sectors. Reading trade publications and magazines not only provides a good source of information of marketing research relevance, but it is also a good source of information on changing trends in an industry. There are also industry-specific and other organizations that collect information which is then available to members of the association and often to others as well. Some organizations, e.g. British Rate and Data (BRAD), publish their information, which is available in reference libraries, and also available on-line at http://www.brad.co.uk. Government departments provide information and statistics on the economic environment, inflation, unemployment and other economic indicators that may be of use for marketing research. Government publications are usually available in reference libraries and increasingly over the internet, e.g. the Department of Trade and Industry (UK) website is available at http://www.dti.gov.uk. Newspapers and magazine publishers generate circulation, readership and other information which may be useful in marketing research. Usually such information is available without charge.

Field research refers to the collection of information and data through primary research, e.g. direct contact (interview, focus group, survey) with people. It is usually recommended that this kind of research be undertaken by independent market research organizations. Primary or field research is extremely time-consuming and often respondents/informants are more open, honest and forthright with a third party than if you were asking them about your own products/services.

Whether you choose to do desk or primary research, to do the research yourself or use the services of a professional market research organization, you need to have solid information on which to base decisions to advertise. Advertising is expensive and must be effective or it could even have a negative, rather than a positive, impact on your organization.

MAKING THE DECISION TO ADVERTISE

Advertising requires careful planning and preparation. Use communicator strategy to help sort out what it is that you want to achieve from your advertising. What are your advertising objectives? Can you identify them in qualitative or quantitative terms? For example, you might try to set sales

TABLE 11.1 *Advertising goals for current and potential customers*

Current and potential customers	Advertising goal
Loyal Customers (they only buy from us)	Encourage continued loyalty
Frequent Customers (generally buy from us but occasionally from others)	Encourage complete loyalty
Infrequent Customers (mainly buy from competitors but occasionally buy from us)	Encourage change in buying behaviour
Uniformed Prospects (competiotors' customers who have never heard of us)	Stimulate initial interest
Ill-informed Prospects (competitors' customers who know us but have never bought from us)	Stimulate interest and encourage change in buying behaviour

growth targets for each product/service that you plan on advertising over a fixed time period. Next, link up your growth targets with your estimated increases in business from existing customers or new business from potential new customers in order to achieve those targets. Do your objectives and growth targets require you to advertise in order to achieve those goals or can it be done some other way? Using column 1 of Table 11.1, ask yourself and your management team which of the groups of current and potential customers have the greatest scope to help realize your objectives.

The table is structured in increasing order of difficulty of persuasion/appeal. In other words, it is likely to be easier to advertise to and persuade current, loyal customers than it would be to appeal to ill-informed prospects. It would also seem likely that each of these categories of current and potential customers would require different approaches in order to get their business or to increase sales to them. Column 2 of Table 11.1 suggests the different ways to appeal to the different groups of customers. Research suggests that targeting all current and potential customers simultaneously tends to be ineffective. You, therefore, must decide in terms of cost/benefit and goals which of these groups offer the most potential for sales growth at a reasonable cost.

CHOOSING THE RIGHT CHANNEL FOR ADVERTISING

Channel strategy would clearly be part of your communication strategy related to advertising. In this section we set out some of the choices that exist for advertising. Alternatives include advertising through:

- directories (telephone, trade, internet directories, etc.)
- magazines

- newspapers (display or classified): national, regional, local

- posters and billboards

- direct mail

- television

- commercial radio

- exhibitions and trade fairs

- merchandising and point-of-sale advertising

- product placement in cinema/theatre

- sponsorship of sporting and other events

- internet.

Successful advertising is targeted not only at a specific group of customers, but must be done using the communication channels to which your target audience is most likely to respond and to which it pays the most attention. Understanding the target audience and the strengths and weaknesses of each communication channel is essential for effective advertising. We will not discuss all of the available channels here (consult Further Reading for more information) but will outline some considerations regarding the key channels of newspapers/magazines, radio and television.

Newspapers and magazines

In the UK newspapers and magazines are the most widely used advertising channel. There are over 4000 publications in the UK from which to choose. A magazine or newspaper ideally suited to delivering messages to nearly any target audience probably exists. Different newspapers and magazines have different advantages for advertising communications. National newspapers in the UK have a circulation of about 14 million per day which permits wide coverage that can be targeted regionally, demographically and socio-economically. Specialist magazines are best, however, at targeting those with specific interests. For example, *Bonsai Today* might be the ideal place if you wanted to advertise to bonsai enthusiasts or to those supplying the industry.

Newspaper and magazine advertising has advantages over other channels in terms of:

- coverage

- flexibility

- credibility.

With a circulation of about 14 million copies a day and even higher readership (more than one person reads most copies) newspapers and magazines have wide coverage. For many people the weekly or daily reading of a paper is a habit. Most readers are not interested in every section of the paper so audiences can be targeted by placing advertisements in appropriate sections. Most papers cater to geographic, socio-economic and political audiences. Special-interest magazines similarly permit the targeting of specific audiences. People also expect to see advertising in their newspapers and magazines and some actually purchase specific publications just to read advertisements for products and services they wish to purchase.

Press (newspaper/magazine) advertising is flexible in terms of:

- cost

- appearance

- content

- positioning

- timing

- engagement with the reader.

Depending upon use of colour, the size and positioning of an advert and the circulation of the publication, you can usually find a combination that fits your particular budget which gives flexibility in cost. While large ads are usually quite expensive, it might actually be more effective to use a series of small advertisements rather than one large one to generate impact or to keep your products in front of your audience. It is cheaper to have an ad placed 'run of paper' which means that you will have no control over where it appears. This might be an option if you are on a tight budget or if placement does not matter in terms of targeting your audience.

The message conveyed by your advertisement can be very broad or contain detailed information. In fact, as an advertiser you have just about total control over appearance and content. Text, images, colours, layout can all be designed to appeal to your audience. Newspaper and magazine advertising can be designed using virtually any colours. Adverts can include illustrations, logos and photographs which enables flexibility in appearance.

The advert can appear in specific positions within the publication, e.g., if your target audience tends to be football fans, you could position your advert in the sports section of a newspaper or you might want it in the travel section if your target audience tends to be people who travel a lot.

Timing can be important for delivery of your message to a target audience. Press advertising has the flexibility that it allows advertisers to reach audiences in a timely way. Most people's calendars are peppered with special days or key shopping periods. Festive seasons, peak shopping periods, the beginning of the gardening season, autumn when people think about preparing their home or car for winter are all examples of key shopping periods that advertisers can capitalize upon due to the immediacy of newspaper advertising. Additionally, ads can usually be inserted in papers at short notice and changes to copy can often be made quickly.

Finally, newspaper and especially magazine advertising offers great flexibility in terms of engagement with the target audience. Unlike radio and television ads, for example, which require that the person be tuned in at a specific time to get the message and even then once it is delivered it is gone, newspaper and magazine ads are always there in the publication. Many people keep or pass on their magazines or leave them on coffee tables for convenient revisiting. Readers can look through paper-based communications at their leisure. If they spot an advertisement for a product or service they need they can cut it out and carry it with them.

The print media still retain credibility among readers. This is partly because regional and local newspapers and special-interest magazines have a community image with which people associate themselves. For this reason people engage with the local paper or their hobby magazine which makes for a favourable advertising context. The advertising, by extension, seems more credible and less intrusive to readers.

We have already mentioned cost in terms of flexibility. Newspaper and magazine advertising is also cost-effective. If advertisers can link their target customers with what those customers read, they can achieve low levels of what is called 'readership wastage'. That is, the advertising will be where target customers will expect to find it. The targeting will be efficient, therefore, in terms of the cost per potential customer reached. Targeted advertising is often much more cost-effective than a broad-based 'shotgun' approach.

Radio

Radio advertising (usually 30-second or 60-second spots, or in the form of sponsorship of programmes such as newscasts) can be a very effective form of communicating with customers. Radio has the following advantages:

- audience targeting

- high acceptance

- low cost compared with television

- low production costs

- production time to air is short.

As part of your audience analysis, if you know the kinds of music or information radio stations to which your target audience listens, then you have the information to enable you to target your message by selecting the appropriate stations. Similarly, there are many regional radio stations so messages can be targeted geographically as well. Messages that are broadcast on a target audience's favourite station generally have good acceptance which increases if the messages are repeated. Radio advertising uses the human voice and is often backed up by music. These can work independently or more powerfully together to generate authority, credibility and emotional responses. This can make radio advertising strong and memorable. Compared to television advertising, radio adverts cost less to produce and get on air. Relatively little time is required to produce radio messages and it is often possible to have them aired with little lead time, which means that messages can be topical.

Television

Television has advantages too. Some of those advantages are:

- flexibility

- product demonstration

- high prestige

- high visibility and impact – strong image/branding

- mass audience

- targeting.

The power of television advertising is not only its ubiquity but its richness. Television is a multi-media communication channel that uses colour, movement, and visual and audio stimuli. This means that it is extremely flexible. It can use not only the symbols (words, sounds, colours) of all the other media but can combine them with movement as well. Through the use of such multi-sensory representation, television can generate viewer involvement and interest unparalleled in other channels.

Advertisers can even position their advertisements within programmes that reinforce or link to their products/services, e.g. trainers and other sporting goods advertised during sporting events in which some of the athletes are using the branded equipment. This also means the products can be demonstrated within contexts: the audience can see the product actually being used or can see representations of higher-quality living by using a product/service. Television can, therefore, be very powerful in terms of generating a strong brand image.

Building a strong image or brand requires high-impact advertising that has high visibility. Television has just such characteristics. It is a highly prestigious form of advertising. Only those firms with 'deep pockets' generally can advertise their products on television, though the cost per viewer is not out of line with other forms of advertising. Simply being on television transmits the image that a company and/or its products are successful. This sets up a positive spiral of impact and visibility.

That visibility is consequential given that television enables organizations to reach mass audiences. It is estimated that over 80 per cent of the population in the UK watches television every day. While television is a mass communications channel, targeting is possible through station and programme selection, viewing times, regional newscasts, and so on. In some parts of the world, e.g. North America, there are regional/local programmes that permit very narrow geographic and ethnic-group targeting because some local programming is in minority languages specifically for minority language groups. In Calgary, Canada, for example, which is predominantly English-speaking, there are local television programmes broadcast in Hindi, French, Spanish, German and other minority languages.

A key disadvantage of television advertising is its high cost both in terms of production and air time compared with other channels. Indeed, all forms of advertising must be viewed as an investment from which positive results are expected. It is important, therefore, that the effectiveness of advertising be assessed.

HOW EFFECTIVE IS YOUR ADVERTISING?

You will want to have some way to measure the effectiveness of your advertising. There is no point in investing time and money into a process if it does not produce results. The use of discount coupons in newspaper and magazine advertising helps to keep track of the immediate success. Similarly, the use of references (numbers or key words) linked to discounts helps track effectiveness of particular channels. For example, a radio advertisement could have a tag whereby the reader says something like 'Tell them you heard it on BusComFM and receive a 10 per cent discount'. The most popular way to test effectiveness is through pre-testing advertising and marketing campaigns, that is, before the full budget is spent. Advertisements can be pilot-tested by interviewing or having focus group sessions with small groups of consumers. Many companies deny themselves useful information by not using post-testing, which is examining the impact of the advertising after the campaign is finished. Regardless of how you test you should have some way to test the effectiveness of your efforts for one or more of the following reasons:

- lower monetary and communication risks for future advertising

- better advertisements in future

- cost savings through avoiding ineffective advertising

- increased experiential learning.

Good evaluation provides experience and learning that enables more effective advertising in future. You can consult with publishers and other advertising channel representatives about testing how effective your advertising is. It is clearly in their best interests to be as helpful as they can.

EFFECTIVE ADVERTISING STYLES

After decades of research into advertising and its impact, we know very little about precisely how advertising works. We do have part of the picture. Part of what makes advertising effective is the style used to present or 'package' the message.

Some currently popular formats are:

- Aspiration and product-image transference – through images of persons or lifestyles to which the target audience might aspire, the implicit message with this style is that if you use the advertised products/services you will become that to which you aspire. For example, the implicit image in some automobile advertising where the car is placed in an aspirational context (outside a top-class restaurant in an exotic locale) is that if you purchase the car you will become (or will be demonstrating that you already are) successful in life. This format suggests that there is a 'magical' transfer of the qualities of the context, e.g. the expensive exotic locale that only the successful can afford, to the purchaser.

- Daily life/lifestyle – these themes often show a situation with which the target audience would identify and then places the product 'naturally' in that setting in a way that suggests that the product improves the quality of daily life or enhances lifestyle. Microwave oven advertising, for example, would show a normal kitchen made better by having a microwave oven.

- Product information – this format focuses on the product (usually with an image) and provides information about the product and its performance. The 'demonstration' format is a variant of this style.

- Demonstration – sometimes new products need to be demonstrated to show how they work. If the marketing research suggests that people perceive the product might be difficult to use, this kind of advertising might show a child using the product. The message is 'even a child can do it, so surely you can'.

- Endorsement – one of the preferred ways to sell sporting goods or kit is to have the product recommended by a famous sports star. Similarly, celebrities of just about any type can be used to motivate a target audience. If over-50s watch a gardening show on television and your product (though nothing to do with gardening) would appeal to that age group, you could use the star of the gardening show to endorse your product. This is a very effective, if expensive, advertising style.

- Humour – people tend to remember and to repeat humorous stories and it is no different in advertising. Advertising that can utilize tasteful humour is often successful but there is not a direct correlation between humour and product sales (Zang and Zinkhan 1991) though there is a link with humour and the likeability of the advert.

- Art – because some target audiences are so visually literate, there is an increase in the use of advertising inspired by post-modern, surreal and other art. Sometimes the message is not immediately clear, which makes audiences think about the advertisement, mentally searching for the link between the images/sounds/text and the product. Keeping the advert in audiences' minds makes for successful advertising for particular target audiences.

Public relations and image building

All business communications – advertising, customer contact and communications with suppliers, employees, shareholders, the press, government regulatory agencies and the general public – are not only event- or message-specific, but also communicate an image of your organization. That is, advertising not only does something (promotes the product), it also says something (it presents an image of the company). Managers must reflect on the kinds of images their organization is embedding in its advertising messages and the messages it sends when it deals with various external stakeholder groups (also called 'publics' in public relations jargon).

Public relations can be defined as 'the management of communication between an organization and its publics' (Hunt and Grunig 1994: 6). Some examples of publics are:

- customers – past, present, potential

- consumers (not necessarily the same as customers since an organization could sell to a customer who in turn sells it on to its customer who is the consumer)

- opinion leaders – people and institutions in the community, industry or government or general public who can influence others' opinions

- media – television, radio, newspapers, magazines

- general public

- industry

- pressure groups – e.g. environmental groups, consumer associations.

Public relations refers to two-way communication between an organization and the publics in its external environment. This means that press releases, communications with regulators, handling of complaints from customers, interactions with suppliers and competitors, etc., all have an impact on corporate image which also impacts product/service image. Figure 11.2 represents the overlapping and reinforcing nature of product/service advertising and public relations.

An integrated public relations/advertising function should, therefore, concern itself with:

- Advertising – this includes not only products, but also advertising for employment vacancies, sub-contractors, etc. Advertising can be carefully controlled and should reflect an integrated corporate image.

- Corporate communications – includes communications with suppliers, buyers, regulators and competitors.

- Crisis management – means, in its simplest form, having contingency plans to handle both large- and small-scale disasters of many kinds ranging from loss of electrical power in the corporate head office to hostage taking, environmental disasters, product tampering and so on. How a company responds in a crisis leaves a lasting impression on publics, so organizations should in advance – as best they can – plan

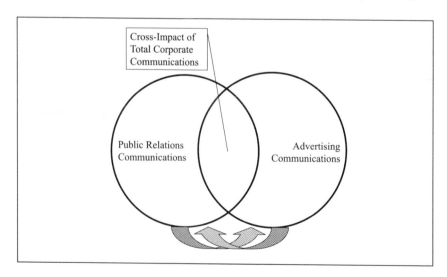

FIGURE 11.2 *Cross-impact of PR and advertising*

precisely how they would respond to disasters that may befall their organization.

- Donations and sponsorships – can convey a message of good corporate citizenship. Many organizations donate to local, regional and national charities. Organizations must be careful, however, that their donations be seen to be sincere or negative publicity can result. Sponsorship can be of local or national/international events and is often tied in with the qualities or uses of the company's products, e.g. a petroleum company sponsoring auto-racing.

- Community relations – are linked to donations and sponsorships, but are more than that. The environmental friendliness (or otherwise) of an operation, the level of local employment, participation in local events and local social/economic development are all part of community relations.

- General publicity – can be a powerful form of positive communication for an organization. This is especially so if the publicity comes from a third party that is considered credible and unbiased, e.g. a newspaper.

- Media relations – should be designed to encourage positive impressions of the company and its products/services. Part of this function would be to ensure that journalists receive relevant information in a timely way, that press releases are factual and timely, that photos or videos are available for media use, and that public relations managers develop and maintain good relationships with key journalists and editors.

- Corporate publications – include product brochures, project proposals, annual reports and organization-promoting literature. These should reflect the image the organization wishes to promote of itself.

- Internet sites – are an increasingly popular form of public relations and advertising. The internet is being used to promote and sell products as well as functioning as a medium through which firms can build and reinforce their corporate images and reputations.

An integrated public relations/advertising function contributes to the overall image of an organization and its products/services.

Reputation, communication and competitive advantage

Public relations and advertising both function to construct an organization's reputation. Reputation is becoming, therefore, increasingly important for organizations. The research into reputation suggests that both a good corporate reputation and good brand reputation (image) can be sources of competitive advantage. Both of these forms of reputation (brand and corporate) are a subset of what is known in strategic management as 'intangible resources'.

Resources are capital equipment, raw materials, organizational processes and attributes, information, expertise and all assets that are used and controlled by the organization (Wernerfelt 1984). Tangible resources are those resources and assets that can be seen, e.g. the buildings and land, financial resources, raw materials, capital equipment and so on. Intangible resources are those resources that cannot be easily seen. Processes, technologies, expertise and know-how are examples of intangible resources. Reputation and brand image are also considered intangible resources that are often referred to as 'reputational assets' (Grant 1991).

The image of a brand is the entire set of perceptions, expectations and values which buyers/consumers hold about a particular product/service. It is the totality of the product's reputation. Similarly, corporate image or reputation is the entire set of perceptions, expectations and values which publics hold concerning a particular organization. There is no denying that brands are important. Alan Palmer (1997), marketing director for Cadbury Ltd, estimates that the Cadbury brand is worth £1.3 billion in the UK alone compared to £1.2 billion for Coca-Cola (UK) and Walkers at £500 million. Brands are built not only through advertising and packaging which communicate with customers but also as represented in Figure 11.2 (page 240) through the corporate image.

We often speak of corporate image or reputation as if it were a single perception. Given the differences in an organization's various publics, it should not be surprising that organizations tend to have reputations (in the plural) rather than merely one reputation. Some perceptions among publics cannot be controlled but it is in organizations' best interests to try to have consistency in its communications in an effort to promote as consistent an image as possible.

Reputation goes beyond product sales. It also functions as a key element in an organization's ability to position itself within its operating environment. For example, reputation has an impact on an organization's ability to attract and retain good employees. Firms should be concerned that they have an image of relative permanence within a community as opposed to being seen as a 'fly-by-night' operation. They will want to be seen as offering competitive remuneration and working conditions, and as concerned with employees and the environment. Organizations will want to have a reputation among suppliers as being fair, paying their invoices on time and working with their suppliers in various ways, such as giving advance notice where possible of increased demand. Intel, for example, needs the best and brightest people to continue to dominate its industry so it focuses on ensuring that it has a reputation as a good place to work. Intel is rated by those polled for *Fortune* magazine as one of the world's best companies.

Corporations are also keen to ensure that they maintain their reputations for fairness and honest dealings in joint ventures and strategic alliances. In the oil exploration industry, for example, joint ventures are a common risk-sharing strategy among firms. Companies who 'cheat' in their agreements soon discover that they are no longer able to find exploration or other partners because information about an organization that has cheated becomes communicated widely in an industry (Granovetter 1985).

All of these examples of brand image and corporate reputation speak to the competitive advantage that can accrue to organizations who hold such intangible resources. This relationship between reputation and competitive advantage is represented in Figure 11.3.

In strategic management, competitive advantage is analysed using what is known as the 'resource-based view' (Wernerfelt 1984). The resource-based view suggests that competitive advantage can be assessed by isolating specific resources or assets and asking the following questions (Barney 1997):

- Value – does the resource generate value for the organization?

- Rarity – is the resource rare or narrowly distributed among competitors in an industry?

- Inimitability – is the resource inimitable and non-substitutable or can others copy it but only at a greater cost?

- Organization – is it organized to leverage or exploit the resource?

If the answer to these four questions is 'yes', then the resource-based view suggests that the resource could be a core source of competitive advantage. Brand image and corporate reputation both meet these criteria. Research

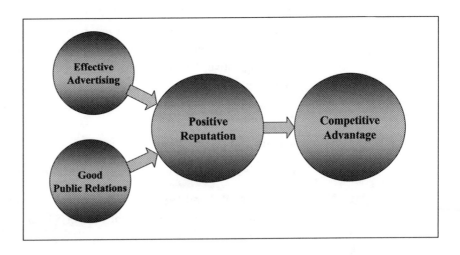

FIGURE 11.3

Relationship between reputation and competitive advantage

suggests that reputation among customers and suppliers (Porter 1980; Klein and Leffler 1981) not only adds value, but is socially complex, so that it is difficult for others to imitate – further, a particular reputation is not usually shared by others in an industry, so it is rare. In fact, it has been argued that nothing is more difficult to try to imitate or duplicate than an organization's reputation (Barney 1997). Reputation (whether brand or corporate image) is based on years of commitment, experience, trust, social and communications investment, and interaction. Reputations cannot be built quickly. They cannot be purchased. Organizations with positive reputations enjoy competitive advantages that reflect themselves in sales and profits and in relationships with suppliers, government, customers and others.

Companies are finding that their 'true' competitive advantages are to be found in intangible resources such as reputation. Interestingly, the scope for leverage of something like reputation is not limited. Unlike tangible resources (e.g. raw materials), reputation does not get used up by a consumer. In fact, positive reputation increases as it is passed from person to person and the larger the network, the greater the benefit (Hitt, Ireland and Hoskisson 2001).

Here, we want to take this concept of competitive advantage from intangible resources even further to include business/organizational communication as a source of competitive advantage. Research evidence suggests that both internal and external communications may be linked with organizational success.

General Motors (GM) in the United States began a formal communications enhancement programme in 1982. The steps and results have been documented by several authors (McKeans 1990; Smith 1991; Tourish and Hargie 2000). GM began by encouraging managers to immerse themselves in reading about effective communications. They then introduced internal newsletters including one written with the trade union. Video news 'magazines' containing relevant business information were introduced and shown during meetings. Managers increased meetings with staff especially in smaller groups, during which even sensitive issues were discussed. They introduced regular communications audits. While some of the results are more suggestive than demonstrably causally linked, it is worth noting the following:

- sales doubled over seven years

- costs dropped by about 3 per cent per year

- part delivery delays were almost totally eliminated

- between 1982 and 1986 employees' trust of manager-supplied information rose from less than 50 per cent to over 80 per cent

- savings to the company from its employee suggestion scheme rose from US$864 per employee in 1981 to US$5748 in 1987.

An Institute of Directors (UK) report (Dawson-Sheperd and White 1994) suggests that companies with internal communications programmes credited those programmes with improved productivity (65 per cent), fewer industrial disputes (68 per cent) and improvements in loyalty (80 per cent). Performance as measured by levels of innovation is linked with internal and external communication in another study (Kanter 1988).

Kao Corporation (Butler and Ghoshal 1991) is another case in point. Kao was formed in 1890 as the Kao Soap Company and by 1990, with sales of US$3.9 billion, was an international corporation competing with firms such as Procter & Gamble. Kao's success is directly attributed to its success as a learning and communicating organization. The company believed that its only source of advantage was in information. Information was therefore shared at all levels. The organization was structured to make interactive communication easier, they instituted a fortnightly internal newspaper, there was internal open access to the company's databases and there was no 'classified' information – equal access to information was available to all. With the advent of computers, terminals throughout the company ensured that any employee could see current data on sales for any product and up-to-date findings from continuing R&D were available on-line to any employee who wanted to see what was going on. Similarly, current inventories and production data were available. Kao executives were not concerned that competitors might somehow get access to the information because Kao was learning and moving forward so quickly that by the time competitors had learned what Kao knew, Kao had integrated, synthesized and used the information in new ways and moved on. Any leaked information was for all intents and purposes obsolete information. Internal communication is cited as one of Kao's core sources of competitive advantage.

The application of the resource-based view may help us consider whether communications could be a source of competitive advantage. Begin with the question of value. Good internal and external communications clearly are valuable to organizations. Next, given what we know about the paucity of attention paid generally to internal and external communications in most organizations as compared with the finance function, for example, it would seem that effective business communications are rare. Are they inimitable? In Kao's case it would be difficult to copy the depth of communications and information sharing in the organization and even if it could be copied it would be expensive to try to duplicate. Finally, business/organizational communications are central to effective organization. It would seem then that there may be a case for claiming that communications could be a core source of competitive advantage for organizations.

Summary

In this chapter we discussed the wider social and economic issues related to advertising and the steps for developing effective advertising campaigns. We then related that discussion to the characteristics of some key advertising channels, notably newspapers and magazines, radio, television and the internet. We identified that all advertising not only promotes goods and services but also communicates messages about the organization, which led us to a wider discussion of public relations and its function with advertising in building brand image and organizational reputation.

Reputation and brands were identified as sources of competitive advantage from the perspective of the resource-based view of the firm. Through analysing resources such as reputational assets in terms of whether they were valuable, rare, inimitable and organized, we were able to suggest that some resources could be sources of advantage. We then applied similar thinking to business and organizational communications and decided that effective communications could be a core source of an organization's competitive advantage.

Discussion questions

1. There are several criticisms of advertising, including claims that it creates false demand and false needs. Based on your own experience as a consumer, what is your opinion?

2. A key positive feature of advertising is that it functions to lower prices of goods and services. How can that be so when advertising costs money?

3. How does communication strategy relate to effective advertising and marketing campaigns?

4. Choose an industry about which you have some knowledge (perhaps retailing, or a manufacturing industry). Based on your knowledge of that industry would it be most effective to target loyal customers or uninformed prospects in order to hit your sales targets and why?

5. The internet is a powerful channel for effective brand image advertising. Do you agree and if so, why?

6. From your own experience or reading, describe an organization that has demonstrated that it is at a competitive disadvantage as a result of ineffective business communications.

References

Advertising Age (1989) *Advertising Age*, 15 May, Ad Age Group, Detroit.

Barney, J. (1997) *Gaining and Sustaining Competitive Advantage*, Addison-Wesley, Harlow.

Butler, C. and Ghoshal, S. (1991) Kao Corporation, in H. Mintzberg, J. Quinn and S. Ghoshal (1998) *The Strategy Process*: revised European edition, Prentice Hall, London.

Dawson-Sheperd, A. and White, J. (1994) Communication: why UK managers are shooting themselves in the foot, *Business News*, May, p. 6.

Driver, J. and Foxall, G. (1984) *Advertising Policy and Practice*, Holt, Rinehart and Winston, London.

Galbraith, J. (1958) *The Affluent Society*, Houghton Mifflin, Boston.

Galbraith, J. (1967) *The New Industrial State*, Houghton Mifflin, Boston.

Granovetter, M. (1985) Economic action and social structure: the problem of embeddedness, *American Journal of Sociology*, 91, 481–510.

Grant, R. (1991) A resource based theory of competitive advantage: implications for strategy formulation, *California Management Review*, 33(3), 114–135.

Hitt, M., Ireland, R. and Hoskisson, R. (2001) *Strategic Management: Competitiveness and Globalization*, South-Western, Cincinnati, OH.

Hunt, T. and Grunig, J. (1994) *Public Relations Techniques*, Harcourt Brace, Forth Worth, TX.

Kanter, R. (1988) Three tiers for innovation research, *Communication Research*, 15, 509–523.

Key, W. (1976) *Subliminal Seduction*, Signet, New York.

Klein, B. and Leffler, K. (1981) The role of market forces in assuring contractual performance, *Journal of Political Economy*, 89, 615–641.

Leiss, W., Kline, S. and Jhally, S. (1997) *Social Communication in Advertising: Persons, Products and Images of Well-Being*, Routledge, London.

McKeans, P. (1990) GM division builds a classic system to share internal information, *Public Relations Journal*, 46, 24–41.

Marcuse, H. (1964) *One Dimensional Man: Studies in the Ideology of Advanced Industrial Society*, Beacon Books, Boston.

Palmer, A. (1997) Cadbury Ltd: harnessing the strengths of the corporate brand, in F. Gilmore (ed.), *Brand Warriors: Corporate Leaders Share Their Winning Strategies*, pp. 145–159, HarperCollins Business, London.

Porter, M. (1980) *Competitive Strategy*, Free Press, New York.

Smith, A. (1991) *Innovative Employee Communication: New Approaches to Improving Trust, Teamwork and Performance*, Prentice Hall, London.

Tourish, D. and Hargie, O. (2000) Communication and organizational success, in O. Hargie and D. Tourish (eds) *Handbook of Communication Audits for Organizations*, pp. 3–21, Routledge, London.

Wernerfelt, B. (1984) A resource-based view of the firm, *Strategic Management Journal*, 5, 171–180.

Zang, Y. and Zinkhan, G. (1991) Humor in television advertising – the effect of repetition and social setting, *Advances in Consumer Research*, 18, 813–818.

Further reading

Ewen, S. (1988) *All Consuming Images*, McGraw-Hill, New York.

Ewen, S. and Ewen, E. (1982) *Channels of Desire*, McGraw-Hill, New York.

Fox, R. W. and Lears, T. J. (1983) *The Culture of Consumption*, Pantheon, New York.

Gilmore, F. (ed.) (1997) *Brand Warriors: Corporate Leaders Share Their Winning Strategies*, HarperCollins Business, London.

Goldman, R. (1987) Marketing fragrances: advertising and the production of commodity signs, *Theory, Culture and Society*, 4, 691–725.

Haug, W. F. (1987) *Commodity Aesthetics, Ideology and Culture*, International General, Paris.

Jhally, S. (1987) *Codes of Advertising: Fetishism and the Political Economy of Meaning in the Consumer Society*, Saint Martin's, New York.

Kellner, D. (1990) *Television and the Crisis of Democracy*, Westview Press, Boulder, CO.

Pickton, D. and Broderick, A. (2001) *Integrated Marketing Communications*, Prentice Hall, Harlow.

chapter twelve

Communicating across boundaries

Introduction

ORGANIZATIONS COMMUNICATE their products and their image. They also engage in continuous communications with a wide range of institutions, groups and individuals outside of their organizational boundaries. Some of these stakeholders are suppliers, customers or government. Organizations also have to communicate within their boundaries too. They have to maintain relations with employees and shareholders who also have a stake in the company. Effective communications requires different approaches to dealing with different groups. In this chapter we provide a deeper understanding of stakeholders and explore their related communications issues.

Some corporations are in the process of globalizing their businesses or are already global players. Such organizations have to communicate across cultures which brings a different set of contingencies and issues. In this chapter we examine national culture and explore some issues related to cross-cultural communications for the corporation.

LEARNING OBJECTIVES

After studying this chapter you should be able to:

- Define the term 'stakeholder'
- Identify stakeholders of an organization and then plot them on a stakeholder map
- Decide how best to communicate with stakeholders
- Identify some key national cultural variables
- State the rationale for studying national cultures
- Apply the principles of effective cross-cultural communications
- Discuss the issues related to stereotyping.

Stakeholders: boundary-spanning communications

In Chapter Eleven we introduced the public relations term 'publics' and in communication strategy the term 'audience'. Here we want to introduce another term that is very similar to these: 'stakeholder'. Publics, audience and stakeholder are not exactly the same concept. Audience, you will recall from Chapter Four, refers to those with whom you plan to or do communicate, e.g. the person you telephone, the organization to which you write, the potential customers who are the targets of your advertising. Publics refers to individuals, groups and organizations in the external environment that hold a perception of your organization and/or its products. A **stakeholder** is a person or group inside or outside an organization that has an interest or stake in what the organization does and how it performs. Thus, when you send a communication to employees they are both 'audience' (receiver of a specific communication) and a 'stakeholder' (their continued employment depends upon organizational survival) but they are not a 'public' (they are internal, not external).

You will recall from Chapter One that organizations have been defined as society's way to generate value that individuals cannot generate on their own. Clearly, organizations generate many qualitatively different kinds of value. Profit, employment, need-fulfilling products, personal satisfaction, return on investment, careers, promotion and so on are all examples of some of the value being created by organizations. That value is distributed among stakeholders.

Stakeholders are, however, diverse: e.g. creditors, customers, employees, managers, governments, suppliers and shareholders. Given this diversity of stakeholders, not all can be fully satisfied all the time and the interests of some stakeholders must be privileged over others in most situations. For example, reducing the workforce during recession means that shareholder wealth is protected but at the expense of the needs and desires of another stakeholder group, the employees.

Different stakeholders are interested in different kinds of value. Public-sector organizations such as the government and its agencies have an even greater problem because they are perceived to exist for the interests of all. If stakeholder theory is taken to its logical extreme there could be different performance and other expectations associated with every stakeholder (Barney 1997). This is an important observation because it means that there are different communications criteria associated with diverse stake-holder groups. In other words, organizations communicate differently with different stakeholders.

In order to identify, describe, categorize and think about relevant stakeholders, Mitchell, Agle and Wood (1997) combine three elements:

- power

- legitimacy

- urgency.

Power in the model can be described as the ability of one person or group to influence or force change in another's behavior. Following Etzioni (1964), power can be coercive (based on physical threat or force), utilitarian (based on control of financial or other resources) or normative (based on symbolic resources such as reputation).

Legitimacy is defined by the behavior or status of individuals, groups or other organizations that are socially accepted as being proper or appropriate. For example, a village that is situated downwind from a polluting smoke-stack would be seen as a stakeholder based on legitimacy because, in Western European countries, it is recognized by the social system's values and beliefs that villagers have a moral right to be a stakeholder since they are recipients of some negative consequences of the company's actions – pollution. Similarly, shareholders would have legitimacy because they place something at risk with the company (financial capital).

Urgency refers to the idea that stakeholders have variable degrees of urgent claim on some of the value being generated by an organization. For example, employees who work all week have an urgent claim on an organization for a week's wages for work already done and time already spent working for the company.

The Venn diagram (Figure 12.1) illustrates that any person or group that does not possess power, legitimacy or urgency, firstly, will not be recognized as a stakeholder – they simply do not appear on the map. The very process of identifying those individuals, groups or other organizations that hold at least one of the three attributes is the process of identifying stakeholders – but all stakeholders are not equal. Some have more salience than others. Salience refers to perceptions of importance or prominence, which is simply to say that some stakeholders are perceived to be more important than others. Of those stakeholders that are represented in the circles, there are three broad categorizations that we have labelled following Rouse (2000) as:

- value takers – those that have one attribute

- value negotiators – those with two attributes

- value makers – those with all three attributes.

Value takers are stakeholders (numbers 5, 6, 7 in Figure 12.1) who, because they are perceived to hold only one of the three attributes, may find that their claims on organizational value and to management's attention may generally be given little consideration. With only one attribute they are likely

FIGURE 12.1

*Stakeholder model
(adapted from
Mitchell, Agle and
Wood 1997)*

Power   2   Legitimacy

5   1   6

4   3

Urgency

7

to tend to have little to prompt management to recognize their claims for attention or value delivery. They would have to take the value that is given them with little opportunity to influence the quantity or quality of value they receive.

Value negotiators are stakeholders perceived to have two of the three attributes (numbers 2, 3, 4 in Figure 12.1). They may have sufficient salience to make demands on the focal organization and in the process may be able to negotiate for their share of the value generated. They may not have to settle for the amount, quality or type of value offered. They presumably can, but do not necessarily, engage in negotiations for their share of generated value to varying degrees.

Value makers are stakeholders with all three attributes (number 1 in Figure 12.1). Since those possessing both power and legitimacy may tend to receive considerable management attention, the addition of urgency of claim makes the demands of this group a high priority for management. Management has such a clear, high-priority mandate to serve this group that programmes and initiatives are often made especially to deliver value to, or in the interest of, these stakeholders.

Power, legitimacy and urgency as criteria for assessing stakeholder identification is particularly useful in communications because the categorizing and consideration of stakeholders and management's perception of their salience makes a difference in how organizations do or should communicate with particular stakeholders. This is represented three-dimen-

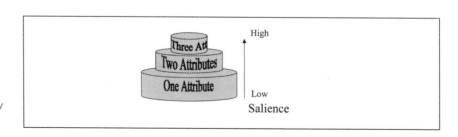

FIGURE 12.2 *Hierarchy
of salience/attributes*

sionally in Figure 12.2 as a set of stacked cylinders. The more attributes held, the higher a stakeholder is in Figure 12.2 and the more salience or importance they will be perceived to have. Stakeholder salience within a particular organizational context should then be reflected in organization–stakeholder dynamics, differential value outcomes and differing communication styles and strategies. That is, the relative position of stakeholders in terms of their identification and salience should explain and predict how a focal organization deals and communicates with its stakeholders.

Stakeholder mapping is a powerful way to think about, organize and implement stakeholder communication. The stakeholder mapping process has three steps:

1. Identify stakeholders

2. Map stakeholders

3. Identify values of interest.

The first step is to identify which individuals, groups or other organizations in the external and internal environments:

• have some degree of power over your organization

• are perceived to have legitimacy

• have a relatively urgent claim on value generated by your organization.

An example of this step is represented in Table 12.1 where we identify just a few of the many stakeholders of a petroleum company.

TABLE 12.1 *Identifying stakeholders by attribute*

Stakeholder	Power	Legitimacy	Urgency
Employees		✓	✓
Top management team	✓	✓	✓
Shareholders	✓	✓	✓
Local community		✓	
Customers		✓	✓
Suppliers			✓
Government regulator	✓	✓	
Local unemployed		✓	
International environmentalist	✓		

Step 2 is to map the stakeholders identified onto the stakeholder Venn diagram. Figure 12.3 shows the result based on the identification of stakeholders in Table 12.1.

Step 3 is to decide what are the primary and secondary (or even tertiary) organizational values or negative consequences (e.g. jobs, profit, self-fulfilment, return on investment, environmental degradation) of interest to each of the stakeholders identified in the mapping exercise. Table 12.2 suggests what the key areas of interest might be for the stakeholders identified in our example.

As is demonstrated in communication strategy (Chapter Four) organizations have a choice about what they over-communicate and what they under-communicate to particular audiences. With a deep understanding of stakeholders and their attributes and interests, an organization can ensure that its stakeholder communications are effective. When a business organization communicates with stakeholders the organization has to make decisions about:

- kinds of information to transmit

- quality of the communication

- frequency of communication

- originating hierarchical level.

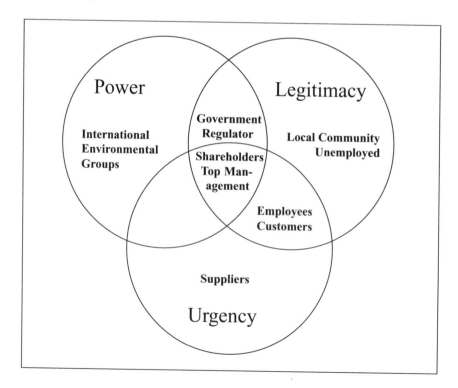

FIGURE 12.3

Stakeholder map

TABLE 12.2 *Stakeholders' key interests/performance indicators*

Stakeholder	Key values/performance sought
Employees	Job security, remuneration, skills enhancement
Top management team	Growth, perquisites, security, profits, career progression
Shareholders	Return on investment, profit, growth
Local community	Local jobs, stability, controlled growth, corporate contribution to local quality of life
Customers	Value-for-money products/services
Suppliers	Invoices paid, continued business, growth
Government regulator	Laws obeyed
Local unemployed	Jobs
International environmentalists	Environmentally friendly operations, low/no growth, corporate social responsibility

Organizations do not communicate all information to all stakeholders. Clearly there is a hierarchy of information from simple product and other public-knowledge kinds of information to very detailed financial and strategic planning information. The kind of information that is communicated to value makers (those with power, legitimacy and urgency) would be of a different kind from that sent to value takers (those with solely one attribute). Organizations communicate who they are, what they do and where they stand when they do it (Chapter Eleven). In other words, organizations communicate an image of themselves. That image, the ethics, products, goals and performance of the organization must fit with and be acceptable to stakeholders.

Similarly the quality of information in terms of how it is presented, packaged and delivered would differ depending upon the salience of the stakeholder. These characteristics of communications vary and are represented in Figure 12.4 where we plot the number of attributes (1, 2 or 3) along the horizontal axis and plot the concomitant level of salience on the vertical axis. The result is an indication of the kind and quality of information for different levels of stakeholder salience. The grid also represents other communication characteristics such as how the frequency of communication should increase with salience. Further, it would make sense that the hierarchical level in the organization from which communications originate

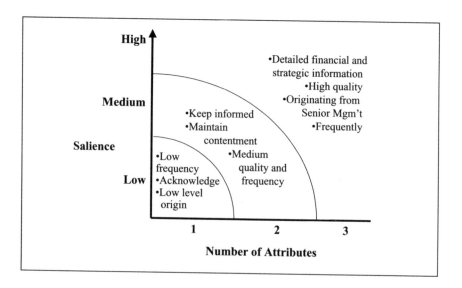

FIGURE 12.4
*Stakeholder salience
and information
intensity*

should change as a function of salience. When dealing with shareholders (value makers according to our stakeholder map, Figure 12.3) it would be most effective for communications to originate from the senior management level.

From Figure 12.4, it can be seen that low-salience stakeholders need to be acknowledged. Communication with them can be of low frequency and from less senior levels of management in the organizational hierarchy. Communication can be low-contact in many cases and might be letters or simply communication through the information on web pages or through general public relations.

Stakeholders with medium salience are those that need to be kept informed. Their level of contentment with the organization and the value it delivers must be reinforced and maintained in communications. These stakeholders would receive all or most of the information made available to low-salient stakeholders plus more detailed information. For example, a government regulator would be sent more, and more detailed, information about occupational health and safety issues than would suppliers or environmental groups. That information would also be packaged and delivered in a customized way for the individual stakeholder, probably at the middle-management level of the organization. Middle managers probably would also have access to the necessary information and hold responsibility for relationships with those medium-salience stakeholders.

Stakeholders with high salience, such as shareholders for private corporations or government for public-sector organizations, would receive key communications from senior levels of management. That information would be detailed and delivered in a high-quality way, including colourful reports and even oral presentations in addition to the quality and type of information available to lower-salience stakeholders. This level of communication would be considered high-intensity and high-quality and would symbolize that management was paying attention to and working in the interests of those high-salience stakeholders who are mapped as value makers.

There are some ethical considerations that must go with this kind of analysis and application. Organizations and the top management team must think carefully about their stakeholders to ensure that they are not ignoring those that do have a stake in the organization. Since the stakeholder identification process is subjective, managers must ensure that their perceptions of legitimacy, power and urgency are not constrained by their cultural filters. To that end, it is most useful to do the stakeholder identification using a diversified group of people from several levels of the organization. It is even more effective if external people or groups are involved in the process. Those that clearly are stakeholders might even be ideal candidates for inclusion in a boundary-spanning assessment team whose task it is to determine other stakeholders. This, additionally, would symbolically communicate the organization's interest in and respect for those stakeholders on the assessment team.

Such boundary-spanning interaction and communication has some similarities with communicating across other boundaries. We now turn our attention to cross-cultural communication.

Cross-cultural communication

International business and global events affect not only those corporations that we normally think of as global competitors (e.g. Ford, Toyota, Sony, Coca-Cola, General Electric, General Motors, BP, etc.), but affect nearly all businesses and some public-sector and not-for-profit organizations as well. Even medium and small businesses are finding it in their best interests to expand internationally. There are several reasons for internationalization:

- it increases sales especially if domestic markets have settled into low-growth

- it generates growth less expensively than gaining market share in the domestic market

- it realizes higher profits in markets that have advantageous market conditions

- it acquires resources at lower prices or of higher quality

- it minimizes competitive risk by doing business across international economies.

Internationalization is increasing. Around the world trade barriers are dropping, people are being exposed to new products, places and services, and new technologies in transportation and communication are making internationalization more and more attractive for more and more companies. We seem to be witnessing the emergence of a commercial global village where companies, project teams and individuals communicate and do business around the world using a full suite of traditional and electronic technologies. It is now common for people from different countries to communicate over mobile phones and the internet at any time, day or night. Familiar products and services are available the world over and we are witnessing the internationalization of production whereby product components are built in many places and assembled in another.

Success for corporations doing business globally depends upon several factors such as: competitive environments, political and legal contexts, economic forces, differences in climate and geography, and, of course, differences in cultures. A key element to being successful that spans and facilitates all of the above is cross-cultural communication.

Global corporations have to deal with foreign legal and political systems, differences in the nature of competition and how competition is waged, and, of course, corporations have to deal with employees, suppliers and buyers, and other stakeholders in foreign countries. Finally, in order to build an international brand corporations have to be able successfully to advertise and market in foreign countries. Just as communication is essential to doing business domestically, so too it is in the global marketplace. There is little doubt, given the increasing cross-cultural contact between firms and their staff, about the importance of understanding cross-cultural communication.

Cross-cultural communication refers to the process of sending and receiving messages between people who are in different cultural contexts. This means that communications between a company in the UK and a company in Canada is cross-cultural communication even though the communication is in English and both countries share some cultural similarities. Similarly, communication between the US division of an American company and the French division of that same American company is also cross-cultural communication. When a manager from the UK is transferred to Indonesia to be the UK company's representative in Jakarta, that person (called an 'expatriate') would be continually engaged in cross-cultural communication as part of day-to-day work. It is not easy communicating across cultures. Communicating effectively in one's own culture is difficult enough. It is even more so when everything seems different.

Culture shock occurs when consciously, but especially subconsciously, people realize that nearly everything about a host country and its ways of doing things is different. They become uncertain about meaning, and interpretation of symbols. Behaviour is indeterminate and there are symbols and behaviour for which there is no readily available frame of reference. Communication in either direction, to or from others, seems fraught with misunderstanding and difficulties. Anxiety increases. They feel like they are taking in too much information and cannot cope with the information overload – and that is precisely what is happening. The mind is struggling to make sense of its environment.

To some extent people experience mild doses of culture shock when they travel on their holidays. Suddenly the smells are different. The language is different. People dress and behave differently. There might be different architecture, different cars. The money is confusing. We are unsure about conventions such as how much to tip a waiter or taxi driver or whether to tip at all. For many this is part of the excitement of travel.

For those who are expatriate managers on a foreign assignment for their company, the first few weeks might hold that same excitement the tourist experiences, but then the manager realizes that the differences in the host country go much deeper than those on the surface. The anxiety heightens. Anxiety may lead to feelings of homesickness, frustration, alienation and isolation or it can lead to depression and many managers become depressed to the point of not being able to function in their post – this, in its mild to its severe form, is culture shock. Unfortunately some managers have to return home if the culture shock creates depression because they cannot cope. Most, though, do cope and learn to accept the host country's culture in its own terms and to adapt to and feel more comfortable in the foreign culture.

The deep-rootedness of the home culture is clearly the culprit in culture shock. One of the best ways to minimize the impact of culture shock and to hasten acceptance and adaptation is through cultural understanding, and realizing that the painful process of moving from culture shock to cultural adaptation is a normal process (Figure 12.5) that everyone goes through when working in another culture.

We discussed culture at some length in Chapter Three in terms of language and symbolic communication. Here we need to extend some of

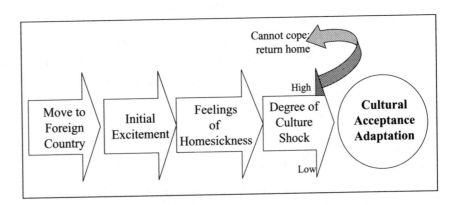

FIGURE 12.5 *Culture shock to adaptation*

those concepts as they relate to communication not merely within a culture but across cultures. Enhanced cultural understanding is critical to preparing for and getting through culture shock, and for communicating and engaging in international business that is conducted across national boundaries.

National culture is a relevant concept in international business communications even though many anthropologists might voice disagreement with the concept. We have suggested (Chapter Three) that culture 'naturally' develops as people spend time together and as they solve their problems of external adaptation and internal integration. Nationhood tends to define which people spend time together, in which internal context, and national boundaries also help to define the external environment. For example, by defining those within a particular boundary (even if seemingly arbitrary or based on historical contingency or accident) as those constituting a nation of people, frames for those people an idea of nationality – the in-group (our nationality) versus the out-group (other nationalities). Within national boundaries people are subject to national laws, enjoy the availability of particular types of food, shelter, climate, education, certain choices in religions, are taught particular histories and engage in or are spectators of nationally favoured sports. They share political and economic environments, get similar management education and so on. In other words, the people constitute the nation and in turn are constituted by it. To the extent that they are constituted by nationality it is reasonable to speak of national culture.

In saying that people within nations share cultural elements, we are not saying that all people are the same. In fact, there is tremendous variation within nations. There are differences in religion, values, beliefs, food, rituals, social practices, history and language which tend to confound the sense of national culture and yet, at some level, it is meaningful to say that there is something recognizable as British culture as distinct from Canadian culture or American or French or Indian culture. Coming to grips with international communications requires that we have some means to talk about the differences that seem to have real consequences for international business and communications. National culture, while not entirely robust from an anthropological perspective, does provide a starting point. In order to talk about national cultures and the impact they have on communications we will briefly discuss the impact of and cultural role played by:

- language

- five key variables of national culture

- sub-culture

- variations in information requirements.

LANGUAGE

Language, as was discussed in Chapter Three, is a core element of culture even though visual and other forms of symbolic communication have grown. There are somewhere between 8000 and 10,000 languages spoken in the world. Most businesses will communicate using only a few of these. Obviously, some markets such as Canada which officially is bilingual (English and French) require that organizations be able to communicate in both official languages, e.g. packaging has to be in both languages. Switzerland has four official languages none of which is English. South Africa has eleven officially recognized languages: English, Afrikaans, Zulu, Xhosa, Sepedi, Setswana, Sesotho, Zitsonga, Siswati, Tshibenda and Ndebele, though English is generally the language of business and functions as a *lingua franca*.

Many countries have minority languages which, while not officially required, are nonetheless important for business communications. In the UK, for example, Welsh is an important minority language (especially in North Wales). Spanish is becoming indispensable in some parts of the US and may in a few years become the majority language in some states. Many companies doing business in the US find it useful to have fluent Spanish-speaking managers on their staff.

Even though English is the international language of business, it is always appreciated by host countries if corporate representatives make the effort to speak in the host country's language even if they are not particularly fluent. Such effort is symbolically important even if the actual business is done in English. In some countries, e.g. France, there can be understandable resentment if English is automatically assumed as the language of communication. International managers (especially in Europe) are increasingly fluent in several languages, notably French, German and Spanish. Effective business communications may depend upon the language skills the company has at its disposal. Alternatively, companies can use agents in the host country who can communicate on behalf of the international company.

KEY VARIABLES IN NATIONAL CULTURE

Communication strategy (Chapter Four) begins with examining the sender (communicator strategy) of a message and then looks at the receiver, the audience. When communications are across cultures, those analyses need carefully to explore cultural differences. Culture is difficult to measure. Its dynamism and complexity make it very difficult to specify, but while it is recognized that culture cannot really be reduced to a few dimensions, it is worthwhile examining cultures in terms of empirically relevant dimensions to increase our understanding.

One of the most cited studies is Geert Hofstede's (1980, 1981) research based on questionnaire data from 80,000 IBM employees in 66 countries. He reduced his data to four (later five) key dimensions of culture with each represented as a continuum or a scale. Those dimensions are:

1. individualism–collectivism

2. achievement–relationship

3. power distance

4. uncertainty avoidance

5. time orientation.

Individualism–Collectivism

Individualism–collectivism is defined as the degree to which individuals' behaviours are influenced and defined by their relationships with others. As represented on a continuum (Figure 12.6) individualism and collectivism are polar extremes to which no culture would perfectly fit (this notion of polar extremes representing unattainable 'ideal' types holds for other continua as well). Rather, all societies have some degree or elements of both polar extremes but tend towards one side more than the other.

People from cultures rated as individualistic tend to put their own interests and those of their nuclear families first. They tend to have higher degrees of independence and self-respect. It is not unusual for people to consider personal careers and personal interests ahead of that which is best for their organization. They prefer to be self-sufficient and have social networks that are not as important as their immediate families. Hofstede's research suggests that Americans, the British, Australians, Canadians, New Zealanders and the Dutch rate the highest on the individualism end of the continuum. They tend to be task-oriented. Individualists also tend to be more enthusiastic about relocation than those who come from a more collectivist culture.

Those who have a collectivist orientation tend to give more recognition to their group-based roles and their obligations to that group. Within the

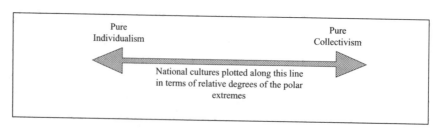

FIGURE 12.6

Individualism–

collectivism continuum

group, relationships with others in the group may take precedence over the task itself. Collectivist societies have tighter social networks and more extended perceptions of the family. They tend to put the interests of the group ahead of their own self-interest. Job mobility is problematic not only because of the tight social networks that might have to be left behind with relocation, but also because others might perceive them as disloyal to the company and therefore to them, if they left to join another firm. Cultures rated highly on the collectivism scale include those of Mexico, Greece, Hong Kong, Pakistan, Peru, Singapore and Taiwan.

In terms of communications strategy, there are implications for which elements of a message are over-communicated or under-communicated given expectations on this dimension. For example, when communicating with those holding a collectivist orientation it would most likely be effective to emphasize group benefits rather than individual benefits. For another example, communicating to an overseas colleague that favourable results of the project could lead to an overseas posting (assuming it is true) would be effective if that colleague was socialized in an individualistic culture. Remember, the purpose of a strategy is not to lie or to mislead. The purpose is to use your understanding, analysis and synthesis to generate messages that get results.

Achievement–Relationship

The achievement–relationship continuum measures perceptions of goals and quality of life issues. Achievement cultures are those cultures that score high in terms of their desire to seek goals that may be described as aggressive success, their propensity to engage in high degrees of competition, and who tend to be assertive. Money and material possessions are rated highly. Achievement-oriented cultures also tend to have relatively rigid gender-based norms. For example, men are encouraged to pursue traditionally male occupations and to be the 'breadwinners', whereas it is assumed that women should focus on home and family, and if they do work they are expected to take careers in fields traditionally dominated by women. Originally Hofstede labelled this continuum 'masculine–feminine', but because those labels have the potential to communicate sexism we have decided to relabel it achievement–relationship. Japan is rated quite highly in achievement orientation, as are Austria, Switzerland and Venezuela, with Germany, Italy, Mexico, the UK and the United States being rated as moderately achievement-oriented.

Cultures that are rated highly on the relationship end of the continuum focus on group solidarity and relationships. They tend to stress quality of life issues, concern for others, compromise in situations of conflict, and tend to be relatively modest and under-selling of themselves. The cultures rated relatively high at the relationship end are those of the Netherlands, Norway, Sweden, Denmark and Finland.

As part of an audience analysis, when the question is asked, 'How can I appeal to my audience?', the answer may well depend upon whether the audience is achievement-oriented or relationship-oriented. If it is the former, then the way to appeal to that audience may be through rewards, promotions, money or material possessions, etc. (assuming it is ethical and appropriate to offer them). On the other hand, if you are communicating with an audience that is relationship-oriented and the context of the communication is a situation of trying to resolve a conflict, then your analysis may lead you to think that compromise might be an acceptable way forward.

Power distance

Power distance refers to the beliefs that people hold with regard to the legitimacy and acceptability of the unequal power differences in society and in business. Cultures that score high on the power distance scale tend to perceive formal hierarchies and power differences as legitimate. Here communication of information is expected to be formalized and restricted, and relations between those with more and those with less power are expected to be formal. The power of superiors is perceived to be legitimate even if based solely on their position in a hierarchy. It is taken as natural that those at the top have the right to make decisions and those at the bottom expect decisions to be taken by superiors. The Philippines, Indonesia, Mexico, Venezuela, Singapore, Brazil, Spain and France all scored towards the high end of the power distance continuum.

Cultures scoring at the lower end of the power distance scale tend to endorse more egalitarian approaches to organization. They tend to be more open and informal, and tend to perceive that information channels should be relatively unrestricted and functional. Businesses in cultures at this end of the continuum tend to display flatter organizational structures, have less autocratic leaders and tend to engage in consultation across levels. Austria, Denmark, Ireland and New Zealand are at this end of the continuum.

There are implications here for marketing and for communications generally. Advertising in countries that score at the high end of the power distance scale might, for instance, use more informative-type adverts or those that have high status endorsements. As an example of the implications for communications style (part of message strategy), an audience from a culture scoring low in terms of power distance might respond well to a consultative style message. If your audience is at the high end of the scale, it could be advantageous in terms of establishing or enhancing credibility to stress the status of the communicator or the prestige of the organization.

Uncertainty avoidance

Uncertainty avoidance refers to the scale that represents how people within a culture prefer to resolve issues of uncertainty and how they react to ambiguous situations. Cultures that rate high on this scale tend to avoid uncertainty and develop ways of doing things so that uncertainty is controlled as much as possible. Change is seen as generally undesirable whereas social and organizational structures that tend to maintain consistency are seen as positive. These cultures therefore prefer rules and bureaucracy. In some cases people in these cultures would prefer to stick to the rules even it meant that so doing was not in the organization's best interest. Cultures that score higher at this end of the continuum include Austria, France, Germany, Japan, Italy and Peru.

Cultures scoring low in uncertainty avoidance tend to be peopled by those that are stimulated by change and even see ambiguity as a context for opportunities in which an individual can grow and develop. They prefer flexibility, personal choice, risk-taking, and tend to be more accepting of outsiders. They may find environments characterized by certainty and bureaucratic rule to be routine and boring. Cultures rated low on the uncertainty avoidance scale are Australia, Canada, Denmark, Hong Kong, Singapore, Sweden and the United States.

Time orientation

Time orientation refers to some cultures' preference for a long-term or a short-term outlook on life and work. Some cultures are much more future-oriented than others. For example, Hong Kong, Japan and Taiwan have a future orientation. At the other end of the continuum we find those such as Pakistan and some West African cultures where the focus is more present- and past-oriented than oriented towards the future. These cultures tend to have a great respect for tradition. Canada, Germany and the United States are in the middle. Compared to North Americans the British tend to emphasize the past much more.

Time has other dimensions, too. Time has been characterized by Hall and Hall (1987) as either monochronic or polychronic. 'Monochronic time' refers to the preference in some cultures for doing only one thing at a time. 'Polychronic time', on the other hand, refers to doing or paying attention to many things at once.

In cultures characterized as monochronic, time is assumed to be linear – it is like an arrow, straight and clearly pointing in one direction. Time is divided into segments that can be modularized and scheduled so that only one thing needs to be handled at one time. Time is perceived as a resource that can be spent or saved, wasted or lost. Many Western cultures such as those of Germany, Canada, the United States and the Scandinavian countries tend to be predominantly monochronic cultures.

Polychronic cultures perceive time in the opposite way. Many things can and do happen at the same time. They tend to put more importance on completing their current business or communication than in terminating it

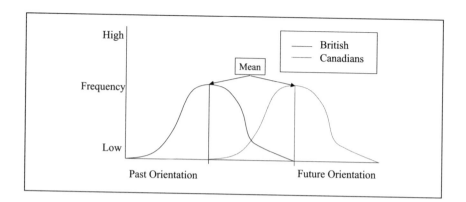

FIGURE 12.7 *Cultural differences in time orientation*

abruptly in order to start the next. Time commitments are more of an objective to be achieved if possible than a rigid schedule to which one must stick. Plans change frequently and relatively easily compared to monochronic cultures. Many Latin American cultures are characterized by a tendency towards polychronic time. Interestingly, according to Hall and Hall (1987), Japanese culture tends to be divided between monochronic time which is used when dealing with foreigners, and polychronic time which is invoked when dealing with other Japanese.

All of these key elements of national culture come from studies that are very limited in scope. They are useful for thinking about national cultures and have provided more information than we have had in the past. Be careful, however, in interpreting the information. While the British are perceived to be past-oriented and Canadians future-oriented, it is the case that within Britain there are those who are future-oriented and in Canada there are those who are oriented towards the past. Figure 12.7 illustrates how even though it can be said that the cultural average for the British (represented by the mean line) is past-oriented compared to the Canadian average, there are still Canadians who are more past-oriented than some British and *vice versa* as represented by the overlapping areas under the curves.

SUB-CULTURE

Sub-culture (as defined in Chapter Three) refers to a system of perceptions, values, beliefs and assumptions that are different from those of the dominant culture. Nation states generally contain many sub-cultures that may be based on religion, region, occupation, social class, ethnicity or even lifestyle. Sub-cultures can display key national culture dimensions (time orientation, power distance, etc.) in ways different from the dominant culture. For example, in Canada, Canadian culture on average may tend to be low in terms of uncertainty avoidance, but Canada has the largest population of

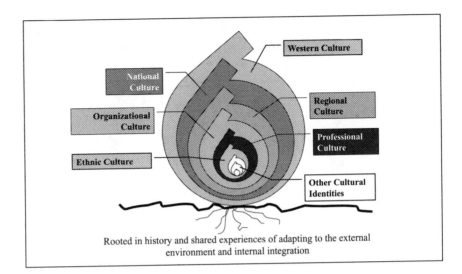

Rooted in history and shared experiences of adapting to the external
environment and internal integration

FIGURE 12.8 *Levels of culture and sub-cultures*

Chileans outside of Chile and Chileans as a sub-cultural group tend to score high on the uncertainty avoidance scale.

Sub-cultural groups can be highly relevant to international business and communications. Marketing campaigns in parts of the US, for example, that do not recognize Spanish as the first language of many of its target audience might be ineffective. Most of the discussions in this chapter about culture and communications are considerations that need to be analysed at the sub-cultural level as well as the national level. Metaphorically, culture is rather like an onion (Figure 12.8). At one level there is something definable as Western culture based on history, technology, philosophical underpinnings and so on. At another level we can recognize national culture. There are sub-cultures too and they can be regional, linguistic, ethnic, etc. We also have evidence of community cultures, and there are organizational cultures, professional cultures, or other types of sub- and sub-sub-cultures. For our purposes here we are dealing predominantly with national cultures as key variables in international business communications though consideration has to be given to these variables as they might apply to other levels, too.

INFORMATION REQUIREMENTS

In international communications whether in meetings, negotiations, text-based or other communications, the amount and kind of information that is exchanged hinges – as you would expect – on culture. In terms of information requirements, cultures can be arranged on a continuum representing degrees of what Hall and Hall (1987, 1990) call 'high context' or 'low context'.

A high-context culture at one end of the continuum relies on interpersonal relations and extensive social networks for information. People in these cultures do not require and do not expect to receive in-depth background information about business decisions because they make it their responsibility to find out ahead of time. They have in-depth information about anyone who may be involved in the discussions, the business or the negotiations. They tend to use many more cultural cues to interpret communications rather than relying heavily on the actual words used. National cultures such as the Japanese, Koreans, Chinese, Vietnamese and those of the Arab nations tend to be high-context cultures (Figure 12.9).

A low-context culture is the opposite. Generally, the actual words used in a communication are considered to carry weight. Low-context cultures require a great deal of background information and data upon which to base a decision. They prefer to get the information first-hand and even then only if it is directly relevant to the issue at hand. Germans, Canadians, Swiss, Scandinavians, Americans and the British (Figure 12.9) all tend to be low-context. They do not have the extensive personal networks of the high-context cultures and prefer to have information compartmentalized for modularized analysis so that they can deal with specific information at the specific appointed time. Even advertising in low-context cultures tends to be more fact-oriented too. The terms and conditions of specific transactions are given high importance and there is very little time given at meetings to 'small talk'.

All cultures have elements of both low and high context. For example, at work a manager from a low-context culture could be part of a colleague's personal network and they could have a considerable amount of information about each other. Nonetheless, they would still tend to seek background information for projects on which they were working together which to them would seem natural. To someone from a high-context culture, this would seem strange. In negotiations, as an example, the insistence by, say, Americans (low-context) for lawyers to be present in the early stages of negotiations to ensure that the precise meanings and words are carefully chosen might well be interpreted as evidence of distrust by Japanese negotiators. While this response by the Japanese might seem unreasonable from an American perspective given their purpose and their interpreation of a

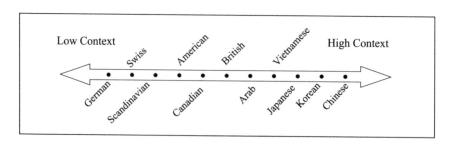

FIGURE 12.9 *Context variation*

lawyer's presence, it is consequentially the symbolic interpretation of the Japanese that carries the day. The presence of the lawyers might well prompt an early end of the negotiations without an agreement. The Japanese would have seen the early rounds of the negotiations as a time to build a relationship, not the time to nail down the details of a contract.

The use within a culture of low- and high-context symbols is a powerful form of communication. The movement from a low-context-type relationship where only relevant information is exchanged to a high-context relationship where detailed, wide-ranging and peripheral contextual information is exchanged signals increased trust. It signals an invitation into an interpersonal network of trusted confidants. Of course the opposite is true. When the contextualizing information stops coming, the relationship is cooling.

Whether the audience is high-context-oriented or low-context-oriented has an impact in other areas of communication as well. When writing, for example, to someone from a high-context culture, be sure to provide information about who is involved. With low-context audiences it is more important to over-communicate what is involved. It is also a good strategy to be concise and to the point with a clear, well-structured communication.

Management of international communication networks

Thus far we have identified some key variables affecting international communications across cultures. The complexity of the cultural universe creates problems for international communications and global commerce in terms of marketing products, dealing with suppliers and government regulators, managing workforces, and even with intra-company but cross-country communication. In order to get a handle on the issues and to manage international communications, information must be organized and then made available to managers.

One way to begin to organize cultural information of relevance to international communications is through cultural–country clustering. There are not only differences between countries across a wide range of variables, but there are similarities as well. In order to organize the information it is useful to focus on the similarities. A cultural–country cluster or group is constructed from cultural similarities shared by nation states. For example, we know intuitively that there are similarities between the UK, Ireland, Canada, New Zealand, Australia and the United States. The most obvious similarity is language. There are other variables in addition to those discussed above for global business that can be used to group countries: economic development, ethnicity, geographic location, job satisfaction, technological development, religion, social roles. Using dimensions that measure work goals, values, needs and job attitudes, Ronen and Shenkar (1985) generated groupings of countries based on cultural variables that clustered consistently on the basis of language, religion and geography. They clustered selected countries into eight groups with four independent countries that did not fit well with the others. The four independents are Brazil, India, Israel and Japan. The eight clusters are listed in Table 12.3.

Language does seem to be a fairly dominant organizing principle as is evident in the clustering of the Anglo, Latin American and Germanic groups. For other cultural–country clusters other variables work better. Clearly, one can take issue with some of the clusters. For example, Brazil has many cultural similarities with other Latin American nations and those nations in turn have many cultural similarities with the United States. Still, this particular cultural–country clustering is useful for international business decision-making and its inherent communication issues.

For example, UK firms find it easier to communicate with and to understand Americans, Canadians or Australians than the Japanese. It is not surprising then that UK businesses prefer to expand to and find more

TABLE 12.3 *Country–culture clusters*

Anglo	Germanic	Nordic	Latin American
Australia	Austria	Denmark	Argentina
Canada	Germany	Finland	Chile
Ireland	Switzerland	Norway	Columbia
New Zealand		Sweden	Mexico
South Africa			Peru
United Kingdom			Venezuela
United States			

Latin European	Near Eastern	Arab	Far Eastern
Belgium	Greece	Abu Dhabi	Hong Kong
France	Iran	Bahrain	Indonesia
Italy	Turkey	Kuwait	Malaysia
Portugal		Oman	Philippines
Spain		Saudi Arabia	Singapore
		United Arab Emirates	Taiwan
			Thailand
			Vietnam

success (especially for first forays into globalization) when they expand within the Anglo group. Similarly Spanish companies find it easier to communicate with and to expand into Latin America. Communication is less problematic when it is across countries with the least cultural distance between them. **Culture distance** refers to the magnitude of difference between cultural variables such as language. Caution must be exercised here, too. The similarities within cultural–country clusters can mislead managers into thinking that countries are more similar than they are. There are a host of other important cultural variables that can be masked by such coarse-grained clustering methods. Use culture–country clusters as an initial guide, but then more depth of information is required for business and communications with a particular country and region.

Access to information is central, therefore, to preparing for overseas expansion and for managing the international communications network. Through modern technology there is information available over the internet of a quality and degree of sophistication and depth that only a few years ago was solely held by large multinational corporations. Trade Partners UK, for example, (at http://www.tradepartners.gov.uk) provides a single point of access to a full range of support for international business both in Britain and through their commercial and diplomatic teams in more than 200 countries. Through the internet, companies of all sizes can capture large amounts of relevant data on foreign countries, foreign business data and opportunities.

More than being just a storehouse of business data, corporate networks can contain a record of an organization's experiences in a country. Records of the annual cycle of consumption patterns, trade fairs, climatic/economic cycles and social events are of immense importance for communicating to visitors from head office, for newly transferred managers, and for project teams and others visiting an overseas operation. Cultural details can also be recorded for purposes of marketing research and advertising. The corporate communications network is responsible for retaining and making available much of the organizational learning that occurs as companies expand overseas.

The corporate network can also be invaluable for allowing expatriate managers to keep in touch with the home office and to receive support and information. Overseas managers do face the risk of feeling that they are 'out of the loop' for career progression by virtue of being away from head office. To keep expatriates from feeling forgotten, the corporate communications network has the additional function of keeping those managers in the loop, which means better retention of overseas-experienced executives and better-quality information on which they and the home office can make decisions.

International organizations and firms planning to globalize need to think carefully about their communications network and how information capture and information sharing can be a competitive advantage. Global corporations that communicate and operate successfully have discovered that as they increase their foreign operations they also need to increase their cultural knowledge. There usually is a dramatic increase in the amount of cultural knowledge required as businesses and corporations move from operating in countries with similar cultures to their own, to operating in dissimilar foreign contexts. Clearly, the deeper the involvement in a foreign country the deeper the cultural knowledge needed. By strategically managing the international communications network as they grow, organizations can build capabilities in cross-cultural communication.

CROSS-CULTURAL COMMUNICATION CAPABILITIES

Learning about culture and at least something about the language of communication in the host country are necessary for successful cross-cultural communication. First must come the realization that it is the expatriate manager or the globalizing company that is the foreigner. Knowing this will help frame the experience and the realization that it is the manager/company which has to change, perhaps not in all ways, but certainly in many ways, in order to be effective. Change will require learning about a host culture. One of the best ways to engage in cultural learning is through experience. There is simply no substitute for actually being immersed in another culture.

It is also extremely helpful to study their language. Managers and corporate representatives do not necessarily have to become fluent, but the more of a language that is learnt the more can be understood about the culture. It is also the case that a sincere effort to speak the language is looked on favourably by the host country. It shows sincerity for cultural learning and it shows respect for the culture. These are positive signals.

Learning about the host culture is necessary even for the basic level of understanding required to engage in appropriate greetings and physical contact. Physical touching is always a tricky area inter-culturally. Should a handshake be quite firm and vigorous as in America, somewhat firm but with little vertical movement as in the UK, or a very light partial grasp as in Indonesia, and used mostly on business occasions, or on all occasions as in France? How acceptable is back-slapping when leaving the company of other men, and when is it appropriate for men to hug? Whom do you kiss, when and how many times? In Paris it is one peck on each cheek but in other parts of France it is two on each cheek. But do not try kissing in a business context in most parts of the US unless you are relatively good friends and then only if you are both female and the business context is relatively informal. The point here is that there is much to be learned not only about physical touching that is culturally specific but many other cultural idiosyncrasies as well.

Knowing about general cultural variables is useful, but as can be seen from relatively simple norms related to greetings, detailed cultural information about the specific culture in which a manager is working and communicating is essential. Many multinational corporations provide cultural training programmes not only for expatriate managers but also for their marketing, advertising and general communications teams. Culture-specific information can be obtained from a variety of published sources. Detailed information on 101 countries can be found on the United States Country Studies website at http://memory.loc.gov/frd/cs/cshome.html. And there are other internet sites that can provide useful information for cultural study.

Another important element for acquiring cross-cultural capabilities is interpersonal skills. Integration into the host community is facilitated by managers who have the skills to form relationships. This requires sensitivity and good communication skills. It is important for building trust, improving knowledge transfer, facilitating co-ordination and control, and all of these are intimately linked with communications. Expatriate managers also tend to settle in better when they have the skills to make friends and develop relationships. It also helps if expatriates have a sense of humour. A sense of humour seems to go with good interpersonal skills and helps people cope during the difficult period of culture shock.

Learning about another culture also requires a certain amount of patience as well as the ability to deal with uncertainty. Often this requires the ability clearly to see that one's own behaviours are culturally driven. This makes it easier to appreciate others' behaviours and other ways of doing things. Without sufficient respect for the other culture, cross-cultural learning is very difficult and effective communication just about impossible.

One of the things that we have found in our research and business experiences around the world is that people everywhere are just people. They are not all alike culturally, of course, but almost everywhere we go we find people that are warm, and friendly, and forgiving. As long as you demonstrate a sincere interest in and make a sincere effort to understand others' cultural ways, most people will be polite and helpful and will not take offence if cultural mistakes are made. It would be unforgivable, though, not to know to remove your shoes before entering a mosque. It would be rude and just bad business to travel to Japan without business cards.

Of course, the goal of cultural studies is to enable informed decision-making and communications in foreign countries. By developing cross-cultural capabilities organizations and managers will be better equipped to market their goods and services, procure resources, deal with culture shock for managers away from home, and in the final analysis to generate value through their business activities both for themselves and for the host nation.

STEREOTYPES

One of the real dangers of national culture studies is in the tendency of people to develop stereotypes. The word **stereotype** comes from the history of printing when sections of text or other images were cast in metal plates so that the identical text or image could be used whenever necessary. In a similar way stereotyping among people refers to a stock image of a person or group based on cultural, national, racial or other characteristics. Stereotypes that are used unthinkingly can create discriminatory practices, cloud judgement and relationships, and may act as barriers to communication. It is one thing to know something about a culture so that one is prepared for certain customs, practices and behaviours that generally (in the statistical sense) are found in a particular culture, but it is something else to allow stereotypes to cloud judgement and prevent interaction with individuals.

Stereotyping used to be considered as very negative and as being irrational and founded upon prejudice. Now, we know that we all use stereotypes as simply mental models that develop as part of cognitive processes. In order to avoid information overload and to enable shortened mental processing we all categorize everything in our environments in order to try to make sense. Developing stereotypes of groups of people is really no different in that respect. Where stereotyping becomes a problem is when stereotypes are used to be biased or make judgements about specific individuals whether we have had any contact with those persons or not. A stereotype is a mental representation of an 'average social person' based solely on your exposure to selected information about an identifiable group. You will never find that 'average social person'. It is a construct. Everyone is both more and less than a stereotypical image.

Stereotypes are inevitable. They are a form of cultural information. Cultural knowledge is preparation for contexts in which and during which judgements can then be developed about individuals and their companies. You will find that though you have prepared for and witness, for example, that many Japanese are collectivistic you must be open to the fact that not all Japanese people you meet will be collectivistic. Indeed, there are more differences within what we analytically construct and call cultures, than between cultures. Be very careful that you do not allow stereotypes to prevent you from seeing and dealing with people as individuals – to do otherwise is not only unfounded and morally suspect, but bad business practice and results in ineffective communications.

Discussion questions

1. Why is it that shareholders are generally better informed than the employees who actually work in a company?

2. Ethically, organizations should communicate fully and truthfully with all of their stakeholders. Do you agree and what are the reasons for your answer?

3. What are the communications implications of overseas managers suffering from culture shock?

4. How might differences in time orientation between cultures affect international business communications?

5. Adapting communications and marketing efforts based on cultural differences is time-consuming and expensive. The whole world over people choose the best products so cultural differences are irrelevant. Would you support these statements? Why or why not?

References

Barney, J. (1997) *Gaining and Sustaining Competitive Advantage*, Addison-Wesley, New York.

Etzioni, A. (1964) *Modern Organizations*, Prentice Hall, Englewood Cliffs, NJ.

Hall, E. and Hall, M. (1987) *Hidden Differences: Doing Business with the Japanese*, Anchor Press, Garden City, NY.

Hall, E. and Hall, M. (1990) *Understanding Cultural Differences*, Intercultural Press, Yarmouth, ME.

Hofstede, G. (1980) *Culture's Consequences: International Differences in Work-related Values*, Sage, Beverly Hills, CA.

Hofstede, G. (1981) *Cultures and Organizations: Software of the Mind*, Harper-Collins, London.

Mitchell, R, Agle, B. and Wood, D. (1997) Toward a theory of stakeholder identification and salience: defining the principle of who and what really counts, *Academy of Management Review*, 22, 853–886.

Ronen, S. and Shenkar, O. (1985) Clustering countries on attitudinal dimensions: a review and synthesis, *Academy of Management Review*, 10(3), 435–455.

Rouse, M. (2000) *Oil sands and organizational cultures: strategy and stakeholder dynamics in an environmental public consultation process*, Unpublished Ph.D. Dissertation, University of Calgary, Canada.

Further reading

Ferraro, G. (1990) *The Cultural Dimension of International Business*, Prentice Hall, Englewood Cliffs, NJ.

Freeman, R. (1984) *Strategic Management: A Stakeholder Approach*, Pitman, Boston.

Gudykunst, W. and Kim, Y. (1992) *Communicating with Strangers: An Approach to Intercultural Communications*, 2nd edn, McGraw-Hill, New York.

Hickson, D. and Pugh, D. (1995) *Management Worldwide: The Impact of Societal Culture on Organizations around the Globe*, Penguin, London.

Näsi, J. (ed.) (1995) *Understanding Stakeholder Thinking*, LSR-Julkaisut, Helsinki.

Terpstra, V. and David, K. (1985) *The Cultural Environment of International Business*, Western College Publishing, Cincinnati, OH.

Trenholme, J. and Daggatt, W. (1990) *The Global Negotiator*, Harper Business, New York.

Wierzbicka, A. (1991) *Cross-cultural Pragmatics: The Semantics of Human Interaction*, Mouton de Gruyter, Berlin.

Glossary

Advertising refers to communications that effectively and efficiently provide persuasive messages about products/services for potential consumers or buyers of those products/services.

Bounded rationality means we are limited by our cognitive powers in the amount of information we can process at one time.

Channel refers to the particular technology or method used to get the message to the receiver.

Coercive power is the power to force compliance by means of physical, psychological, economic or emotional threat.

Communication is the process of transmitting information from one person to another.

Connotations are additional word meanings that come from the context of a communication as opposed to denotations which refer to dictionary definitions.

Cross-cultural communication refers to the process of sending and receiving messages between people who are in different cultural contexts.

Culture distance refers to the magnitude of difference between cultural variables such as language.

Culture shock occurs when consciously or subconsciously, people realize that nearly everything about a host country and its ways of doing things is different.

Data are raw facts and figures defined within a narrow context (note: the word 'data' is plural, the singular is 'datum').

Decoding is the act of interpreting an encoded message.

Denotation refers to what a word means as in a dictionary definition.

Division of labour is defined as the way in which a company allocates people to functional organizational tasks and responsibilities in order to generate value.

Effective communication means that the information is received as accurately in terms of content and meaning as was intended by the sender.

Encoding is the act of converting formulated thoughts into spoken or written words.

Ethics refers to principles of right or wrong conduct.

Ethnocentrism is seeing one's own culture as the only valid one and finding all others lacking by comparison.

Expert power comes from knowledge, information or expertise in some area.

Feedback is a response from the receiver of a message.

Information is data in a meaningful form.

Leader is someone who can influence the behaviors of others without resorting to force, but a leader could also be someone whom others accept as being their leader.

Leadership is a process of non-coercive influence that shapes a group's or an organization's goals, motivates people's behavior towards the attainment of those goals, and helps define organizational culture.

Legitimate power is power individuals hold by virtue of their position in the management hierarchy.

Medium refers to the way in which a message is encoded.

Metaphors link two expressions from different semantic domains.

Metonyms are parts that stand for a whole, e.g. the crown stands for the monarchy.

Morphemes are the smallest units in a language that have meaning.

Morphology is the word structure of a language.

Multivocality (literally 'speaking with many voices') means that symbols can have meaning on different levels.

Negotiation can be defined as a social process of interaction and communication between people with the purpose of obtaining a lasting agreement based on some common interests for the purpose of achieving goals and avoiding conflict.

Noise is anything that interrupts or distorts a message.

Non-verbal communication refers to all intended and unintended meanings that are not in the form of written or spoken words.

Oral communication refers to conversations in which the spoken word is the major code for communication.

Organizational structure is the formal organizing framework created to achieve the organization's goals.

Organizations are society's way to generate value that individuals cannot generate on their own.

Over-learning is knowing a subject well beyond the point of mastery.

Paralanguage refers to vocalizations (other than words) and pauses associated with speech, such as pitch, volume (loud or soft), intensity and hardness, or what people generally refer to as 'tone of voice'.

Phonemes are the smallest sound units that have meaning in a language.

Phonology is the system of sounds (phonemes) in a language.

Political behaviour refers to actions and activities for the specific purpose of acquiring, developing and using power and other resources in order to obtain preferred outcomes.

Power is the ability to affect others' behaviors.

Prototypes in linguistics are experiences that a society sees as typical and uses as a baseline for judging whether other experiences are typical.

Public relations is the management of communications between organizations and their external stakeholders.

Referent power is based on charisma, imitation, loyalty or identification with a leader.

Resources are capital equipment, raw materials, organizational processes and attributes, information, expertise and all assets that are used and controlled by the organization.

Reward power is the power to grant or to withhold valued rewards.

Role theory of leadership suggests that there are certain roles that must be performed within a group or organization for successful results and that those who perform those roles are the leaders.

Semantic domains are domains of experience that are culturally meaningful.

Semantics is the study of meaning.

Sign in linguistics refers to anything that transmits information such as a word, an object, a gesture, a picture or a sound.

Social norms are tacit or informal 'rules' about what is done, how, when, where and by whom.

Stakeholder is a person or group inside or outside an organization that has an interest or stake in what the organization does and how it performs.

Stereotype refers to a stock image of a person or group based on cultural, national, racial or other characteristics.

Stereotyping is the attempt to predict people's behaviour based on their membership of a particular group.

Subliminal advertising is the insertion into a film, television programme, or other audio or visual media, of a 'subliminal' message which exerts subconscious influences on purchasing behavior.

Symbol a sign with arbitrary meanings.

Syntax is an aspect of grammar that has to do with how words are arranged to form phrases and sentences.

Trait theory suggests that there are certain qualities or traits that people have that make them good leaders.

INDEX